Feminism, Violence Against Women, and Law Reform

Offering an important addition to existing critiques of governance feminism and carceral expansion based mainly on experiences from the Global North, this book critically addresses feminist law reform on violence against women, from a decolonial perspective.

Challenging the consensus that penal expansion is mainly associated with the co-option of feminist campaigns to counteract violence against women in the context of neoliberal globalisation, this book shows that long-standing colonial narratives underlie many of today's dominant legal discourses justifying criminalisation, even in countries whose governments have called themselves "leftist" and "post-neoliberal". Mapping the history of law reform on violence against women in Ecuador, the book reveals how the conciliation between feminist campaigns and criminalisation strategies takes place through liberal legality, the language of human rights, and the discourse of constitutional guarantees, across the political spectrum. Whilst human rights make violence against women intelligible in mainstream legal terms, the book shows that the emergence of a "rights-based penality" produces a benign, formally innocuous criminal law, which can be presented as progressive, but in practice reproduces colonial and postcolonial paradigms that limit and reshape feminist demands. The book raises new questions on the complex social and political factors that impact on feminist law reform projects, as it demonstrates how colonial assumptions about gender, race, class, and the family remain embedded in liberal criminal law.

This theoretically and empirically informed analysis makes an innovative contribution to feminist legal theory, postcolonial studies, and criminal law; and will be of interest to activists, scholars, and policymakers working at the intersections between gender equality, law, and violence in Latin America and beyond.

Silvana Tapia Tapia is Assistant Professor of Law at Universidad del Azuay (Ecuador). She holds a PhD in Socio-Legal Studies from the University of Kent (United Kingdom), a Master's in Criminal Law, and a Bachelor's in Law from the Universidad del Azuay (Ecuador). In 2021 she was awarded a Leverhulme Early Career Fellowship to conduct research on violence against women and human rights penality, hosted by the University of Birmingham (United Kingdom).

Part of the SOCIAL JUSTICE series

series editors

Sarah Keenan, Birkbeck College, University of London, UK
Davina Cooper, University of Kent, UK
Sarah Lamble, Birkbeck College, University of London, UK

for information about the series and details of previous and forthcoming titles, see https://www.routledge.com/Social-Justice/book-series/RCSOCJ

a GlassHouse book

Feminism, Violence Against Women, and Law Reform

Decolonial Lessons from Ecuador

Silvana Tapia Tapia

Routledge
Taylor & Francis Group
a GlassHouse Book

First published 2022
by Routledge
4 Park Square, Milton Park, Abingdon, Oxon OX14 4RN

and by Routledge
605 Third Avenue, New York, NY 10158

a GlassHouse book

Routledge is an imprint of the Taylor & Francis Group, an informa business

British Library Cataloguing-in-Publication Data
A catalogue record for this book is available from the British Library

Library of Congress Cataloging-in-Publication Data
A catalog record has been requested for this book

ISBN: 978-0-367-56647-0 (hbk)
ISBN: 978-0-367-56650-0 (pbk)
ISBN: 978-1-003-09879-9 (ebk)

DOI: 10.4324/9781003098799

Typeset in Bembo
by Deanta Global Publishing Services, Chennai, India

"*Feminism, Violence Against Women, and Law Reform* is a testament to the power of feminist decolonial thinking in a resiliently patriarchal, colonial, and violent world. Its central argument is devastating. Whether in the form of reactionary criminalisation or in the apparently more progressive guise of human rights advocacy, liberal legality continues to dominate the public debate about violence against women. Indeed, neither the demise of formal colonialism nor the effort to transcend neoliberalism has done anything to undermine this dominance, let alone the impervious levels of violence that women all over the world continue to face. What then? An epistemic break in the form of a decolonial feminist abolitionist agenda – this is Tapia Tapia's answer. To get there and beyond is everyone's task."

Luis Eslava, *Reader in International Law, Kent Law School, University of Kent*

"In this innovative and wide-ranging socio-legal history of initiatives tackling violence against women in Ecuador, Silvana Tapia Tapia makes a key contribution to the growing field of post-colonial legal studies. In her illuminating analysis of the Ecuadorian case, she problematizes what has been taken in much literature to be an analytic association between neoliberalism and the feminist embrace of penality, suggesting instead that, even in the context of left-wing governments, penal expansion in the field of violence against women has been fed by both colonial discourses and, ironically, the appeal to human rights. Her book has important implications both across and beyond Latin America."

Nicola Lacey, *School Professor of Law, Gender and Social Policy, LSE*

"Tapia Tapia's excellent book is a vital intervention on a contemporary topic of the utmost importance and urgency: the deployment of carcerality in the name of liberation. Focusing on the feminist alliance with the State's carceral power over the course of significant political change in Ecuador, the study's account of the process, pitfalls, and alternatives to this alignment is based on painstaking research and remarkable critical insight. Tapia Tapia's findings, particularly regarding the lure and ramifications of penality for progressive agendas, are sensitive to the context in which her research is embedded, but also carry significant implications for anyone seeking to understand and fight oppression anywhere. Ultimately, the author eloquently delivers a call to 'unlearn' and undo rights-based penality, embracing a counter-carceral approach that transcends the pull of liberal legality and reimagines both emancipation and protection through a decolonial feminist lens."

Natasa Mavronicola, *Reader in Law, Birmingham Law School, University of Birmingham*

For Adrian and Svein.

Contents

Figures

Tables

Foreword

What are feminists to make of the growing turn to criminal law as a solution to gender inequality? Whether manifest in World Bank gender equality rankings that identify the criminalisation of sexual harassment as progress, or in social movement demands that an end to impunity for rape requires the death penalty, the imbrication between enhancing women's rights and punishment is tightening. How do we make sense of this? How do we ascertain whether such strategies are working to reduce violence against women? What is our role, as feminists, in producing this carceral response, and how might we produce other, better responses?

Feminism, Violence Against Women, and Law Reform: Decolonial Lessons from Ecuador offers several original insights to scholars and activists interested in this intersection between gender equality, law, and violence. Moreover, while offering us lessons from Ecuador, it is less a case study of Ecuador, and more a vital new account of gender, law, and penality, with wide-reaching theoretical implications.

When I first encountered the ideas in this book, I was beginning to think about why, how, and with what effect the turn to law within international development had reframed our conversations about gender equality. I was not looking at violence, or criminal law. I was exploring initiatives oriented to economic empowerment, and their imbrication with a faith in legal reform as a marker of progress that seemed strange to me. One of the key insights I have taken from Silvana Tapia Tapia's work over the years is that this sense of strangeness is shared by many others, including those who focus on violence against women. For experts in gender, violence, criminal law, and Latin America, the book is indispensable: but it also contains crucial insights in a range of other areas.

Firstly, by foregrounding the experience of Ecuador, the book decentres the USA, and the Global North, within our debates about feminism's complex and contested relationship to neoliberalism, penality, and carcerality, while offering general lessons that stretch far beyond the case study. It offers an in-depth account of a country – one among many in the Latin American region[1] – that

1 Other countries considered part of this tide included Argentina, Bolivia, Uruguay, and Venezuela.

explicitly embarked on an anti-neoliberal path in the early years of the new century. The broader 'pink tide' context within which Ecuador's 2007–2017 Citizen's Revolution is located means that the country's experiences are of relevance far beyond its borders: although a tiny country geographically, Tapia Tapia makes it a giant, analytically speaking.

One key advantage of the Ecuadorian focus, in my view, is that it prompts us to question the often-assumed association between neoliberalism and penal expansion, including by identifying the investment that left-leaning regimes and social movements, with human rights as their lingua franca, may have in criminalisation. The book focuses in depth on the way that transnational human rights instruments justify, or even require, carcerality, with campaigns against impunity focusing heavily on the creation and enforcement of new offences.[2] While this produces a "rights-based penality" that appears to soften the power of punishment, it does not, in Ecuador, actually expand the number of people imprisoned for violence against women. It does, however, result in a limited state response to such violence, fixated on the criminal trial, and ineffective for most survivors.

In this regard, the book's multi-method and interdisciplinary approach is another key strength. It combines archival research with close reading of parliamentary records, constitutional law, current legislation, and case law, alongside in-depth interviews with those leading the struggle for gender equality in Ecuador. Having explored the narrowing of political debates about violence against women in the 2014 Penal Code, for example, in the final chapter Tapia Tapia draws on fieldwork to explore the experiences that violence survivors have of the new specialized procedures linked to that code. This focus on the perspectives of women who turn to the courts for support is paired with deep historical and doctrinal expertise, giving us, as readers, a comprehensive account of the reasons behind the turn to penal solutions, and the concrete implications this turn has for survivors and others.

Historical curiosity also shapes the book, especially in its attention to the way that family law was informed by the racialised nature of colonial and early republican nation-making projects. Criminal law has, Tapia Tapia notes, "long been used to manage populations and 'optimise the race', including by reprehending 'excessive' violence against women and children" (Chapter 1). She also meticulously shows that law was generally seen as "foe" by a range of different women's movements; even among upper middle-class women there was limited interest in using criminalisation to protect women prior to the 1990s. We learn that the turn to criminal justice as the key solution to violence against women, in Ecuador and elsewhere, relied in part on a transnational and regional convergence of discourses including public health, psychology, women in development, and human rights. However, the book also shows

2 Her critical account of the Belem do Pará convention, where state accountability primarily takes the form of legal measures and criminalisation commitments, is particularly thought-provoking.

that domestic political debates were key. Conservative government officials reframed feminist campaigns against gendered violence into initiatives designed to protect the family, and erased feminist priorities relating to state provision of social services from draft bills. Again, close attention to Ecuador's past experience is used to provide a re-theorisation of transnationality, law, and feminist social movements anchored in the country, but resonating far beyond its borders and history. I was particularly struck by the careful argument against the assumption that women's movements were coopted by neoliberal and conservative sectors: the attention shown to unequal power relations is refreshing, including as manifest in the imposition of party discipline against those supporting abortion rights.

This historical curiosity notwithstanding, by tracing a continuity between earlier and more recent criminalising responses to domestic violence Tapia Tapia notes resonances that –she insists – can only be understood through the lens of coloniality. This lens rejects a temporally delimited framing of European imperialism bookended by conquest. Instead, it centres the continuity of colonial power, including in terms of how legal and political elites define and understand concepts of modernity, statehood, gender, law, and humanity itself. While Ecuador's 2008 Constitution purported to offer a radical departure from colonial and postcolonial paradigms, in its recognition of plurinationality and legal pluralism, and its grounding in the Andean concept of Sumak Kawsay, ultimately its decolonising potential was undercut by the Constitutional Court's on-going commitment to the penal and coercive dimensions of human rights. In short, the post-neoliberal programme was not decolonial enough. This blunt assessment of the colonial limits that rights-based penality places on our legal and political horizons extends existing conversations about feminism and carcerality into new directions, complicating the analytical association between neoliberalism and penal expansion that is common to much other work.

Taken together, these insights underpin a provocative, carefully argued book, generously spirited in its engagements with other scholars, and meticulous in its attentiveness to historical archive, legal doctrine, critical scholarship, and contemporary lived experience. Far more than an application, or critique, of existing literature via a country case study, in the best tradition of radical empirical work it upends some core assumptions of that literature. It offers a retheorising of the relationship between law, gender, coloniality, human rights, and neoliberalism that is sure to inspire considerable further research, in Ecuador and many other places.

Kate Bedford
Professor of Law, University of Birmingham

Acknowledgements

I am indebted to innumerable people and institutions that have made this book possible. This is an attempt at naming most.

First, I owe this work to the women who shared their experiences of feminist activism and gender-based violence with me, and authorised me to write about them. I am especially thankful to *Cabildo por las Mujeres*, *Casa de Acogida María Amor*, and the now defunct *Corporación Mujer a Mujer*, for facilitating my work with violence survivors. I shall also acknowledge the amazing work of the collectives *Mujeres de Frente*, *Corredores Migratorios*, and *Alianza Contra las Prisiones* in Ecuador. I have learnt so much from their ethical approach to activism and scholarship.

I am immensely grateful to Tatiana Padrón Palacios for her research assistance and diligence in coding part of the data for Chapter 6. She also formatted large sections of this manuscript and helped me keep track of the checklists involved in the publication process, while being a loyal and reliable friend all the time.

I am forever thankful to Kate Bedford for her limitless generosity, guidance, advice, friendship, hospitality, encouragement, solidarity, and feminist comradery. *Gracias, siempre.*

I am lucky to have worked with Vinita Joseph as a coach. With her, I learned to organise my time and prioritise that which is truly important. A lotus for you.

Luis Eslava, Natasa Mavronicola, and Nicola Lacey have given me their continued support, mentorship, and feedback for this and many other academic projects. I will pay it forward!

Various parts of this book were presented as papers at the Law and Society Association, and the Socio-Legal Studies Association annual conferences. I received invaluable feedback at these fora. I also benefited from participating in the Scholars' Academy of the Harvard Institute for Global Law and Policy, and the Stanford Junior Faculty Forum, where I discussed and improved my work.

Sebastián López Hidalgo and María Caridad Sánchez Palacios (Universidad del Azuay) compiled a portion of the primary data for Chapter 6.

Genaro Tapia Tapia transcribed several interviews and gifted me with his long-standing comradeship. ¡*Venceremos*!

The series editors, Davina Cooper, Sarah Lamble, and Sarah Keenan, offered invaluable and thoughtful feedback on earlier versions of this monograph. Thank you for engaging so generously with my work and helping me improve it.

Colin Perrin provided prompt and clear advice during all the stages leading to the publication of this book.

A large part of the research for this book was funded by Ecuador's Secretary for Higher Education, Science, and Technology (SENESCYT).

Kent Law School provided most of the logistics and training required to finish this project. In particular, I am grateful to Donatella Alessandrini, Emily Grabham, Maria Drakopoulou, and Sinéad Ring (now at Maynooth University) for their guidance and advice. I am also indebted to my doctoral cohort at Kent Law School, especially Aravinda Kosaraju, Laura Binger, and Serena Natile, not only for our engaging scholarly discussions, but primarily for their sincere friendship.

The Birmingham Institute for Global Innovation funded the research on women's experiences of using specialised courts, whose findings appear in Chapter 6. Dr Caroline Bradbury-Jones, from Birmingham's School of Nursing, also contributed with valuable input on the methodology.

Part of this monograph was written with the support of Universidad del Azuay. I am especially grateful to Jacinto Guillén García, Vice-Rector of Research, for his continued trust. The staff at the university's law clinic was helpful and cooperative when I carried out documentary research and interviews at their premises.

Most of this book was written up during a severe global crisis due to the COVID-19 pandemic. I would not have had the calm and inner peace required to finish this project without my practice with the World Inter-being Sangha, and the teachings of Thich Nhat Hahn.

My friends María Elisa Durán and Belén Abad have always been there for me, even when I disappeared for long periods to conduct research or write.

My parents, María and Genaro Tapia, have always supported my career, trips, moves, changes, absences, bad temper, and stubbornness. Thank you.

My son Adrian provided the laughs, joy, awe, and affection I needed to make sense of my work, life, love, and the cosmos. In you I see the courage of the Cañari, the Vikings, and the Sami. Be free.

Most of all, I thank Svein Tuven, who has been walking with me for over a decade, unconditionally, making sure I have the time, space, and resources required to develop my projects. None of them matter if you are not there, fighting by my side. I love you.

Abbreviations

AFE	*Alianza Femenina Ecuatoriana* Ecuadorian Feminine Alliance
AMM	*Acción por el movimiento de mujeres* Action for the women's movement
AP	*Alianza País* Fatherland Alliance
CEDAW	Convention on the Elimination of all Forms of Discrimination Against Women Latin American and Caribbean Committee for the Defense of Women's Rights
CEPAM	*Centro ecuatoriano para la promoción de la mujer* Ecuadorian centre for the promotion of women
CIM	*Comisión Interamericana de Mujeres* Inter-American Women's Commission
CLADEM	*Comité de América Latina y el Caribe para la Defensa de los Derechos de las Mujeres*
CONAIE	*Confederación de Nacionalidades Indígenas del Ecuador* Confederation of Indigenous Nationalities of Ecuador
CONAMU	*Consejo Nacional de las Mujeres* National Council of Women
CSW	United Nations Commission on the Status of Women
CWGL	Center for Women's Global Leadership
DINAMU	*Dirección Nacional de las Mujeres* National Directorate of Women
ECOSOC	United Nations' Economic and Social Council
ECtHR	European Court of Human Rights
EFLAC	Encuentro Feminista Latinoamericano y del Caribe
ENDEMAIN	*Encuesta demográfica de salud materna e infantil* Demographic Survey of Maternal and Infant Health
FLACSO	*Facultad Latinoamericana de Ciencias Sociales* Latin American Faculty of Social Sciences
IACHR	Inter-American Commission on Human Rights

IACtHR	Inter-American Court of Human Rights
INEC	*Instituto Ecuatoriano de Estadística y Censos* Ecuadorian Institute of Statistics and Censuses
LOIPEV	*Ley Orgánica Integral para Erradicar y Prevenir la Violencia contra las Mujeres* Comprehensive Law to Eradicate and Prevent Violence Against Women
OAS	Organization of American States
OFNAMU	*Oficina Nacional de la Mujer* National Office for Women
PAHO	*Pan-American Health Organization*
SENDAS	*Servicio para el Desarrollo Alternativo del Sur* Service for the Alternative Development of the South
UN	United Nations
UNESCO	United Nations Educational, Scientific and Cultural Organization
USAID	United States Agency for International Development
VAW	violence against women

Introduction

Toward a decolonial feminist critique of penality

A carceral world

We live in a highly incarcerated world: it is estimated that if all the people imprisoned in only three nations: the United States (US), China, and Russia, were to stand next to each other, the resulting line would stretch across the surface of the planet (Scott, 2013). We also live in a racist world: non-white minorities are overrepressented in prisons, including in the countries with the highest incarceration rates (Davis, 2000; Gilmore, 2007; Hart et al., 2020; Richie, 2012; Sudbury, 2005). And we live in a world where poverty is gendered and criminalised: women's prisons in Ecuador, for instance, are populated mainly by persons who committed low-level, non-violent offences, such as small-scale robbery and drug micro-trafficking (Aguirre Salas et al., 2020; Fleetwood, 2014; Torres Angarita, 2007). The effects of this expanding penality[1] are not felt only within the prison's walls: families, friends, partners, and children are part of the penalised communities that suffer the violence of incarceration. Various strands of scholarship and activism have addressed these phenomena from fields such as critical criminology, feminist legal studies, critical legal anthropology, and critical international law. Anti-carceral collectives like *Mujeres de Frente* in Ecuador; Critical Resistance and Incite! in the US; Empty Cages and Bent Bars in the United Kingdom (UK); *Hermanas en la Sombra* in Mexico; and *Actoras de Cambio* in Guatemala, are ensembles of activists, scholars, and people deprived of their freedom, inside and outside the prison's walls, who are articulating counter-hegemonic strategies to resist the carceral, patriarchal, racist, and classist state.

Within the anti-carceral tradition, a rich body of literature on the political economy of punishment has unveiled a structural relation between penal expansion and the transformations of late capitalism (Amar, 2013; Christie, 2000; Davis, 2000; Garland, 2012; Gilmore, 2017; Simon, 2007; Wacquant,

1 In this book, I use the term "penality" to refer to the broader penal field, including its laws, discourse, institutions, and sanctions. That is, the term is inclusive of criminal law, criminal justice, the penal system, and carceral punishment (Garland, 1985; Howe, 1994; Pinto, 2020).

DOI: 10.4324/9781003098799-1

2009). This literature has also revealed puzzling paradoxes: for instance, that emancipatory social movements and progressive scholarship, including feminists, have fuelled the penal apparatus by demanding more criminal laws and harsher penalties for offences like hate crimes and gender-based violence; often without assessing the power dynamics involved in such strategies, nor the limited efficacy they have (Gottschalk, 2006; Pérez, 2019; Pérez & Radi, 2020; Richie, 2012). Some authors have even identified a "carceral feminism", that is, a set of discourses and practices, frequently deployed by "governance feminists", based on the belief that criminal justice can alleviate gender-based violence by criminalising, prosecuting, and incarcerating offenders (Bernstein, 2010; Halley et al., 2018; Kim, 2019; Law, 2014; Terwiel, 2020; Whalley & Hackett, 2017). According to these accounts, feminist advocacy groups have become complicit in the build-up of mass incarceration by endorsing law-and-order responses to social conflict.

At the same time, as the Ecuadorian case confirms, the passing of criminal laws has not resulted in a reduction of gender-based violence. Feminist researchers have long known that criminal justice is intricate, onerous, revictimising, and seldom provides reparations for violence survivors (Goodmark, 2018; Richie, 2012; Snider, 1998). In Ecuador, specialised criminal courts for violence against women (henceforth VAW) were established in 2013, VAW misdemeanours became criminal offences in 2014, and a new specialised law on VAW passed in 2018. Yet, the 2019 national survey on VAW shows an increase of the phenomenon compared to the rates of 2012: 64% of Ecuadorian women have experienced some form of gender-based violence throughout their lives, with provinces where incidence is as high as 79% (INEC, 2019). Around 36% of violent deaths between 2014 and 2019 were femicides, mostly perpetrated by an intimate partner (Tupiza Aldaz & Guerra Páez, 2019). However, my empirical research has shown that only 11.1% of all cases heard by the specialised courts between 2014 and 2019 resulted in a conviction. Almost 56% of the cases never reach a resolution (see Chapter 6). Still, Ecuador scored 100/100 in legally protecting women from violence, in a 2018 World Bank report (Iqbal, 2018).

This book addresses these socio-legal phenomena, introducing some analytical innovations that have emerged from my empirical work in Ecuador. These contribute to our understanding of the relationship between penal expansion, mainstream feminism, and coloniality, beyond neoliberalism and co-optation as the main explanatory factors for feminist "complicity" in expanding penality. I unearth the role of coloniality, human rights, and liberal criminal law in reconciling feminist agendas with criminal justice. Rather than reasserting how governance feminism contributes to penal expansion, I focus on how liberal legalism produces a "rights-based penality" that is embraced by left-leaning and progressive sectors, including feminists. At the same time, this rights-based penality does not challenge the colonial paradigms that govern women's sexuality and social roles. Furthermore, the rights-based penality has produced a legal and judicial system specialising in VAW, which acts as a proxy for state action, leaving most violence survivors unprotected and without access to the services they require.

One of this book's starting points is that "carceral feminism" is a matter of debate. As I demonstrate empirically, trials on VAW very rarely result in the imprisonment of defendants (Tapia Tapia, 2021; Taylor, 2018). In addition, the anti-statism that characterises some anti-carceral feminist work has been questioned, because it could open a door to reprivatise VAW and obscure the state's duty to perform economic redistribution (Gotell, 2015; Masson, 2020). Thus, this book considers various aspects that might have been overlooked by the existing literature: for instance, that criminal laws on VAW do not often produce more carcerality, that feminist legislators and policy-makers *do* resist various forms of penal discourse,[2] that human rights, due process, and the idea of a constitutional criminal law play a significant role in producing criminalisation as the main response to gender-based violence, and that the coloniality of power, gender, and penality can thrive even under left-leaning and anticolonial regimes that intend to challenge it, often disguised by human rights and liberal legal discourse.

A rights-based penality

My interest in criminal justice and VAW began when I was a master's student. The programme I studied was decidedly liberal: the materials promoted a minimal criminal law; that is, an *ultima ratio* (last resort) approach to contain the state's punitive power by limiting it through constitutional guarantees. I also explored the "theory of penal guarantees" (*garantismo penal*), a rights-based model mainly introduced by European jurists,[3] which emphasises due process as an antidote to illegitimate prosecutions and wrongful convictions. Anglo-American authors have referred to this as "constitutionalized procedural criminal law" (Dubber, 2004). As I finished my master's, feminist groups were discussing the implications of a new penal code. I was intrigued by their demands to criminalise, or harshen the sanctions for, gender-based violence. My sense was that feminists needed to incorporate more penal guarantees and human rights principles into

2 While this book confirms that Ecuadorian mainstream feminism has largely been built around ideas brought in by international cooperation to development, and the know-how of agencies like the Organization of American States (OAS) and the United Nations (UN), it also acknowledges that those perspectives have been resisted, and that many legal outcomes of feminist proposals have been reshaped by the national legislature.

3 *Garantismo penal* in contemporary criminal doctrine generally refers to the use of the term by Italian scholars Luigi Ferrajoli and Norberto Bobbio. For Ferrajoli, penal principles are the deontological basis of criminal law, the rational foundation of the law: they mark the direction that law must take and they acquire operability through the configuration of penal guarantees. The State and the law are cultural creations whose purpose is to guarantee human rights.

their proposals. However, a couple of years into my doctoral research and after conducting fieldwork, I had come to a very different understanding of the problem: penal minimalism, human rights, and constitutional criminal law were precisely what feminists were invoking to demand criminalisation. By then, I had become familiar with Global North literature on neoliberalism, carceral expansion, and the "prison-industrial-complex". Many of these analyses scrutinised the relationship between the "carceral turn" and late-capitalist political economy, broadly arguing that carcerality serves as a governmental tool to manage deviant populations that may interfere with the free flow of capital. Yet, as compelling as they were, I thought that these accounts did not suffice to explain the feminist engagements with criminal law in Latin America.

In the region, some left-leaning governments came to power between the late 1990s and 2000s (a phenomenon known as the "Pink Tide"[4]) and implemented various measures for social redistribution. The 2007–2017 government of Ecuador called itself the "Citizen's Revolution" and adopted an anti-neoliberal rhetoric. While penal expansion has often been connected to the decline of the welfare state, the redistributive Pink Tide policies did not result in a reduction of the incarcerated population. Furthermore, researchers observed a rapid increase in incarceration rates[5] in the region during these periods (Sozzo, 2016; Valarezo, 2021). In this book I show how appeals to penality, including by feminists, have emerged from the entire political spectrum, from left to right(s). This argument, in the Latin American context, differs from the idea of a "progressive punitivism" coined in the US to refer to an academic and popular discourse that advocates "turning the cannons of the punitive machine against the powerful" (Aviram, 2020, p. 201). I still am referring to discourses targeting "common criminals", who are often impoverished and racialised. Furthermore, in "post-neoliberal" Ecuador, conservative and progressive politicians frequently speak about women's sexuality in eerily similar ways, while the colonial history of human rights remains uninterrogated by almost everyone. In the light of these reflections, my focus became the role of what I term "rights-based penality", a framework that explains the prevalence of criminalisation as the central response to gender-based violence, even during a period when an anti-neoliberal and anticolonial discourse thrived.

This book posits novel arguments on the coloniality of liberal law and rights-based penality: human rights have been complicit in smoothing the path of feminist appeals to criminalisation and punishment. They have also displaced

4 Some countries, including Argentina, Bolivia, Brazil, Ecuador, Nicaragua, Uruguay, and Venezuela, have been called the "Pink Tide" (Kampwirth, 2011) of Latin America to convey a form of leftist politics that is not socialist "enough" to be considered "red". Other terms used to refer to these regimes were "new left", "socialism of the 21st century", and "post-neoliberal" (Borón, 2003; Dieterich, 2009). Some of these countries, including Ecuador, currently have governments that moved back to right-wing politics.

5 For data on Ecuador's incarcerated population and carceral expansion see Valarezo (2021).

non-Western conceptions of justice and facilitated the framing of criminal prosecution as the only adequate response to human rights violations – even through left-leaning government programmes. I also unmask other drawbacks of rights-based penality; for instance, how feminist proposals are mediated, taken up, and reshaped by their political interlocutors, how liberal legality facilitates the erasure of violence survivors' day-to-day experiences, and how law reform and specialised criminal justice hide the absence of social services and effective protection for women. These are crucial matters to address if we are to rethink law reform, feminist anti-violence work, and the paradox of "carceral feminism". Further, if we are to imagine a "post-neoliberal future" even the most benign legal discourses –including what Mavronicola and Lavrysen (2020) have termed "coercive human rights" – should be vehemently interrogated. In the following sections, I explain how this book engages with the existing literature and what analytical tools it introduces.

Gender, race, and coloniality

Acknowledging Latin America's long postcolonial history is indispensable to understanding how dominant discourses on gender, family, and race, inform current approaches to VAW. The Spanish and Portuguese invasion of Abya Yala,[6] perpetrated between the 16th and 19th centuries, generated resistance from the outset: already in the early colonial period we can find counter-narratives of the European occupation from the standpoint of the colonised.[7] Later, when the new republics had been established, thinkers like José Carlos Mariátegui (1928) linked colonialism to the development of capitalism, emphasising that racial hierarchies and the racial division of labour were constitutive of capitalist dispossession.

Contemporary critics have continued to scrutinise the effects of colonisation, which has resulted in a shift in Latin American critical thought, known as the "decolonial turn". Decolonial theory proposes a rereading of the past to trace the continuity of colonial power after the end of colonialism. Aníbal Quijano stated that coloniality is above all, epistemic: it is realised through the dominance of Eurocentric epistemes, legal apparatuses, and categories such as gender, race, and class (FLACSO Ecuador, 2015). Accordingly, decolonial studies run counter to great modernist narratives such as Christianity, liberalism, and Marxism, locating their inquiry at the borders of the systems

6 Abya Yala is a term in Kuna language which roughly translates as "earth alive" or "ripen earth". The Bolivian Aymara leader Takir Mamani argues for the use of the term "Abya Yala" in the official declarations of indigenous peoples' governing bodies; today, many indigenous movements across the continent are claiming "Abya Yala" as the name of the lands they inhabit. For more on the origin of the idea of Latin America see Walter Mignolo (2005).

7 See the chronicles of Garcilaso de la Vega (2000), Guamán Poma de Ayala (1980), and Pachacuti Yamqui Salcamaygua (1993).

of thought, with an aim to foreground non-Eurocentric modes of thinking (Escobar, 2013). For instance, *andar preguntando* (to go around asking), is one of the maxims that define Zapatista politics, which is very different from the *andar predicando* (to go around preaching) of the Judeo-Christian-Western cosmology. Zapatistas do not set off from an abstract universal model or ideal (socialism, communism, democracy, the nation, etc.); rather, they "go around asking" to produce a working plan that results from mutual listening. In this way, political strategy can include the epistemic diversity and the demands of all of the oppressed (Grosfoguel, 2007).

Decolonial social theorists first introduced the concept "coloniality of power" (Mignolo, 2000; Moraña et al., 2008; Quijano, 2000) to characterise world capitalism as a racialised system. With the invasion of the Americas, indigenous peoples and enslaved Africans were relegated to the realm of the subhuman and the non-human. This hierarchical division is at the core of the colonial project. Slavery and servitude formed a new global pattern of labour control, alongside a new pattern of power (Segato, 2014). Thereby, skin colour defines the status of people and continues to dictate who has access to full citizenship (Mendoza, 2016; Quijano, 2000). Non-European world orderings were deemed absurd, monstrous, and uncivilised; a manoeuvre that has continued to permeate Latin American societies. Researchers have corroborated the connections between the colonial ordering, colonised subjectivities, and the formation of juridical fields, including the carceral regimes that persist to this day (Salvatore & Aguirre, 1996; Vidal López, 2003).

Decolonial feminists have revised and enriched these theories to frame gender "as a central category, capable of illuminating all other aspects of the transformation imposed on the life of the communities as they [were] captured by the new modern colonial order" (Segato, 2016, p. 111). Not only race, but also gender, were inflicted through colonisation. Precisely, Maria Lugones (2007, 2010) coined the term "coloniality of gender" to convey that gender and race are co-constitutive producers of the "modern/colonial gender system". To decolonial feminists, modernity is a violent process tied to the construction and imposition of race and gender hierarchies (Mendoza, 2016). In Lugones's words: "Unlike colonization, the coloniality of gender is still with us; it is what lies at the intersection of gender/class/race as central constructs of the capitalist world system of power" (2010, p. 746). These divisions were violently imposed as "natural" and "universal" upon indigenous and African ontologies and epistemes. For instance, Andean cosmology conceived gender as the effect of a relational dynamic that produces complementarity and reciprocity (Dean, 2001; Lugones, 2009), a vision that was overridden by the gender binarism that colonisation introduced. This was essential to produce the colonial *Other* (Segato, 2016).[8] These processes

8 Segato has argued, however, that a "low intensity patriarchy" did exist in indigenous and African societies, although it was different from the Western subordination of the feminine.

provoked, for instance, women's exclusion from public life and the economy. The history of the public sphere, of the state sphere, is in reality the history of gender.

As we see, the coloniality of gender operates at various levels: it encompasses the subordination of white women to white men, and the dehumanisation of non-white women and men, whereby the female is further hyper-sexualised and confined to the lowest level of the race-gender power structure. This subordination informed the governance of domestic and public life in colonial Latin America and did not disappear after independence. I employ the coloniality of gender as an analytical category to historicise postcolonial legal institutions and trace how they reproduce racial categories and models of femininity and masculinity. In this way, the coloniality of gender lets us unveil the limits of contesting gender norms when coloniality is not challenged as well.

Also, this type of inquiry has enabled me to obtain a nuanced picture of women's movements in Latin America and Ecuador, which has, in turn, allowed me to recognise and celebrate the often hidden struggles of those who have resisted state violence, such as Ecuadorian indigenous leaders. With this backdrop, I analytically link postcolonial family-protection discourses to the framing of VAW as a human rights matter that requires a penal response. I also show that human rights have not undermined the coloniality of gender in Latin America; rather they have converged with earlier, colonial penal approaches to family violence. To better explain these associations, I address the coloniality of liberal law below.

The coloniality of liberal law

Having outlined the coloniality of gender as a tool to historicise power, governance, and social hierarchies, I now propose a workable framework to address "liberal legalism",[9] using colonial and postcolonial theories of gender and power, as well as some feminist readings of Foucault's governmentality (Dean, 2002; Drakopoulou, 2008; Foucault, 1991; Oksala, 2013; Stoler, 1995). Through these lenses, I situate liberal law as a governmental technology that exerts epistemic violence (Spivak, 1988) and reproduces colonial dividing practices. These include gender norms and other standards intended to ensure social cohesion.

Liberal legalism is founded on philosophical presuppositions that are presented as universal, such as a binary ontology, a sovereign, pre-social subject, and an understanding of liberty as an individual asset that materialises in rights such as private property. At the same time, liberal legal doctrine ignores the way in which legal systems and processes are inserted in colonial or postcolonial

9 I use "liberal legalism" and "liberal legality", following Rosemary Hunter (2013), to refer to a set of assumptions found within law in societies and regimes in which liberalism is the dominant political philosophy.

relations of domination (Hernández Castillo, 2017). Thus, the universalising discourse of liberal law is colonial: it privileges Western ontologies and epistemologies, excluding from the realm of the juridical that which does not conform to the liberal paradigm. If, from a decolonial standpoint, race, gender, and class define who can produce knowledge and what counts as truth, then coloniality also determines what counts as justice. Consequently, legal coloniality produces patterns of thought and action that shape the strategies that political actors can use to address their interlocutors. More concretely, liberal legalism is the interpretive schema through which feminists channel their demands for justice and make sense of criminal law, thinking about it as an adequate institution to defend women's rights.

In Kapur's view, liberal legality, when used by those who have been excluded from the protection of law, conveys "precarious desires", which reproduce the same normative framework underlying the precarisation of the excluded group (2015, 2018). In her words: "[liberal] human rights advance a specific script of freedom" (2018, p. 46). That is, they reinscribe subordinate subjectivities in the hierarchies that enable colonial oppression because human rights are founded on a "narrow liberal ontology" (Golder, 2014, p. 79). Along these lines, human rights have been interpellated as devices that reproduce heteronormative, binarised, and asymmetrical scripts of sex/gender, while privileging certain lives over others (Kapur, 2015; McNeilly, 2014). Here, I add that human rights have historically sped up the erasure of non-Western forms of knowledge on gender, violence, and justice. Not only does rights-based penality justify punitivism; the liberal juridical field defines when and how women deserve to be protected and, in so doing, it alienates those who do not comply with the paradigm of the liberal adversarial subject. To benefit from law, as other researchers have suggested, one ought to conform to the dominant understandings of subjectivity and citizenship (Merry, 2003, 2006; Sieder & Sierra, 2011). In practice, litigation requires material and immaterial resources that are not accessible to those excluded from full citizenship. As I show in this book, human rights have expedited the dissemination of approaches to VAW that are abstract, non-redistributive, and adversarial.

This book also argues that liberal legal discourse facilitates three fundamental processes: (1) Encouraging/compelling the state to penally respond when women's human rights are violated; (2) Presenting the penal apparatus as a benign and rational system under principles that limit the state's punitive power; (3) Masking that penality prolongs the coloniality of gender and hinders women's access to protection and reparations. In the next subsection, I refer to the colonial dimensions of rights-based penality in particular, as developed in this book.

The colonial roots of rights-based penality

Critical historians have identified criminal law and policy as (re)producers of "normal and deviant" subjectivities in Latin America, beyond colonial rule

(Campos, 1996; Salvatore, 2001; Vidal López, 2003). Indeed, the penal apparatus has been a great ally to institutionalise colonial family paradigms, including through the surveillance of women's sexuality (Díaz, 2001; Guy, 2000; Rodríguez, 2000). The penal apparatus can thus be framed as a colonial system, not only because it legitimised imperial expansion, but also because it has continued to fix norms and make claims to truth based on principles that privilege Western norms.

While the universalisation of modern human rights is a post-Cold War phenomenon (Engle, 2015; Meister, 2011; Moyn, 2012), the use of criminal law to tackle VAW in Latin America is much older: Canonical Law and the Catholic Church have intervened in "marital disputes" since colonial times. In the early republican period, law prosecuted and punished violent husbands to ensure the preservation of family harmony. There is, indeed, a chronological and ideological convergence between human rights and neoliberalism but, in this book, I make the case for looking into older narratives on protecting women, to identify the colonial elements that may explain the contemporary, relatively easy reception, by the Ecuadorian legislature, of proposals to criminalise VAW. I contend that various rationales underpinning colonial and early republican laws on women and the family are present in today's legislation, often renovated by the human rights/penality assemblage. The construction of gender-based violence as a criminal offence, this book shows, is connected to the coloniality of gender. At the same time, human rights have not challenged the colonial continuities that underlie penality.

Presently, human rights have become the universal language to voice political demands and pursue social justice (Golder, 2014; Kennedy, 2004). Feminists operate in that globalised context. Unlike the Ecuadorian feminist and indigenous leaders who denounced legal violence in the mid-20th century (see Chapter 2), today's feminists almost never condemn gender-based violence without appealing to law and human rights. In Karen Engle's words: "since the beginning of the 21st century, the human rights movement has been almost synonymous with the fight against impunity" (2015, p. 1070). A key element of this rights-based penality is the idea that fighting impunity is essential to protect rights and ensure reparations. This has led to the centring of juridical mechanisms – namely, law reform and litigation – as strategies to obtain gender justice. In this way, advocacy documents such as the Shadow Reports to the CEDAW (an alternative account of women's status in a member state by non-governmental organisations), appeal to human rights, legal reform, and penalisation, in nearly every area of concern they address.[10]

Despite existing critiques of human rights as reproducers of a market-oriented model (Beckett, 2016; Douzinas, 2013; Harvey, 2005) and imperialist

10 See, for instance, Ecuador's 2015 Shadow Reports to the CEDAW (Coalición Nacional de Mujeres, 2014).

politics (Kennedy, 2004; Orford, 2003), progressive actors do not usually identify them as devices that carry patriarchal, neoliberal, or colonial connotations. To a great extent, this is because human rights provide "a universalist, moral, and supposedly neutral language that individuals can use in order to oppose the unjust exercise of state power" (Golder, 2015, p. 151). This book shows how feminists acknowledge some shortcomings of criminal justice, yet do not question human rights-based strategies to address VAW. Even Ecuador's 2008 Constitution, an ambitious political project that challenged neoliberalism and coloniality, did not scrutinise human rights as an element of the system it opposed. Of course, it has become impossible to allege democratic legitimacy without endorsing the punishment of human rights violations. Human rights thus play a decisive role in solving feminist ambivalence toward law reform and criminalisation. As I show in this book, human rights deliver a benign portrayal of criminal law, which renders prosecution and punishment conceptually coherent with protecting women.

Correspondingly, human rights are taken for granted as effective tools to moderate punitive power through a "constitutionalised" criminal law that respects due process (Ávila, 2013; Dubber, 2004; Ferrajoli, 1995). The double function of human rights as "shield and sword" regarding state force has been posited as a potentially irresolvable paradox (Tulkens, 2011). However, this book shows that it *is* the shield that enables the sword. Thinking of penality as progressive, democratic, and constitutional, makes it *desirable*. Then, once the sword has been enabled, it proves very difficult to contain, including at the level of carceral violence.

Importantly, this book does not deny that human rights can deliver powerful social messages and bring relief to those who pursue the legal recognition of their struggles (Lemaitre, 2009). Yet, revelling in the fruits of law should not weaken our caution when we use the "master's tools" (Lorde, 2018). Centring human rights and criminal justice may debilitate and displace radical critiques of power, and efface the experience of the most marginalised (Golder, 2015; Kapur, 2015; Kennedy, 2004). Therefore, it is still necessary to assess what the human rights-based juridification of gender justice brings to the day-to-day lives of underprivileged women. Violence survivors often experience law, courts, and litigation as providers of very precarious forms of protection that do not facilitate the overcoming of violence and can even make matters worse.

Overall, I posit rights-based penality as a colonial device through which women's demands are continuously mistranslated, by a liberal legal apparatus, into demands for law reform, criminalisation, and punishment. These mistranslations are colonial because they subdue the alternative knowledges that could decentre penality. Pursuing a criminal conviction requires, not only financial and social resources, but also a will to give up one's own understanding of fairness to accept what the criminal law offers: survivors' desire for protection is mistranslated, through rights-based penality, into an obligation to litigate. What is more, when women are unable or unwilling to advance a criminal trial, they are depicted as "deserters" of the law. Desiring something that is not penally coherent is seen as abandoning one's own right to access justice.

At this point, I shall remind the reader that, in Ecuador, many criminal law reforms on VAW and its judicial system have occurred during a time that has been considered "post-neoliberal". A time when many social and legal institutions were expected to be radically transformed. That context enables an interesting enquiry into the journey of penality into progressive politics. Next, I describe the ten-year period that this book centres as a key backdrop to understanding penality's pervasiveness.

Neoliberalism and the "post-neoliberal" alternative

In this subsection, I address my use of the term "post-neoliberal" to refer to the Citizen's Revolution in Ecuador (2007–2017). The term is important, not only as a chronological marker, but also because it designates a period when many policies that have been connected to neoliberal globalisation were, at least to some extent, reverted.

In Latin America, "neoliberalism" commonly alludes to the financing packages and restructuring requirements of the "Washington consensus", a rubric coined in 1989 to identify the views on development associated with Washington-based institutions such as the International Monetary Fund, the World Bank, and the United States Treasury (Serra et al., 2008). It was first proposed to describe policies that would replace the "old ideas of development economics that had governed Latin American economic policies since the 1950s" (Williamson, 2009, p. 7). Broadly, the measures comprise financial liberalisation, privatisation, openness to foreign investment, lower taxes, and small government (Tabb, 2004). These conditions are usually tied to lendings from international financial institutions. In Ecuador, after the return to democracy in the late 1970s, successive governments set out to "modernise the state", which translated into the privatisation of public services and the reduction of social welfare expenditure (Bedford, 2009; Endara, 1999). Paying the external debt was prioritised, and the budget for public education, health, and other services never amounted to the minimums established by law. This is the context in which the term "post-neoliberal" acquires significance.

For its part, post-neoliberalism is associated with the rise of a Latin American "New Left" (Grugel & Riggirozzi, 2012), a movement that shifted development thinking, by "systematically confront[ing] the mantras of neoliberal privatisation, state roll-back, and selective social programmes" (Radcliffe, 2012, p. 240). In Ecuador, the post-neoliberal era began with the rise to power of Rafael Correa, in 2007. His government endorsed what was then called the "socialism of living well":

> The Socialism of Living Well questions the hegemonic accumulation pattern, that is, the neoliberal way to produce, grow and distribute. We propose the transition to a society where life is the supreme good. We affirm the supremacy of labour – the goal itself of production and the basis to deploy talent – over capital. Through labour we recognise ourselves as social beings and creative actors, exercising rights and liberties.
>
> (SENPLADES, 2013)

Of course, there are complex debates regarding the extent to which the Citizen's Revolution was "truly" or "fully" anti-capitalist (Acosta & Cajas Guijarro, 2016; Álvarez et al., 2013; Dávalos, 2014). However, various authors have acknowledged that this period brought political stability to a country that had had too many ephemeral presidencies during the previous decade (Santos, 2015). The Citizen's Revolution also strengthened social welfare and reduced poverty by applying redistributive measures, including an increase of economic aids for impoverished people, external debt payment suspension, increase of financial aids for housing, increase of investments in public health, education and social security, and other courses of action that expanded public expenditure (Grugel & Riggirozzi, 2012; Grupo Banco Mundial, 2020; Ordóñez et al., 2015; Ospina, 2009). While I do not delve into the inner contradictions of the post-neoliberal government, I do write based on the assumption that the political shift was observable and merits asking questions about the prevalence of a punitive model during that period. Thus, I retain the terms "neoliberalism" and "post-neoliberalism" to emphasise how the case of Ecuador illustrates that redistributive agendas and punitive ones can very well coexist or even be the same.

To be clear, I am aware that neoliberalism has been posited as a form of "governmentality", that is, a rationality of governance that produces new kinds of political subjects and a new organisation of the social realm (Brown, 2005; Foucault, 2008; Oksala, 2013). From these perspectives, neoliberalism exceeds the realm of the economy and is extended to institutions and social practices. In that sense, the Citizen's Revolution could not be called "a-neoliberal". A pertinent question would be, for instance, whether neoliberal subjectivities were fully or partially contested in post-neoliberal Ecuador. However, the sense in which I use the term neoliberalism in this book is economic, historical, and legal: I am interested in the potential continuities between neoliberal and post-neoliberal legal frameworks, through colonial discourses and institutions. The post-neoliberal shift may or may not have resulted in fully formed "post-neoliberal subjectivities", but the prolongation of the legal institutions that had consolidated before and during the neoliberal years, and how they shaped current constructions of gender, is what this book brings to the forefront.

Interestingly, some of Ecuador's neoliberal governments are associated with the forced disappearances which occurred in the 1980s and 1990s, and which have been catalogued as state terrorism (Montúfar, 2000). Ecuadorian history does suggest that there is a nexus between neoliberalism, "tough on crime" programmes, and state violence. Yet, Ecuador's 2014 Penal Code, enacted during Correa's period, introduced over 70 new criminal offences, including "violence against women and the family unit". Correa himself accused some judges of being too lenient with people in preventive detention (Presidencia de la República, 2014). Carceral population increased exponentially thereafter (Valarezo, 2021). At the same time, many feminists promoting the criminalisation of VAW – and, interestingly, the decriminalisation of abortion – were militants of the Citizen's Revolution. This case, which can be seen as a mirror of other Latin American processes, requires us to complicate the question around the historical, social, and political factors that have made state penality central to feminist lawmaking in the field of VAW.

What a decolonial feminist critique of rights-based penality adds to the literature on "carceral feminism"

As noted above, "carceral feminism" refers to feminist theories and practices that have helped bolster the carceral state by demanding harsh penalties for gender-based violence. However, many feminist traditions have broadly questioned state policy as a route for feminist struggles,[11] and argued that investing in law reform may contribute to reproducing hegemonic power (Correa, 2008; Corrigan, 2006; Drakopoulou, 2008; Mendoza, 2002; Oksala, 2012; Smart, 1989). From these perspectives, law plays a role in perpetuating oppression by reinforcing and reproducing the categories and hierarchies that subordinate women. Criminal law presents even more challenges, because it is based on forms of coercion and sanction that are especially harmful to women. In this sense, strands of US-based black feminism have adopted an anticarceral/abolitionist stance, denouncing that carcerality oppresses already underprivileged groups, especially non-white minorities (Davis, 2000; Gilmore, 2007; Richie, 2012; Sudbury, 2005).

Ruth Gilmore (2007) has argued that penal expansion is not only a technique to manage the "surplus" population that results from capitalist dispossession, but is also a form of political "vengeance" against unruly subjectivities. This implies that there is more to penality than economic instrumentality. I widely agree with this stance; nevertheless, this book's findings do not indicate that certain men are being stigmatised as non-conforming subjects via criminal legislation on VAW. Prosecutions are usually initiated by a private complainant, and very rarely result in a conviction. The effects of criminalising VAW are different from other areas of criminal policy: the penal framing of VAW has not resulted in an enhanced surveillance of racialised/impoverished

11 For discussions of diverse feminist engagements with the state see Kantola (2006) and Kantola & Dahl (2005).

men; rather, hegemonic masculinity facilitates the dismissal, by police, of many reports and emergency calls on domestic violence. Yet, the pernicious effects of an expanding penality are severe: they translate into a common sense by which offering the possibility of a criminal trial equates to offering justice and protection, while no allocation of social services takes place.

These types of shortcomings have been addressed by Beth Richie (2012), who shows that a punitive legal system, promoted by conservative actors, prevents many black women from accessing services and protection from male violence. I agree that issues of race and class have not been sufficiently considered by mainstream feminist projects, though I augment that critique by emphasising how progressive politics *also* can, via rights-based penality, contribute to making women's access to services and protection more difficult.

In this sense, Naomi Murakawa (2014) has challenged the framing that links conservative politics to "tough on crime" right-wing discourses only. She reveals the associations between the US civil rights procedural justice reforms and prison expansion. In the same vein, in *The Prison and the Gallows* Marie Gottschalk (2006) argued that the victims' movement, the women's movement, the prisoners' rights movement, and opponents of the death penalty – "not the usual suspects" – have contributed to building the US carceral state. I make an argument that resonates with these critiques when I contend that feminist uses of penality are more connected to liberal criminal law and women's human rights than "dominance feminism" (Halley, 2008). However, my work diversifies the debate by centring the colonial history of Latin America as a key precedent of today's penal "common sense". I emphasise the coloniality of liberal legalism, its ability to frame and reshape feminist demands, and its inability to challenge colonial constructions of femininity and justice. Overall, my contribution is to show that human rights can curb the decolonial potential of post-neoliberal projects, including through VAW legislation.

A decolonial feminist approach provides a lens to inspect a non-neoliberal, but still colonial, endorsement of penality. In Ecuador, penality thrived through a programme that prioritised social redistribution and rejected neoliberalism, while incorporating self-identified feminists into various governing agencies. Moreover, penality thrived through a post-neoliberal Constitution that used anticolonial language. I hope to show that, if legal coloniality is not pinpointed and interrogated, penality can be portrayed as compatible with, and perhaps constitutive of, a redistributive feminist political project.

Finally, a feminist decolonial lens, paired with empirical methods, throws light on the complex effects of juridifying women's struggles through human rights and criminal law. Here, I demonstrate, via empirical research, that human rights are informing state approaches to VAW that centre litigation. Due to the existence of a specialised legal system that is allegedly responding to women's demands, the state neglects actual economic redistribution. Even when Ecuador's Citizen's Revolution reduced poverty and expanded public services, survivors of gender-based violence remained at the margins of state justice. This book shares a lesson on the role of human rights and liberal law in facilitating these exclusions.

A note on methods

Feminist and socio-legal research coincide in taking social experience and the grounded effects of law as focal points (Hunter, 2019). Law is a set of social processes embedded in historical and political contexts; not a device that operates according to its own internal logic, and outside of social life (Banakar & Travers, 2005; Creutzfeldt et al., 2019; Sarat & Silbey, 1987). My research is situated in this tradition, with an aim to reveal how legal discourses co-produce social reality, limit the scope of what can be said, and privilege some knowledges over others, thereby selectively empowering and disempowering people. In this book, I do not develop a technical analysis of the legislation, nor do I delve into how laws should have been designed. Likewise, I do not dig into the (many) technical inconsistencies of the laws I address. Rather, my methodology emphasises the implications of law and gender in reproducing and sustaining unequal power relations, and unearths how liberal legality moulds social struggles, social life, and social conflict. More specifically, I reveal how criminal law and human rights discourses condition what strategies feminists can use successfully, however radical their stance.

I consider this book's methodology to be itself a contribution to the legal literature on violence against women in Latin America. Much legal research carried out in the region relies on the doctrinal study and commentary of positive legislation and jurisprudence, particularly in criminal law. For my part, I have made an effort to bridge the gap between critical theories and empirical research. The methods I used are multiple and interdisciplinary: I combined document analysis, close readings of historic and current legislation, in-depth interviews, observation, and analyses of quantitative data. Documentary sources include parliamentary records, legal databases, press coverage, and feminist publications. As for fieldwork, between 2015 and 2019, I carried out 52 semi-structured interviews with self-identified feminist legislators and policymakers, non-governmental organisation (NGO) staff, public servers, activists, judges and officers specialising in VAW, caseworkers, and survivors of domestic violence. I also observed the activities of a university law clinic, the first-contact offices of specialised courts in Cuenca, two women's NGOs, and public debates on criminal law reform. This grounded look at the processes by which feminist interventions are articulated, allowed me to identify the diverse voices and narratives that are part of the diffuse power networks in which feminisms exist. These methods also revealed the effect of local political actors' manoeuvres on feminist law reform outcomes. It showed me that VAW legislation does not necessarily produce carceral expansion (though it does have problematic effects), and that feminists have a limited reign over the implementation of the laws they propose.

While conducting fieldwork, I reflected on my own position as a *mestiza* researcher, living in the "borderlands" (Anzaldúa, 1987), and utilising a decolonial approach to understand how law deserts so many women. The feminist networks I came in contact with were mostly composed of professional upper- and middle-class *mestizas*. The research design led me to these groups, because they are the ones that gained spaces as negotiators of legal change. Other collectives, including community-based associations and indigenous and Afro-Ecuadorian organisations, have been protagonists of women's emancipatory struggles; however, they have not prioritised criminal law reform as their strategy, for reasons that this book does address. In addition, although I often thought of myself as an "insider" of the feminist networks I was researching, I recognise that their commitments are different, and often more difficult than mine. As an academic, I have a relative freedom to interrogate mainstream legal doctrine, public policy, and authoritative discourses, given that my occupation does not normally entail negotiating, and implementing law and policy in a highly stratified and non-feminist political context.

Reflexivity became even more crucial when I interviewed violence survivors. I have been brown and female in an intensely racist and sexist society all my life. However, as a *mestiza*, I am somewhat privileged. I can, at times, "pass" as white, if not by way of skin colour, by way of formal education and material resources. I benefit from a position that lets me negotiate my status and resist some forms of power. Thus, I could never claim to speak *for* violence survivors, but I do speak *with* them. Listening to those who attempt to obtain legal protection while fighting abuse and dispossession, is urgent. Violence survivors are often cornered by legal rules and procedures that are not meaningful to them, but they are compelled to use under penalty of being denied legal protection. None of these complexities would have been evident without a decolonial, feminist, and socio-legal approach.

Finally, I will address some ethical issues. All of the interviewed violence survivors have been anonymised, as have most other participants. In some cases, I used the real names of feminist public figures, because they either asked me to, or were aware that they would be identifiable (for instance, the lawmakers that were part of a small legislative commission). All interviews were conducted in Spanish, and all translations are mine. I also translated Ecuadorian laws into English as well as the fragments of academic and advocacy documents not originally written in English. Ethical clearance for fieldwork was provided by the University of Kent and the University of Birmingham, at different stages of this project. Each chapter contains a more detailed description of the research techniques and sources I used.

Book overview

Chapter 1. Protecting women in postcolonial Latin America

This chapter presents a socio-legal framing of domestic violence in Ecuador and Latin America during the late 19th and early 20th centuries. First, I outline the critical and feminist theories on race, whiteness, and *mestizaje* (racial hybridisation) used in the book to address coloniality, domesticity, and penality. Then, based on an examination of historical civil and penal laws, and building on feminist historians' work on colonial and early-republican gender-state relations, I contend that coloniality has long informed the legal framing of family violence, and criminal law has long been used to govern populations and "optimise the race", including by reprehending "excessive" violence against women and children. Women's status as legal subjects historically emphasised their role as mothers with a duty to raise good (white-like) citizens. As a result, they were selectively protected and selectively penalised: white and white-like, middle-class, prudent mothers deserved legal protection, while non-conforming women, such as "adulterous" wives, "dishonest" women, and those who had an abortion, were criminalised. In sum, early legal interventions in the family were underpinned by a colonial regulation of gender, and aspirations to whiteness and Europeanness. These framings produced a "non-violent patriarchy" discourse that subsequent laws on violence against women would reproduce.

Chapter 2. Law was foe: women's movements in Ecuador before human rights

This chapter maps early feminist engagements with criminal law reform in Ecuador, including indigenous women, the Marxist left, the first non-governmental organisations, and the thought of critical legal thinkers in the late 20th century. Until the late 1980s, criminalising male aggression was not a priority for Ecuadorian women's movements: indigenous leaders and leftist feminists in the early 20th century viewed the state and its law as an abusive machinery to resist, while feminist authors and advocacy groups denounced law as a cause and reproducer of women's suffering. Early feminist law reform demands pursued the repeal of the criminal offences that discriminated against women. Appealing to criminal justice as a tool to protect women was not part of the feminist legal imaginary at that point. The chapter concludes that there was a clear "before" the dissemination of international human rights discourses on violence against women, which would later propel feminist uses of criminal law.

Chapter 3. Violence against women, human rights, and the turn to criminal law

This chapter discusses the correlation between the dissemination of women's human rights discourses, and the turn to criminal justice to counteract VAW in Ecuador and Latin America. From the 1990s onwards, many feminists began to view the criminalisation of VAW as indispensable to protect survivors. In addition, fields of study such as public health, psychology, and women in development, contributed to constructing gender-based violence as a social problem that required law reform. The interactions between local NGOs and international organisations enhanced the human rights-based frameworks and solidified the turn to criminal law, resulting in a "boom" of dedicated legislation in Latin America. In Ecuador, specialised commissariats were created in 1994 to process VAW complaints and, in 1995, the first specialised law on VAW passed. Tracing the political and legislative processes by which these legal system came to be, the chapter concludes that public officers and the legislature reframed violence against women as family violence, reshaping feminist demands. There was compatibility between older colonial ideologies and the demand to penalise domestic violence, which was decisive to enact the law.

Chapter 4. From neoliberal to post-neoliberal: the constitutional journey of rights-based penality

This chapter introduces "rights-based penality", a concept that highlights the role of human rights in encouraging penal responses to violence across the political spectrum. I compare two Ecuadorian Constitutions: first, the Constitution of 1998, which many consider emblematic of neoliberalism. This corpus recognised certain women's human rights for the first time, including personal integrity, which became the basis to criminalise gender-based violence. Second, the 2008 Constitution, which emerged as the political antithesis of its predecessor, during the "post-neoliberal" era. Although it introduced innovative insights from Andean cosmology and indigenous justice, its approach to VAW is almost identical to that of 1998. "Rights-based penality" addresses these paradoxes and shows how liberal legality undermines radical thought and indigenous understandings of justice: in Ecuador, constitutional judges have considered that activating the state's penal apparatus is the only legitimate response to human rights violations. The chapter concludes that, in portraying criminal law as a constitutionalised system, rights-based penality "solves" many of the problematic aspects of appealing to the state's coercive force, concealing the colonial underpinnings of criminal justice, and making it amenable to further expansion.

Chapter 5. A new penal code: criminalising violence against women using rights-based penality

This chapter examines how scholarly feminist discourses on VAW have integrated rights-based penality in Ecuador. It then traces the making of the 2014

Penal Code, which coincided with a reconfiguration of the women's movement, after the advent of the Citizen's Revolution. Feminist supporters of the government, who emphasised economic redistribution, were keen on criminalising VAW; for their part, NGO-based and other feminist critics of the officialism were more cautious, as they anticipated that ordinary criminal proceedings would be onerous and complex for complainants. In showing the tensions within the women's movement, the chapter nuances the discussion on carceral feminism and punitiveness as the main ambition of anti-VAW proposals. It also shows how rights-based penality has become a universal field of intelligibility to discuss gender inequality more broadly. However, rights-based penality has done little to disrupt hegemonic discourses on womanhood, domesticity, and sexuality. This was most evident when the initiative to decriminalise abortion in the case of rape was rejected by the legislature, as were other feminist proposals. Overall, the chapter contributes to revealing the concrete perils, for feminism, of rights-based penality as a universalised "progressive" framework to address VAW.

Chapter 6. Report from the field: women's experiences of using the specialised penal courts

This chapter presents the empirical findings of a project on women's experiences of reporting domestic violence to Ecuador's specialised courts. Based on quantitative and qualitative data, the chapter demonstrates that, although the legislation on VAW is not directly causing carceral expansion or enhanced police surveillance, it is failing to protect complainants, while masking the state's disregard of women's expectations and needs. A criminal trial is a cumbersome process that subjects survivors to inadequate police intervention, and subordinates legal protection to their willingness to pursue, and win at, a criminal trial. This is illustrated through the operation of the protection order, an instrument that constitutes the primary motivation for women to file a complaint, but is invalidated if they withdraw from the criminal trial. When complainants refrain from advancing the trial, they are made responsible for their own lack of protection. The chapter concludes that rights-based penality is producing a formalistic system that imposes its discourse and logic on women, while sidelining what they envision as justice, such as protection and access to public services.

Conclusion

In this epilogue, I bring together the various arguments made in the book and conclude that the challenges that law reform presents to feminists are complex and varied. Through a historicised account of liberal legality, looking at Ecuadorian women's engagements with law reform on VAW, this book has shown that penality is a colonial apparatus that has long been used to manage race, gender, and sexuality. In that context, when feminists have participated in governance, their proposals have been reshaped by non-feminist actors, frequently reproducing coloniality. Today, human rights principles are perceived by feminists, including those promoting economic redistribution, as tools that can both moderate punitive power and protect women, which makes the resort to criminal justice compatible with their emancipatory demands. Human rights are deeply entangled in the "punitive" feminist agenda. The turn to criminal law is, however, masking women's abandonment by the state: survivors have formal access to litigation but very few material resources to overcome their predicaments. The book arrives to the conclusion that a decolonial feminist critique of penality should start by interrogating liberal legalism, unlearning the equation between penal responses and legal protection, and questioning human rights' penality, as well as human rights' insufficiency to disrupt coloniality.

References

Acosta, A., & Cajas Guijarro, J. (2016). Ocaso y muerte de una revolución que al parecer nunca nació. *Ecuador Debate, 98*, 7–28.

Aguirre Salas, A., Léon, T., & Ribadeneira González, N.S. (2020). Sistema penitenciario y población penalizada durante la Revolución Ciudadana (2007–2017). *URVIO: Revista Latinoamericana de Estudios de Seguridad, 27*, 94–110.

Álvarez, F., Ávila, R., Castro, C., Cuvi, J., Dávalos, P., Torre, C.D. la, Hidalgo, F., Isch, E., Machado, D., Martínez, E., Martínez, M., Meireles, M., Melo, M., Muñoz, F., Ospina, P., Oviedo, A., Sierra, N., Solíz, F., Unda, M., … Villavicencio, A. (2013). *El correísmo al desnudo* (1st ed.). Montecristi Vive.

Amar, P. (2013). *The security archipelago: Human-security states, sexuality politics, and the end of neoliberalism*. Duke University Press.

Anzaldúa, G. (1987). *Borderlands/La Frontera: The New Mestiza*. Spinsters/Aunt Lute.

Ávila, R. (2013). *La (in)justicia penal en la democracia constitucional de derechos. Una mirada desde el garantismo penal*. Ediciones Legales.

Aviram, H. (2020). Progressive punitivism: Notes on the use of punitive social control to advance social justice ends. *Buffalo Law Review, 68*, 199.

Banakar, R., & Travers, M. (2005). *Law, sociology and method* (R. Banakar & M. Travers (eds.)). Hart Publishing.

Beckett, J. (2016). *Creating poverty* (A. Orford, F. Hoffman, & M. Clark (eds.); pp. 985–1010). Oxford University Press.

Bedford, K. (2009). *Developing partnerships: Gender, sexuality, and the reformed World Bank*. University of Minnesota Press.

Bernstein, E. (2010). Militarized humanitarianism meets carceral feminism: The politics of sex, rights, and freedom in contemporary antitrafficking campaigns. *Signs, 36*(1), 45–72.

Borón, A. (2003). *El pos-neoliberalismo: un proyecto en construcción* (E. Sader & P. Gentili (eds.); pp. 78–83). Consejo Latinoamericano de Ciencias Sociales..

Brown, W. (2005). *Edgework. Critical essays on knowledge and politics*. Princeton University Press

Campos, M.Z. (1996). *Vicious women, virtuous women: The female delinquent and the Santiago de Chile Correctional House, 1860–1900* (R. Salvatore & C. Aguirre (eds.)). University of Texas Press.

Christie, N. (2000). *Crime control as industry. Towards gulags, western style*. Routledge.

Coalición Nacional de Mujeres. (2014). *Informe sombra al comité de la CEDAW. Ecuador-2014*. Coalición Nacional de Mujeres. https://tbinternet.ohchr.org/Treaties/CEDAW/Shared%20Documents/ECU/INT_CEDAW_NGO_ECU_18897_S.pdf

Correa, S. (2008). *Cruzando la línea roja: cuestiones no resueltas en el debate sobre los derechos sexuales* (I. Szasz & G. Salas (eds.); pp. 25–55). El Colegio de México.

Corrigan, R. (2006). Making meaning of Megan's Law. *Law & Social Inquiry: Journal of the American Bar Foundation, 31*(2), 267–312.

Creutzfeldt, N., Mason, M., & McConnachie, K. (2019). *Routledge handbook of socio-legal theory and methods*. Routledge.

Dávalos, P. (2014). *Alianza País o la reinvención del poder*. Ediciones desde abajo.

Davis, A.Y. (2000). Masked racism: Reflections on the prison industrial complex. *Indigenous Law Bulletin, 4*(27). https://doi.org/http://www5.austlii.edu.au/au/journals/IndigLawB/2000/12.html

Dean, C. (2001). *Andean androgyny and the making of men* (C.F. Klein (ed.); pp. 143–177). Dumbarton Oaks Research Library and Collection.

Dean, M. (2002). Powers of life and death beyond governmentality. *Cultural Values, 6*(1–2), 119–138.

de la Vega, G. (2000). *Comentarios reales*. Editorial Castalia.

Díaz, A. (2001). *Women, order and progress in Guzmán Blanco's Venezuela, 1870–1888* (R. Salvatore, C. Aguirre, & J. Guilbert (eds.)). Duke University Press.

Dieterich, H. (2009, March 11). *El gran salto adelante del Socialismo del Siglo XXI*. Rebelión. https://rebelion.org/el-gran-salto-adelante-del-socialismo-del-siglo-xxi/

Douzinas, C. (2013). The paradoxes of human rights. *Constellations, 20*(1), 51–67.

Drakopoulou, M. (2008 01). Feminism, governmentality and the politics of legal reform. *Griffith Law Review, 17*(1), 330–356.

Dubber, M.D. (2004). Toward a constitutional law of crime and punishment. *The Hastings Law Journal, 55*, 1–77.

Endara, X. (1999). *Modernización del Estado y reforma jurídica, Ecuador 1992–1996*. Universidad Andina Simón Bolívar.

Engle, K. (2015). Anti-impunity and the turn to criminal law in human rights. *Cornell Law Review, 100*(5), 1069.

Escobar, A. (2013). Worlds and knowledges otherwise. The Latin American modernity/coloniality research program. In W. Mignolo & A. Escobar (eds.), *Globalization and the decolonial option* (pp. 33–64). Routledge.

Ferrajoli, L. (1995). *Derecho y razón. Teoría del garantismo penal* (Vol. 2). Editorial Trotta.

FLACSO Ecuador. (2015, August 26). *Aníbal Quijano en el III Congreso Latinoamericano y Caribeño de Ciencias Sociales*. Youtube. https://www.youtube.com/watch?v=OxL5KwZGvdY

Fleetwood, J. (2014). *Drug mules: Women in the international cocaine trade*. Palgrave Macmillan.

Foucault, M. (1991). *The Foucault effect: Studies in governmentality*. University of Chicago Press.

Foucault, M. (2008). *The birth of biopolitics: Lectures at the College De France, 1978–79*. Palgrave Macmillan.

Garland, D. (1985). *Punishment and welfare: A history of penal strategies*. Gower.

Garland, D. (2012). *The culture of control: Crime and social order in contemporary society*. University of Chicago Press.

Gilmore, R.W. (2007). *Golden gulag. Prisons, surplus, crisis, and opposition in globalizing California*. University of California Press.
Gilmore, R.W. (2017). In the shadow of the shadow state. In INCITE! (ed.), *The revolution will not be funded. Beyond the non-profit industrial complex*. Duke University Press.
Golder, B. (2014). Beyond redemption? Problematising the critique of human rights in contemporary international legal thought. *London Review of International Law, 2*(1), 77–114.
Golder, B. (2015). *Foucault and the politics of rights*. Stanford University Press.
Goodmark, L. (2018). *Decriminalizing domestic violence: A balanced policy approach to intimate partner violence* (1st ed.). University of California Press.
Gotell, L. (2015). Reassessing the place of criminal law reform in the struggle against sexual violence. In A. Powell, N. Henry, & A. Flynn (eds.), *Rape justice: Beyond the criminal law* (pp. 53–71). Palgrave Macmillan UK.
Gottschalk, M. (2006). *The Prison and the Gallows: The politics of mass incarceration in America*. Cambridge University Press.
Grosfoguel, R. (2007). Descolonizando los universalismos occidentales: el pluri-versalismo transmoderno decolonial desde Aimé Césaire hasta los zapatistas. In S. Castro-Gómez & R. Grosfoguel (eds.), *El giro decolonial. Reflexiones para una diversidad epistémica más allá del capitalismo global* (pp. 63–77). Siglo del Hombre Editores.
Grugel, J., & Riggirozzi, P. (2012). Post-neoliberalism in Latin America: Rebuilding and reclaiming the state after crisis. *Development and Change, 43*(1), 1–21.
Grupo Banco Mundial. (2020, March). *Ecuador*. Banco Mundial. https://datos.bancomundial.org/pais/ecuador
Guamán Poma de Ayala, F. (1980). *La nueva crónica y buen gobierno* (F. Pease García (ed.)). Fundación Librería Ayacucho.
Guy, D.J. (2000). *White slavery and mothers alive and dead: The troubled meeting of sex, gender, public health, and progress in Latin America* (Vol. 5). University of Nebraska Press.
Halley, J. (2008 04). *Split decisions: How and why to take a break from feminism*. Princeton University Press.
Halley, J., Kotiswaran, P., Shamir, H., & Rebouché, R. (2018). *Governance feminism: An introduction*. University of Minnesota Press.
Hart, E.L., Greener, J., & Moth, R. (2020). *Resist the punitive state: Grassroots struggles across welfare, housing, education and prisons*. Pluto Press.
Harvey, D. (2005). *A brief history of neoliberalism*. Oxford University Press.
Hernández Castillo, R.A. (2017). Activismo legal y talleres penitenciarios. Las paradojas de la antropología juridica feminista y del trabajo cultural en espacios de reclusión. In R.A. Hernández Castillo (ed.), *Resistencias penitenciarias. Investigación activista de espacios de reclusión* (pp. 51–82). Juan Pablos Editor.
Howe, A. (1994). *Punish and critique. Towards a feminist analysis of penality*. Routledge.
Hunter, R. (2013). *Contesting the dominant paradigm: Feminist critiques of liberal legalism* (M. Davies & V. Munro (eds.); pp. 13–30). Ashgate.
Hunter, R. (2019). Feminist approaches to socio-legal studies. In N. Creutzfeldt, M. Mason, & K. McConnachie (eds.), *Routledge handbook of socio-legal theory and methods* (p. 260). Routledge.
INEC. (2019). *Violencia de Género*. Instituto Nacional de Estadística Y Censos. https://www.ecuadorencifras.gob.ec/violencia-de-genero/
Iqbal, S. (2018). *Women, business, and the law 2018* (No. 125804; pp. 1–187). The World Bank. http://documents.worldbank.org/curated/en/926401524803880673/Women-Business-and-the-Law-2018

Kampwirth, K. (2011). *Latin America's new left and the politics of gender: Lessons from Nicaragua.* Springer.

Kantola, J. (2006). *Feminists theorize the state.* Palgrave Macmillan.

Kantola, J., & Dahl, H.M. (2005). Gender and the State: From differences between to differences within. *International Feminist Journal of Politics*, 7(1), 49–70.

Kapur, R. (2015). Precarious desires and ungrievable lives: Human rights and postcolonial critiques of legal justice. *London Review of International Law*, *3*(2), 267–294.

Kapur, R. (2018). *Gender, alterity and human rights: Freedom in a fishbowl.* Edward Elgar Publishing Ltd.

Kennedy, D. (2004). *The dark sides of virtue. Reassesing international humanitarianism.* Princeton University Press.

Kim, M.E. (2019). Anti-carceral feminism: The contradictions of progress and the possibilities of counter-hegemonic struggle. *Affilia*, *35*(3), 309–326.

Law, V. (2014). *Against carceral feminism.* Jacobin. https://www.jacobinmag.com/2014/10/against-carceral-feminism/

Lemaitre, J. (2009). *El derecho como conjuro: fetichismo legal, violencia y movimientos sociales.* Siglo del Hombre Editores.

Lorde, A. (2018). *The master's tools will never dismantle the master's house (penguin modern)* (Kindle ed.). Penguin.

Lugones, M. (2007). Heterosexualism and the colonial/modern gender system. *Hypatia*, *22*(1), 186.

Lugones, M. (2009). Hacia una lectura decolonial de Chacha-Warmi. *Reunión Anual de Etnología*, *II*, 153.

Lugones, M. (2010). Toward a decolonial feminism. *Hypatia*, *25*(4), 742–759.

Mariátegui, J.C. (1928/2009). *Siete ensayos de interpretación de la realidad peruana.* Linkgua.

Masson, A. (2020). A critique of anti-carceral feminism. *Journal of International Women's Studies*, *21*(3), 64–76.

Mavronicola, N., & Lavrysen, L. (2020). Coercive human rights: Introducing the sharp edge of the European Convention on Human Rights. In *Coercive human rights: Positive duties to mobilise the criminal law under the ECHR* (pp. 1–26). Hart.

McNeilly, K. (2014). Gendered violence and international human rights: Thinking non-discrimination beyond the sex binary. *Feminist Legal Studies*, *22*(3), 263–283.

Meister, R. (2011). *After evil: A politics of human rights.* Columbia University Press.

Mendoza, B. (2002). Transnational feminisms in question. *Feminist Theory*, *3*(3), 295–314.

Mendoza, B. (2016). Coloniality of gender and power: From postcoloniality to decoloniality. In L. Disch & M. Hawkesworth (eds.), *The Oxford Handbook of Feminist Theory* (p. 100). Oxford University Press.

Merry, S.E. (2003). Rights talk and the experience of law: Implementing women's human rights to protection from violence. *Human Rights Quarterly*, *25*(2), 343–381.

Merry, S.E. (2006). *Human rights and gender violence: Translating international law into local justice.* University of Chicago Press.

Mignolo, W. (2000). *Local histories/global designs: Coloniality, subaltern knowledges, and border thinking.* Princeton University Press.

Mignolo, W. (2005). *The idea of Latin America* (1st ed.). Blackwell Publishing.

Montúfar, C. (2000). *La reconstrucción neoliberal: Febres Cordero o la estatización del neoliberalismo en el Ecuador, 1984–1988.* Abya-Yala.

Moraña, M., Dussel, E., & Jáuregui, C. (2008). *Colonialism and its replicants* (M. Moraña, E. Dussel, & C. Jáuregui (eds.); pp. 1–20). Duke University Press.

Moyn, S. (2012). *The last Utopia: Human rights in history* (Reprint ed.). Belknap Press.

Murakawa, N. (2014). *The first civil right: How liberals built prison America*. Oxford University Press.

Oksala, J. (2012). *Foucault, politics, and violence*. Northwestern University Press.

Oksala, J. (2013). Feminism and neoliberal governmentality. *Foucault Studies, 16*, 32–53.

Ordóñez, A., Samman, E., Mariotti, C., & Borja Borja, I.M. (2015, October). *Sharing the fruits of progress: Poverty reduction in Ecuador*. Overseas Development Institute. https://www.odi.org/publications/9958-sharing-fruits-progress-poverty-reduction-ecuador

Orford, A. (2003). *Reading humanitarian intervention. Human rights and the use of force in international law*. Cambridge University Press.

Ospina, P. (2009). *Historia de un desencuentro: Rafael Correa y los movimientos sociales en el Ecuador (2007–2008)* (R. Hoetmer (ed.); pp. 195–218). Universidad Nacional Mayor de San Marcos.

Pachacuti Yamqui Salcamaygua, J. de S.C. (1993). *Relacion de antiguedades deste reyno del Piru* (P. Duviols & C. Itier (eds.); pp. 117–118). Institut français d'études andines.

Pérez, M. (2019). El antipunitivismo como utopía cotidiana. In XIX Congreso Nacional AFRA, Mar del Plata. https://www.aacademica.org/moira.perez/59

Pérez, M., & Radi, B. (2020). Gender punitivism: Queer perspectives on identity politics in criminal justice. *Criminology & Criminal Justice: The International Journal of Policy and Practice, 20*(5), 523–536, 1748895820941561.

Pinto, M. (2020). Sowing a " Culture of Conviction" what shall domestic criminal justice systems reap from coercive human rights? In L. Lavrysen & N. Mavronicola (eds.), *Coercive human rights: Positive duties to mobilise the criminal law under the ECHR (Hart studies in security and justice)*. Hart Publishing.

Presidencia de la República. (2014). *"Vamos a vencer a la inseguridad": Presidente Correa*. Presidencia de La República Del Ecuador. https://www.presidencia.gob.ec/vamos-a-vencer-a-la-inseguridad-presidente-correa/

Quijano, A. (2000). Colonialidad del poder y clasificación social. *Journal of World-Systems Research, XI*(2), 342–386.

Radcliffe, S.A. (2012). Development for a postneoliberal era? Sumak kawsay, living well and the limits to decolonisation in Ecuador. *Geoforum, 43*(2), 240–249.

Richie, B.E. (2012). *Arrested justice*. New York University Press.

Rodríguez, E. (2000). *Civilizing domestic life in the central valley of Costa Rica, 1750–1850* (E. Dore & M. Molyneux (eds.); pp. 85–107). Duke University Press.

Salvatore, R. (2001). *Death and liberalism: Capital punishment after the fall of Rosas* (R. Salvatore, C. Aguirre, & J. Guilbert (eds.); pp. 308–341). Duke University Press.

Salvatore, R., & Aguirre, C. (eds.). (1996). *The birth of the penitentiary in Latin America*. University of Texas Press.

Santos, B.D.S. (2015). ¿La Revolución ciudadana tiene quién la defienda? *Estudios latinoamericanos, 36*, 133–138.

Sarat, A., & Silbey, S. (1987). Critical traditions in law and society research. *Law & Society Review, 21*(1), 165–174.

Scott, D. (2013). Why Prison? Posing the question. In D. Scott (ed.), *Why prison?* (pp. 1–22). Cambridge University Press.

Segato, R.L. (2014). La perspectiva de la Colonialidad del Poder y el giro descolonial. In J.L. Coraggio & J.-L. Laville (eds.), *Reinventar la izquierda en el siglo XXI. Hacia un diálogo Norte-Sur*. Universidad Nacional de General Sarmiento.

Segato, R.L. (2016). *La guerra contra las mujeres*. Traficantes de Sueños.

SENPLADES. (2013). *Plan Nacional del Buen Vivir 2013–2017 de Ecuador*. Secretaría Nacional de Planificación y Desarrollo.

Serra, N., Spiegel, S., & Stiglitz, J.E. (2008). *Introduction: From the Washington consensus towards a new global governance* (N. Serra & J.E. Stiglitz (eds.); pp. 3–13). Oxford University Press.

Sieder, R., & Sierra, M.T. (2011). *Acceso a la justicia para las mujeres indígenas en América Latina* (WP 2011:2). Michelsen Institute.

Simon, J. (2007). *Governing through crime: How the war on crime transformed American democracy and created a culture of fear*. Oxford University Press.

Smart, C. (1989). *Feminism and the power of law*. Routledge.

Snider, L. (1998). Towards safer societies: Punishment, masculinities and violence against women. *The British Journal of Criminology, 38*(1), 1–39.

Sozzo, M. (2016). *Postneoliberalismo y penalidad en América del Sur. A modo de introducción* (M. Sozzo (ed.); pp. 9–28). CLACSO.

Spivak, G.C. (1988). *Can the subaltern speak?* (C. Nelson & L. Grossberg (eds.)). University of Illinois Press.

Stoler, A.L. (1995). *Race and the education of desire: Foucault's history of sexuality and the colonial order of things*. Duke University Press.

Sudbury, J. (ed.). (2005). *Global lockdown: Race, gender, and the prison-industrial complex*. Routledge.

Tabb, W. (2004). *Economic governance in the age of globalization*. Columbia University Press.

Tapia Tapia, S. (2021). Beyond carceral expansion: Survivors' experiences of using specialised courts for violence against women in Ecuador. *Social & Legal Studies, 30*(6), 848–868, 0964663920973747.

Taylor, C. (2018). Anti-carceral feminism and sexual assault: A defense a critique of the critique of the critique of carceral feminism. *Social Philosophy Today, 34*, 29–49.

Terwiel, A. (2020). What is carceral feminism? *Political Theory, 48*(4), 421–442.

Torres Angarita, A.I. (2007). *Drogas y criminalidad femenina en Ecuador: el amor como un factor explicativo en la experiencia de las mulas* (M. Prieto Noguera (ed.)) [Master in Social Sciences, FLACSO sede Ecuador]. http://repositorio.flacsoandes.edu.ec/handle/10469/1317

Tulkens, F. (2011). The paradoxical relationship between criminal law and human rights. *Journal of International Criminal Justice, 9*(3), 577–595.

Tupiza Aldaz, A., & Guerra Páez, V. (2019). *Boletín criminológico y de estadística delictual. Femicidio*. Fiscalía General del Estado.

Valarezo, G. (2021, January 7). *Análisis y cifras sobre la situación de los derechos humanos en Ecuador*. Grupo Faro. https://elecciones2021.ecuador-decide.org/derechos-humanos-3/

Vidal López, R. (2003). Propuestas para una ciencia social del derecho. In M. García Villegas & C. Rodríguez Garavito (eds.), *Derecho y Sociedad En América Latina: Un Debate Sobre Los Estudios Jurídicos Críticos* (pp. 127–142). Universidad Nacional de Colombia.

Wacquant, L. (2009). *Punishing the poor: The neoliberal government of social insecurity*. Duke University Press.

Whalley, E., & Hackett, C. (2017). Carceral feminisms: The abolitionist project and undoing dominant feminisms. *Contemporary Justice Review, 20*(4), 456–473.

Williamson, J. (2009). A short history of the Washington Consensus. *Law & Business Review of the Americas, 15*(1), 7–23.

Chapter 1

Protecting women in postcolonial Latin America

Introduction

This chapter situates Latin America as a postcolonial site, where colonial ideologies have informed criminal laws on domesticity and the family long before the late 20th century's feminist interventions in violence against women (VAW). The legal construction of women as subjects of legal protection has historically been mediated by the preservation of the traditional family as a goal of law and policy, with an aim to consolidate national identity.[1] This chapter shows that, contrary to the common idea that the state was "blind" to violence in domestic spaces, penal legislation has long been used to reprehend "excessive" violence against women and children since the colonial period, and well into the republican years. Acknowledging the racialised nature of nation-making projects, and the role of domestic violence policy in that context, is indispensable to understand the historical production of gendered political identities and the role of coloniality in contemporary legal discourses on VAW.

Because a deeply conservative bias has characterised Ecuadorian and Latin American historical writing (Murray, 2010), this chapter is based on content analysis of historical legislation and the work of feminist historians who have researched gender–state relations in the 19th and early 20th centuries. Feminist authors have unveiled that nation-building projects in the region featured elements from eugenics to "improve the national race" by purifying it from "poisons" that were associated with racial inferiority (Clark, 2001; Stepan, 1991). In turn, deviance has almost always been construed alongside gender and race (Campos, 1996; Stepan, 1991; Walker, 2001); that is, there is a close link between race, gender, and nation-making (Dore & Molyneux, 2000; Radcliffe & Westwood, 1996). Through these connections, law and policy on domesticity and family life have incorporated and produced hierarchies based on race,

1 The term "national identity" is understood here as a normalising discourse that the state has often utilised to channel power relations, resulting in a continuous constitution and reconstitution of subjectivities and identities which in turn takes place in different, often fragmented sites where space, time, history, and culture are articulated (Radcliffe & Westwood 1993).

DOI: 10.4324/9781003098799-2

sexuality, and class, which have not been questioned after the advent of human rights frameworks. Colonial family ideals, fostered through the legal protection of women's modesty to optimise their role as mothers and wives, have long mediated state responses to domestic violence.

Despite their rhetorical endorsement of liberalism and the concepts of freedom and equality, the *criollo*[2] ruling elites of early republican Latin America did not in practice challenge the social hierarchies that had been established in the colonial period. Rather, they were prone to "denigrate the local and value the West" (Radcliffe & Westwood, 1996, p. 13) and, as Stepan puts it: "the educated classes [...] wished to be white and feared they were not" (1991, p. 45). Colonially imposed distinctions such as caste, profession, and family name, which had structured society prior to the permeation of liberal ideas in the 18th century, remained central to political life (Guy, 2000).

Critical accounts of law and race have emphasised the economic and phenomenological implications of racialised subjectification (Ahmed, 2007; Harris, 1993; Quijano, 2000). In addition, some Latin American theorists have pointed out the moral and cultural connotations of white and non-white identities. According to Ecuadorian-Mexican scholar Bolívar Echeverría (2009), the first instances of modern racism can be found in 16th century Latin America, where a rich and open anthropological-theological discussion revolved around questions such as: "do Indians have a soul?" And, "are Indians fully or only partially human?" (Echeverría, 2009; Radcliffe & Westwood, 1996). The moral connotations of racial division are reflected in Echeverría's definition of racism: it consists of addressing other people through the filter of a previous determination that qualifies their appearance as *ethically* meaningful. Echeverría (2007) argues that "identitarian racism" produces whiteness as an ethical and civilisational order. For instance, a concept of ancient Iberian origin, "honour", has helped rationalise the race and class-based social hierarchy of late-colonial and postcolonial Latin America (Murray, 2010). Modern citizenship requires the whiteness, or "whiteyness" (*blanquitud*) of its members. Nevertheless, whiteyness can be acquired to an extent through education and the modification of behaviour; that is, an ethnically non-white person can become white-like (*blanquearse*) and acquire whiteyness (Echeverría, 2007). *Blanqueamiento* (becoming white-like) is a process that is tied to economic and political relations that also involves culture, identity, and values (Radcliffe & Westwood, 1996). Therefore, the narrative of *mestizaje* (racial hybridisation) in Latin America is, at its heart, an aspiration to whiteness.

2 *Criollo/a* refers to a person of white European descent who was born in the Americas. In Latin America, the ruling classes after the independence wars were formed by Europeans and *criollos*, while indigenous people, Afro-descendants, and sometimes mixed people, were excluded from governing positions.

With this backdrop, we can understand how the idea of racial miscegenation, *mestizaje,* has been incorporated into law and policy in the region. Breny Mendoza (2001) has defined *mestizaje* as a technology of power that interweaves race, gender, sex, and class, and shapes colonial and postcolonial societies. *Mestizaje* is, in its origin, the product of violence: "the Spaniard rapes the Indian woman and then abandons her and the [*mestizo*] child born of this union" (Mendoza, 2001, p. 271). Hence, *mestizaje* produces a masculine-*mestizo* symbolic order, whereby racism, sexuality, and colonial subjugation are intertwined. *Mestizaje* is one of the axes around which power relations based on stratification by race, gender, class, and sexuality have been articulated, from the colonial era to the present.

After the independence wars, the *criollo* and white-*mestizo* elites faced the challenge of bringing together very heterogeneous peoples and communities to build the new nations. The idea of a modern republic included a rhetoric by which *mestizaje* (hybridity) was the norm, and exclusive ethnicities were archaic (Radcliffe & Westwood, 1996). As Mendoza puts it: "almost all traces of [an individual's] biological and social existence are suppressed, even in the demographic censuses, in order to erect a [national identity] based on a supposedly full and total *mestizaje*" (2001, p. 259). In many ways, this narrative erased racism as a governance problem, but the connotations of *mestizaje* were in practice evocative of a desire for social whiteness, and produced various forms of internalised racism.

To me, it is important to remark that the *mestiza*[3] (despite the rhetoric that attempts to use the term as egalitarian or multicultural), is still, primarily, a non-white subject.[4] As a consequence, because most inhabitants of the postcolony are non-white, they are dependent on diverse forms of *blanqueamiento,* with all its class and gender implications, to have full access to citizenship. Darker skin means more indigenous and/or African blood, and thus a longer path to walk to become a citizen. Put in a different way, becoming a citizen is

3 In Latin America, the words *mestiza* and *mestizo* traditionally refer to people of mixed ancestry (white and indigenous). Gloria Anzaldúa has vindicated the word *mestiza.* To her, "new mestizas" inhabit multiple worlds because of their gender, sexuality, colour, class, body, and other life experiences. "Mestiza consciousness" refers to a nonbinary way of thinking and acting that includes a transformational tolerance for contradiction and ambivalence (Keating, 2009). In this chapter, I use *mestizaje* in its more traditional sense, although I do include Afro-descendants under the term, which has not always been the case in the historical use of the word.

4 Some regions in Latin America use the term *trigueño.* This is more evocative of skin colour as such, and usually includes mixed people of African descent alongside white and indigenous ancestry. The term is "part of many Latin Americans' popular imaginary about themselves given the difficulty of knowing where they actually come from, and a label officially endorsed by many states to refer to the bulk of their citizens" (Eslava, 2020, para. 7). For a fascinating ethnographic account of the term in Latin America see Luis Eslava's (forthcoming) chapter on "trigueño international law", in Out of Place: Power, Person and Difference in Socio-Legal Research.

largely to become white-like and being able to use the law for one's benefit, it is necessary to be a citizen.

The governmental practices of producing social and cultural whiteness in the early republican period partly relied on the views of neo-Lamarckian eugenics, including ideas regarding the inheritance of acquired characters. In her landmark work, *The hour of eugenics*, Nancy Stepan (1991) argues that Latin America is significant as a case study because it historically challenged the more common "mainline" (Mendelian) eugenics. Lamarckism developed the idea that changes induced in a living organism from the outside can be handed on to future generations. Following Lamarckian theories, Latin American eugenicists understood many diseases, such as tuberculosis or syphilis, as well as behavioural issues, such as alcoholism, as hereditary (Stern, 2016). They referred to these threats as "racial poisons", a term used in the early 20th century to describe the "contamination" of the race. At the same time, backwardness was associated with indigenous and Afro-descendant identities. Behind the idea of the *raza mestiza* as one "national race", we find practices that regarded *mestizaje* as a pollutant that was conducive to degeneration and degradation. Legislation and public policy were thus expected to provoke a modification of behaviour that could contribute to whitening and "civilising" the population.

In that context, the archetypical family, which aspired to aristocratic, white, and heterosexual models, served as the starting point to form a national identity and an optimal citizenry. The ruling elites saw the family as the nucleus that could give the new independent territories the required stability to build a solid nation-state. In sum, as Donna Guy (1991) puts it: the notion of citizenship in Latin America emerges from the conflation of family and nation. Along these lines, I next outline the legal discourses that produced femininity and domesticity in the early republican period.

Race, gender, and the postcolonial legal field

Given their common colonial history, Latin American countries have considerable legal homogeneity. Precolonial institutions are known to us mainly through the lens of the colonisers' chronicles, and via colonialist social sciences; however, critical historians and anthropologists have shown that complex administrative and legal institutions existed in precolonial empires (Vidal López, 2003). During the colonial period, interlegality (Santos, 1995), that is, a sustained interaction between pre-Hispanic and colonial regulations, produced the Latin American juridical field. Some key legal elements introduced by the European invasion included medieval Spanish Law, Roman Law, and the Canon Law of the Catholic Church.

Later, the independence processes called into question certain aspects of the colonial socio-legal field; for instance, Vidal López (2003) has noted that republican intellectuals pursued a conceptual and political separation from Spain, whilst establishing an intellectual and legal connection with France and, later, with England. Still, the elites and the Catholic Church preserved much of their power after the independence wars. The adoption, via constitutional law, of abstract legal concepts such as the "general will" and "the citizenry" played a legitimising role that sustained liberal legal discourse but did not disrupt the colonial stratification of society, including the servitude of indigenous people and the enslavement of Afro-descendants.

Today, most Latin American countries base their legislation on the continental European Civil Law tradition, which is in turn based on Roman Law and historical legal bodies such as the *Siete Partidas* of King Alfonso "The Wise" and the Napoleonic Civil Code. Unlike common law, civil law systems rely on detailed written legislation, which judges ought to apply "literally", as opposed to creating binding case law. For example, the Civil Code of Ecuador has mandated since 1860:

> Art. 3.- It is only up to the Legislator to explain or interpret the law in a generally mandatory way. Judicial sentences do not have binding force except for the causes in which they are pronounced.
>
> (*Código Civil*, 1860)

> Art. 18.- Judges cannot suspend or deny the administration of justice due to obscurity or lack of law. In such cases they will judge according to the following rules: 1. When the meaning of the law is clear, its *literal* tenor will not be neglected on the pretext of consulting its spirit.
>
> (*Código Civil*, 2005, emphasis added)

Even today, while high courts have the power to review inferior judicial decisions and issue binding judgments, most judges decide only for each individual case. The symbolic power of law is not located at the level of the trial or the judgment, as much as at the level of the written codes and their reform. Because legal change comes about mainly through the legislature, law reform is regarded as a sign of cultural and/or political transformation. García Villegas and Rodríguez Garavito have commented that "we [Latin Americans] hold the idea that social destiny is linked to crucial legal decisions" (2003, p. 23). At the same time, law is perceived in an ambivalent fashion, "not only as an instrument of class domination but also as a future prescription for social redemption. It both evokes resistance and inspires hope" (García Villegas & Rodríguez Garavito, 2003, p. 23).

As mentioned above, optimising the nation in the young republics was posited as a governmental goal that could be achieved by modifying the conduct of "aberrant" individuals. To use Echeverría's (2007) terminology, governments were promoting a "civilizational whiteness". Law played a central role in this process: Latin American states invested in the rhetorical and educational functions of law, originated in the Platonic tradition whereby legislation can produce "virtuous" citizens (Htun, 2003). In that milieu, eugenicists and policymakers were especially concerned with women, and human reproduction became a central arena "for the play of science and social policies" (Stepan, 1991, p. 12). Governments scrutinised the family as the site where healthy citizens should be raised. As a result, women were portrayed as responsible for child development, and encouraged to implement scientific knowledge to raise their children. In this way, mothers could fulfil their "civic duty" to be good wives and raise healthy citizens (Clark, 2001; Guy, 2000; Rendón, 1948/2006). As we see, nation-making was, from the outset, reliant on racialised and gendered normalisation and exclusion. Subsequently, the regulation of gender functioned as a technique that stimulated the intervention of the state in domestic life (Dore & Molyneux, 2000; Guy, 2000; Radcliffe & Westwood, 1996).

These nation-making discourses portrayed women either as conforming subjects who deserved legal protection, or as dangerous subjects to be punished when they stepped outside the boundaries of domestic discipline. Such dichotomy is linked to *marianismo*, a term alluding to the Virgin Mary's abnegation and purity, which, via Spanish Catholicism, became the paradigm of ideal femininity. In this manner, modesty, humility, and submission to male authority were (and still frequently are) regarded as the most desirable virtues of womanhood (Castillo et al., 2010).

Alongside state-led discourses on optimising the race, there were other narratives that shaped postcolonial familial ideologies. The Catholic Church's social doctrine and standpoint on morality and sexuality also impacted on the legal regulation of the family. Although the Church has gradually moved from authorising patriarchal violence to endorsing equality between spouses, the notion of equal rights for men and women is only applied so long as the "proper nature" of the sexes is preserved (Htun, 2003). Therefore, only women who fulfil an adequate role in a legitimate marriage are in practice regarded as deserving protection.

Although early Latin American laws – constitutional law in particular – were symbolic of the new republican order, critics have argued that it was not the individual, but the family, that was most important as a legal subject in the formation of the first Latin American constitutions, although they were presented as liberal (Guy, 2000). Many legal bodies reproduced colonial gender norms: civil legislation, in particular, preserved most colonial institutions. For instance, Spanish law treated women as legal minors, and republican Civil Codes would, for the most part, preserve that formulation. The drive to optimise the family as the nucleus of the new society materialised through the regulation of property, child custody, women's juridical capacity, and the regime of marriage and divorce. Marriage, especially, could significantly bolster women's social aspirations (Murray, 2010), which made it a central institution to legally and ideologically define women's status. In addition, criminal laws penalising deviancy from family norms through crimes such as adultery, prostitution, abortion, homosexuality, and infanticide, aimed at preserving family normalcy and cohesion (see Table 1.1). In this way, Catholic values, alongside racialised nation-building discourses, would inform specific legal interventions in domesticity, as explained in the following section.

Nation-building, race, and sexuality in early civil and penal laws

During the 19th century, Latin America received the influence of positive criminology, such as the work of Cesare Lombroso, which was used by governments to develop a scientific approach to managing crime and penitentiary institutions (Salvatore, 2001). Racialised and gendered family norms, and the elements brought in from eugenics that I described in the previous section, cohabited with criminological developments that scientifically justified imprisoning the deviant.

Women who were viewed as sexual transgressors were targeted, for instance, through policies that regulated prostitution and monitored venereal disease (Guy, 1991; Stern, 2016). Also, penal courts punished women who did not conform to the ideals of domestic morality, as well as men who endangered women's "purity" (Díaz, 2001). In this way, adultery committed by a woman was criminalised for a significant part of Ecuadorian republican history (see Table 1.1), as were rape and the seduction of "modest" women. At the same time, even since colonial times, wives could take husbands to court for habitual or severe physical mistreatment, and sue their spouses for failure to fulfill legitimate husbandly responsibilities, such as guaranteeing the family's access to sufficient food and subsistence (Murray, 2010). These parallels illustrate that the penalisation of certain women coexisted with the protection of feminine modesty and integrity as a strategy to preserve the family. For their part, non-conforming family members (the nation's *Others*) were left outside the law's scope of protection. Legally subordinated subjectivities ranged from single mothers and unmarried women who had a sexual partner, to divorced women, sex workers, indigenous, black, and peasant women, as well as impoverished *mestizas*.

Concrete examples of these ideologies are evident in the first Civil Code of Ecuador (1860), which regulated the effects of marriage, based on Canon Law. The Church was then the authority that registered marriages and births, and legitimate ancestry could only be established through lawful marriage. As a consequence, children were legally categorised as "legitimate", "illegitimate", and "adulterous", to indicate the circumstances of their birth (*Código Civil*, 1860). Regarding marriage itself, the first Civil Code mandated: "Article 124.- Spouses are obliged to remain faithful, to assist and help each other in all circumstances of life. The husband must protect the woman, and the woman must *obey* her husband" (emphasis added). Obedience as a conjugal duty posited alongside fidelity and mutual aid, points at an ethic of conjugal harmony that *requires* the subordination of women to their husbands. Laws that

Table 1.1 1938 Penal Code Provisions on women, domesticity, and the family

Article	*Analysis*
Authorisation to kill an adulterous woman Art. 22.- Nor is there any infraction when one of the spouses kills, injures or hits the other, or the accomplice, at the moment of surprising them in blatant *adultery*, or when a woman commits the same acts in defense of her *modesty*, when seriously threatened.	This provision allowed killing an unfaithful spouse with an aim to protect the integrity of marriage. However, adultery was a criminal offence that could only be committed by women, as the equivalent for men required them to be sustaining continued cohabitation with a mistress. This article also authorised women to injure their attacker when their "modesty" was threatened. That is, rather than protecting women's physical and emotional integrity, it protected their reputation and sexual prudence.
Protection of pregnant defendants Art. 61.- No judgment in which a prison sentence is imposed, will be notified to a pregnant woman, until sixty days after delivery. Nor will anyone who is in a state of insanity or in imminent danger of death due to illness or accident, be notified.	The article aims at protecting pregnant women from suffering emotional distress and/or physical injuries that can result from incarceration, with an aim to protect the pregnancy and, ultimately, motherhood.
Criminalisation of abortion Art. 420.- The woman who has voluntarily consented to have an abortion, or herself causes the abortion, will be punished with imprisonment for one to five years. If she consents to being aborted or causes the abortion herself, to hide her disgrace, she will be punished with six months to two years in prison.	This article, which criminalises abortion, has remained largely unchanged to this day. Interestingly, it mandates a reduction of the punishment if it is evident that the woman performed the abortion to hide her "dishonour" and shame for having become pregnant, presumably, outside of wedlock.
Art. 423.- Abortion practiced by a doctor, with the consent of the pregnant woman, or of her husband or close family members, when she is not able to provide it, will not be punishable: 1.- If it has been done to avoid a danger to the life or health of the mother, and if this danger cannot be avoided by other means; and 2.- If the pregnancy comes from a rape or statutory rape committed on an idiotic or insane woman. In this case, the consent of her legal representative must be required for the abortion.	This article authorises abortion in two cases, when women's life or health are in serious danger, and when pregnancy results from rape, but only if the woman is "idiotic" or "insane" (the terms used at the time). The latter case reveals a eugenic purpose rather than a will to protect women's freedom or integrity.

(*Continued*)

Table 1.1 (Continued)

Article	*Analysis*
Criminalisation of adultery Art. 479.- The following persons shall be punished with imprisonment from six months to two years: 1.- The woman who commits adultery; 2.- The accomplice of the adulterous woman; 3.- The husband when he keeps a concubine inside or outside the conjugal home; and 4.- The husband's concubine.	This article reveals the dominant discourses around male and female sexuality: while committing adultery, that is, having sexual relations outside marriage even on a single occasion, was a prosecutable crime for women, men could not be accused of adultery. They would only be punishable if they kept a concubine, that is, a sexual partner in a continued manner, for an extended period. Concubines were categorised as criminals.

Table designed and produced by the author. Source(s): Lexis Finder database and the author's field notes.

moderated domestic violence, in that context, converged with the Catholic doctrine of marriage indissolubility, which praises the values of conjugal love and affection, but also demands the preservation of the matrimonial tie almost at all costs. Indeed, priests have traditionally offered marriage counselling and support to spouses and families, thus playing a key role in mediating marital disputes and conserving marriages (Rodríguez, 2000). State intervention to moderate violence in the family was upheld by both nationalist and Catholic values.

As the Republic and its judicial apparatus expanded, a more secular approach to family life modulated the doctrine of the Catholic Church, but governments continued to worry about child development, apt motherhood, and responsible fatherhood as necessary to optimise the nation. This favoured the enforcement of family-protection law and policy. Evidently, these laws were intended to preserve family integrity, not to challenge established gender roles. For instance, Article 126 of the 1860 Civil Code stated: "The husband has the right to force his wife to live with him and follow him wherever he transfers his residence. This right ceases when its implementation brings imminent danger to the life of the woman". In this Article, patriarchy is reaffirmed through a husband's right to impose a place of residence upon his wife, a right that was tempered only when the woman's life was at serious risk. That is, gender subordination was tolerated in principle and exceptionally moderated by law to avoid excessive force, without challenging male dominance.

In addition, laws promoted white upper-class ideals related to monogamy, reproductive labour, and child rearing. This family model, by which men were responsible breadwinners and women diligent homemakers, mothers, and wives, did not correspond to the reality of many working-class and destitute families that were struggling to make a living. Such a model was also alien to many indigenous communities and was superimposed over indigenous women's traditional participation in economic and community life, which had been common during pre-Columbian times (Dore, 2000; Jefferson & Lokken, 2011).

While civil law was the main corpus governing women and families, criminal law was also used to penalise those who endangered innocent family members. Early criminal laws aimed at neutralising and punishing non-conforming family members who threatened the integrity of the family, including violent men. Early examples can be found in Mexico, where, as early as 1871, the Penal Code criminalised domestic violence. According to Varley's study (2000), the legislators who promoted this project did not question a husband's right to govern his wife, but presented the subjection of women to men as the effect of a marriage contract that was based on free will and reason – both core liberal principles. The contract, they argued, did not include accepting abuse; therefore, violence within marriage would violate a lawful contract. Earlier family archetypes were rearranged in this way to accommodate newer liberal approaches, but did not really challenge colonial familial norms. Instead, a kind of "non-violent domestic patriarchy" was inscribed in law, and "domestic violence was re-construed as the practice of deviant men" (Varley, 2000, p. 241). Feminist historians examining other Latin American countries have agreed that a "softened" version of patriarchy, centring fatherly responsibility, gradually became exemplar (Tinsman, 2002).

Common legal mechanisms to protect women and children included provisions allowing authorities to arrest violent husbands or send them to correctional houses (Guy 2000; Rodríguez, 2000; Dore, 2000). Although in some cases these were private-law provisions, criminal laws were gradually incorporated. Examples can be found in Ecuador's 1938 Penal Code. As mentioned above, alcoholism was considered a "racial poison" that hindered the construction of a powerful nation (Clark, 2001). At the time, the aetiology of alcoholism was unknown, though it was associated with poverty and regarded as a threat to the family (Stepan, 1991). The Ecuadorian Penal Code of 1938, enacted during a military dictatorship, contained the following Article:

> Art. 607.- Those who, within a period of ninety days, have relapsed in drunkenness four times, will be assigned to a temperance house, or another place to this purpose, to remain in it for a period from six months to two years; this period may be extended or shortened, and the detention may even be revoked, when the detailed examination of the inmate offers sufficient evidence that he has been reformed.
>
> (*Código Penal*, 1938)

This provision involves various intersecting narratives. As we know, scientific discourses framing drunkenness as "racial poison" influenced public policy, while violent fathers and husbands were targeted by various legal bodies. Let us take into account that, frequently, the educated, white elite feared violence and danger from non-white lower-class men, who were commonly portrayed as lazy, undisciplined, sickly, drunk, and vagrant (Stepan, 1991). Criminally repressing conducts that were thought to be characteristic of racial and, therefore, moral inferiority was a strategy to "whiten" the population, as described previously.

It is against that backdrop that the cited provision on alcoholism offered some tools for women who suffered domestic abuse to protect themselves: a good argument to convince police to arrest men under Article 607 was to say that they had become dangerous to their families (Clark, 2001). This exemplifies an early use of the penal apparatus to control family violence, with an underlying racial narrative. What we see is a confluence of nationalistic ideals, family-protection policy, punitive strategies for those deviating from family norms, and aspirations to Europeanness and whiteness. Men would be sanctioned when they deviated from their duties as responsible breadwinners, because such deviation was regarded as dangerous for the family and, as a consequence, the nation.

Table 1.1 presents further criminal law provisions in the 1938 Code, which aimed at controlling women's sexuality in the context of colonial familial ideologies. The examples in Table 1.1 expound criminal law as a technology that, in addition to imposing a racialised control and surveillance, encouraged "civilised" behaviours and punished forms of deviance that could endanger family stability or women's modesty. Some criminal laws, like the one on alcoholism, did give women access to a degree of legal protection and a mitigation of domestic violence, but they were based on understandings of deviance as a threat to the family and the national race, which translated into the criminalisation, not only of alcoholism, but also of adultery, concubinage, and abortion. Regarding the latter, in particular, the eugenic orientation of the Penal Code is evident, as it authorised abortion when pregnancy results from rape, but only if the woman was "idiotic" or "insane".[5]

The patriarchal elements of family protection are also apparent in the criminal laws that condoned or reduced sanctions for men who murdered unfaithful wives.[6] Correspondingly, only women who complied with dominant family norms were deemed worthy of legal protection, and their needs were conflated with those of the family very early on. These rationales have been legally and ideologically enduring. Moreover, some of them are still implicit in legal representations of violence against women, as the next chapters show. Indeed, while there have been several reforms of the Civil Code across the years, a large part of this legal body is still identical to the Code of 1860, a shocking fact considering that many constitutional reforms (some

5 This provision was only reformed by the Constitutional Court of Ecuador very recently, in 2021, to decriminalised abortion in all cases of rape.

6 For a more detailed explanation of how the criminalisation of abortion operated, see Chapter 2.

of them deemed radical) have taken place during Ecuador's republican life. As for the Penal Code, it was only in 2014 that a comprehensive revision occurred (see Chapter 5) – which not only preserved offences but also added many more, while toughening existing punishments. Therefore, it is crucial to have in mind that race and gender hierarchies have continued to implicitly – and sometimes explicitly – sustain the activation of criminal law to intervene in the family, long before women's movements denounced domestic violence.

Conclusion

The use of law to normalise and regulate the family in Latin America can be traced back to colonial and early republican times. Marital dispute was first mediated through canonical law and the practices of the Catholic Church and, after secularisation, through civil and penal codes of law based on European legislation and preexisting colonial rules. Legislative efforts have often aimed at regulating the family as a primary site for nation-building. In the region, the family is a key political subject and an area of normalisation whereby compliance with models of whiteness and Europeanness has been regarded as an indicator of civilisation and progress in nation-building. With this backdrop, early legal interventions in family life and domestic violence reflect racial and gender norms that determined who deserved protection, to what point, and through which mechanisms. Women were, in parallel, either protected or punished by the law depending on their status and whether or not they conformed to their expected roles as mothers and wives. Correspondingly, a racialised and gendered rhetoric that incorporated the scientific discourse of the time was used to distinctively characterise the "deviant" subjectivities that would be targeted by law and policy. A nonviolent patriarchy, whereby violence against women was moderated as a way to protect the family, became part of civil and penal laws that intervened in domesticity very early on.

References

Ahmed, S. (2007). A phenomenology of whiteness. *Feminist Theory, 8*(2), 149–168.

Campos, M.Z. (1996). *Vicious women, virtuous women: The female delinquent and the Santiago de Chile Correctional House, 1860–1900* (R. Salvatore & C. Aguirre (eds.)). University of Texas Press.

Castillo, L.G., Perez, F.V., Castillo, R., & Ghosheh, M.R. (2010). Construction and initial validation of the Marianismo Beliefs Scale. *Counselling Psychology Quarterly, 23*(2), 163–175.

Clark, K. (2001). *Género, raza y nación: La protección a la infancia en el Ecuador (1910–1945)* (G. Herrera (ed.); p. 9). FLACSO Ecuador.

Código Civil, Senado y cámara de representantes del Ecuador (1860). http://www.silec.com.ec/Webtools/LexisFinder/DocumentVisualizer/DocumentVisualizer.aspx?id=HISTORIC-CODIGO_CIVIL_1860&query=c%C3%B3digo%20civil

Código Civil, no. 2005-010, Congreso Nacional del Ecuador (2005). http://www.silec.com.ec/

Código Penal, no. Ley 7, Jefatura Suprema del Ecuador (1938).

Díaz, A. (2001). Women, order and progress in Guzmán Blanco's Venezuela, 1870–1888. In R. Salvatore, C. Aguirre, & J. Guilbert (Eds.), *Crime and punishment in Latin America: Law and society since late colonial times*. Duke University Press.

Dore, E. (2000). One step forward, two steps back: Gender and the state in the long nineteenth century. In E. Dore & M. Molyneux (Eds.), *Hidden histories of gender and the state in Latin America* (pp. 3–32). Duke University Press

Dore, E., & Molyneux, M. (eds.). (2000). *Hidden histories of gender and the state in Latin America*. Duke University Press.

Echeverría, B. (2007). Imágenes de la blanquitud. *Sociedades Icónicas. Historia, Ideología Y Cultura En La Imagen, 21*, 15–32.

Echeverría, B. (2009). "Blanquitud". Considerations on racism as a specifically modern phenomenon. In International Conference On Modernity. Vienna.

Eslava, L. (forthcoming). Trigueño international law: On (most of the world) being (always, somehow) out of place. In L.J. Chua & M.F. Massoud (eds.), *Out of place: Power, person and difference in socio-legal research*.

Eslava, L. (2020, October 29). *Our favourite CRT: Gloria Anzaldúa*. Critical Legal Thinking. https://criticallegalthinking.com/2020/10/29/our-favourite-crt-gloria-anzaldua/

García Villegas, M., & Rodríguez Garavito, C. (2003). Law and society in Latin America: Toward the consolidation of critical sociolegal studies. *Beyond Law, 9*(26), 11–59.

Guy, D.J. (1991). *Sex & danger in Buenos Aires: Prostitution, family, and nation in Argentina* (Vol. 1). University of Nebraska Press.

Guy, D.J. (2000). *White slavery and mothers alive and dead: The troubled meeting of sex, gender, public health, and progress in Latin America* (Vol. 5). University of Nebraska Press.

Harris, C.I. (1993). Whiteness as property. *Harvard Law Review, 106*(8), 1707–1791.

Htun, M. (2003). *Sex and the state: Abortion, divorce, and the family under Latin American dictatorships and democracies*. Cambridge University Press.

Jefferson, A., & Lokken, P. (2011). *Daily life in colonial Latin America*. ABC-CLIO, LLC.

Keating, A. (ed.). (2009). *The Gloria Anzaldúa reader*. Duke University Press.

Mendoza, B. (2001). La desmitologización del mestizaje en Honduras: evaluando nuevos aportes. *Mesoamérica, 42*, 256–278.

Murray, P.S. (2010). *For Glory and Bolívar: The remarkable life of Manuela Sáenz*. University of Texas Press.

Quijano, A. (2000). Colonialidad del poder y clasificación social. *Journal of World-Systems Research, XI*(2), 342–386.

Radcliffe, S.A., & Westwood, S. (1993). Gender, racism and the politics of identities in Latin America. In S.A. Radcliffe & S. Westwood (Eds.), *"Viva". Women and popular protest in Latin America* (pp. 1–29). Routledge.

Radcliffe, S.A., & Westwood, S. (1996). *Remaking the nation: Place, identity and politics in Latin America*. Routledge.

Rendón, Z. (1948/2006). La mujer en los diversos organismos humanos. In A. M. Goetschel (Ed.), *Orígenes del feminismo en el Ecuador* (pp. 93–109). CONAMU, FLACSO Sede Ecuador, Comisión de género y equidad social del MDMQ, UNIFEM.

Rodríguez, E. (2000). Civilizing domestic life in the central valley of Costa Rica, 1750–1850. In E. Dore & M. Molyneux (Eds.), *Hidden histories of gender and the state in Latin America* (pp. 85–107). Duke University Press.

Salvatore, R. (2001). Death and liberalism: Capital punishment after the fall of Rosas. In R. Salvatore, C. Aguirre, & J. Guilbert (Eds.), *Crime and punishment in Latin America. Law and society since late colonial times* (pp. 308–341). Duke University Press.

Santos, B. de S. (1995). *Toward a new common sense: Law, science and politics in the paradigmatic transition*. Routledge.

Stepan, N. (1991). *The hour of eugenics: Race, gender, and nation in Latin America*. Cornell University Press.

Stern, A.M. (2016). Eugenics in Latin America. In S. Webre (Ed.), *Oxford Research Encyclopedia of Latin American History*. Oxford University Press.

Tinsman, H. (2002). *Partners in conflict: The politics of gender, sexuality, and labor in the Chilean agrarian reform, 1950–1973*. Duke University Press.

Varley, A. (2000). Women and the home in Mexican family law. In E. Dore & M. Molyneux (Eds.), *Hidden histories of gender and the state in Latin America* (pp. 238–261). Duke University Press

Vidal López, R. (2003). Propuestas para una ciencia social del derecho. In M. García Villegas & C. Rodríguez Garavito (eds.), *Derecho y Sociedad En América Latina: Un Debate Sobre Los Estudios Jurídicos Críticos* (pp. 127–142). Universidad Nacional de Colombia.

Walker, C. (2001). *Crime in the time of the Great Fear: Indians and the state in the Peruvian Southern Andes* (R. Salvatore, C. Aguirre, & J. Guilbert (eds.); pp. 35–55). Duke University Press.

Chapter 2

Law was foe

Women's movements before the 1990s

Introduction

Having explained, in Chapter 1, how gendered and racialised discourses docked in the late 19th and early 20th century regulation of family life, this chapter is set in a period when the first women's movements formed in Ecuador. I show that before the 1990s "boom" of international agencies and NGOs that promoted development and human rights, the relationship between women's movements and the law was mostly antagonistic. In particular, I identify a period during which criminalisation was not considered instrumental to counteract violence against women (VAW). This is key to understanding the turn to criminal law during the last decades of the 20th century.

This chapter builds on primary sources that include historical legislation, feminist press releases and opinion pieces, and interviews with feminists who participated in the first women's advocacy group from the 1970s onwards. The first part of the chapter describes early organisations, which stemmed from the Marxist left and the indigenous movement during the first half of the 20th century. These groups denounced law and the state as oppressive apparatuses. Next, the chapter addresses maternal feminist demands for law reform that would facilitate the protection of children, and the repeal of laws that co-produced women's suffering. Later on, a strand of feminism emerged from the professionalisation of middle- and upper-class women. These groups obtained the abolition of criminal laws that authorised VAW or discriminated against them; however, feminist campaigns did not aim at creating new legislation, nor criminalising VAW. This chapter is situated in a "pre-penal" past, before the punitive turn. There were no conditions of possibility for an instrumental use of criminal justice in the feminist legal imaginary. Penality and criminal law were mostly regarded as the predicament, not the solution.

Against a violent state: indigenous women and the Marxist left

This section identifies two related streams of the early women's movement, associated with working-class and peasant women struggles. Despite the impact

DOI: 10.4324/9781003098799-3

of their work, mainstream histories of Ecuadorian feminism sometimes overlook them. Here, I examine women workers' unions associated with the Communist Party, and the struggles of the indigenous women who coordinated the first indigenous uprisings.

Marxism is a strand of Western thought that has strongly influenced Latin American social movements. Through the 19th and 20th centuries, Marxist and anarchist theory also informed Latin American feminisms, infusing feminist ideas with a working-class orientation (Chinchilla, 1991; Molyneux, 2003). In Ecuador, socialist and anarchist women's groups stemmed from feminist trade union centres as early as the 1920s (Goetschel, 2006). These unions were considered indispensable to dignify women's living conditions. María Esther Martínez wrote in 1933:

> The creation of unions [is an] urgent interest, in that, by enhancing the sense of personality of the female worker, a careful study of her needs can be carried out to concretise her aspirations, ensuring that laws consider a more humane situation for her, to avoid the exploitation [that female workers] are suffering. If the male worker complains and protests so bitterly about his exploitation, what could the working woman say?
>
> (Martínez, 2006/1933, p. 115)

Published in the magazine *Nuevos Horizontes* (New Horizons), this text also addressed law reform in terms that suggest a drive to demand labour rights for women:

> It is therefore necessary to revise the laws of our country regarding women, in order to assure sufficient conditions that enable them to make use of the rights that have been granted to [women] with so much justice in our Constitution.
>
> (Martínez, 2006/1933, p. 117)

Nela Martínez, another notable feminist who become the first Ecuadorian congresswoman in 1945, was a visible militant of the Communist Party. Her writings, articulated in terms of class struggle, denounced poverty and the precarious conditions that women and children endured. Her work also interrogated the colonial and bourgeois family model (Martínez, 2006/1933). In 1938, the Ecuadorian Feminine Alliance (*Alianza Femenina Ecuatoriana*, AFE), a women's trade union, was founded, with Nela Martínez acting as a secretary. This organisation prioritised demanding better working conditions for women, such as equal salaries, protection for informal workers, better safety conditions for factory workers, and childcare facilities.

Quito newspaper *El Día* published a report of the inaugural meeting of the AFE. One of their aspirations was "a revision of penal laws for female delinquency, with the aspiration to transform prisons and correctional houses into work and education centres for women" (*El Día*, 2006/1938, p. 182). This programmatic goal presupposes a rejection of carcerality and a framing of the prison as a despotic apparatus. Indeed, there was a clear drive to challenge the penal system: feminists of the AFE regarded the prison as oppressive for women and imagined alternatives such as educational and occupational programmes. While they grounded their proposal in the Communist Party's principles, it was crafted by, and targeted at, women. Future mainstream feminist networks would not take up this critical approach to criminal justice.

The Marxist left also facilitated the articulation of the first indigenous uprisings against the monopoly of land property. The term "feminism" is linked to Western theoretical and political developments, and is not always embraced by non-Western women's movements; however, I preserve the term to point at the critical radical ideas from indigenous women vis-à-vis the hegemonic patriarchal order. Imperialist flows of knowledge frame "third world" women as objects of study rather than producers of knowledge (Connell, 2015; Gargallo, 2010; Mendoza, 2002), which has resulted in a disregard of indigenous struggles as conceptual frameworks for feminist analyses. Yet, as shown here, indigenous and peasant women inaugurated a critique of the state's law, framing it as violent, illegitimate, and oppressive. This overruled appealing to penality as a tool for women's vindications. Recognising these stances as forms of critical theory and practice allows us to nuance other mainstream narratives that depict Latin American women's movements as "downloaders" of North American and European feminist trends. It also allows us to identify local forms of feminism whereby law had almost no significance as an emancipatory tool.

Indigenous women founded the first Ecuadorian indigenous organisations with the support of the Communist Party. Dolores Cacuango (1881–1971) was the founder of the Ecuadorian Federation of Indians (*Federación Ecuatoriana de Indios*), in 1944. Cacuango's work led her to collaborate with the trade unions of Quito, which in turn connected her to the Communist Party. She thus established links with the feminists within those organisations. Nela Martínez and Dolores Cacuango were protagonists of the 1944 workers' rebellion that led to the dismantling of the government in power.

Dolores Cacuango's thought has been preserved via oral histories in which she recounted the extreme violence that her people suffered at the hands of landowners, local authorities, the Church, the military, and police. In an interview conducted by José Yánez del Pozo (2006), Dolores Cacuango reminisced about the time of the *huasipungo*,[1] when rural indigenous communities reclaimed ownership of the land where they lived and worked, and denounced

1 *Huasipungo* (from the Kichwa words "huasi" -house- and "pungo" -door-) refers to the small portion of land that indigenous people were allowed to plant and harvest, which was adjacent to the shacks they were allowed to live in, within a landowner's grounds. This parcel of land was given as "salary"

the laws that favoured abusive landowners. This resulted in violent revolts and the burning down of the homes of the protesters. To Dolores, who endured abuse and extortion from landowners and state officials, state action was not legitimate:

> I have fought, comrade. So many, so many people bled. No one defended us, no one. Not the police, nor the commissioner, nor the captain from Quito, nobody. Even worse in Quito, in Ayaguachi, they burnt the tiny houses, the little animals, they destroyed the clothes, they destroyed everything, they took us out of the huasipungo. Where did [my comrades] end up dying? They are dead, poor peasants.
>
> (Yánez del Pozo, 2006, p. 196)

State action, in Dolores Cacuango's view, was not delivering justice, but endorsing the appropriation of the ancestral lands where she and her people lived and worked for centuries. In other words, from the perspective of the state, law was being justly enforced, while indigenous people regarded law as a mechanism used by the state to legitimise its violence.

Another emblematic indigenous leader, who fought with Dolores Cacuango, is Tránsito Amaguaña (1909–2009). In a 1977 interview by Mercedes Prieto, Tránsito reminisced of her childhood. She had worked the land from seven years old. In her words: "there was no justice, there was nothing. At their will they mistreated us, at their will they trampled on us" (Prieto, 1978, p. 15 annex). She recounted a time when, during a 1931 peasant uprising in the haciendas of Pesillo, where she and her family worked, the military arrested her brothers, by order of president Isidro Ayora:

> Overall they destroyed 46 homes, they ruined them, burned them, broke into them with people still inside, with the very Pesillo people inside. Some soldiers... When they broke into my mother's house, my father, my brother José, who is now a teacher, and my brother Venancio Amaguaña, they were all arrested.
>
> (Prieto, 1978, p. 16 annex)

During her life, Tránsito Amaguaña was repeatedly arrested and imprisoned, accused of being a terrorist and of cooperating with the Soviet Union to promote a communist revolution in Ecuador (El Mundo, 2009). Indigenous women like Dolores Cacuango and Tránsito Amaguaña did not conceive the state's punitive power as a tool to halt their abusers and free themselves from exploitation and violence. From their perspective, the state protected those

---

in exchange for the indigenous family's work in the lord's hacienda, reproducing feudalist systems into the republican years.

who exploited indigenous people, and enforced criminal law against peasants. Indigenous women instead focused on organising their own people and attaining cohesion within their communities to resist repression, not on demanding law reform nor promoting the use of criminal law against their abusers. These practices of resistance required decentring law as a channel for emancipation, which precluded direct engagement with criminal law reform. To this day, indigenous women's demands do not prioritise criminalisation.

The thought and practices of indigenous women illustrate that demanding law reform, and more so, resorting to criminal law as a protective tool, requires trust that governing institutions will protect one's people. A proximity between the actors and the law enforcement apparatuses makes resorting to law possible. Appealing to law reform presupposes a degree of inclusion in the structures that define citizenship and allow access to the benefits of the legal system. Without this proximity, which many people cannot attain without a redefinition of citizenship (Merry, 2003; Yashar, 2005), emancipatory hopes cannot be placed in law. Positive experiences with the legal system reinforce rights-based subjectivities, which in part explains why feminist engagements with law reform tend to emerge from groups that are already included in prevailing definitions of citizenship, and could therefore resort to liberal legal concepts, such as individual freedom and legal equality, as I show next.

Zoila Rendón: criminal law and women's suffering

Zoila Rendón's thought is a prominent example of a strand of Ecuadorian feminism that significantly differs from the Marxist and indigenous streams. Rendón was associated with an urban middle class that was more prone to engaging with the state to vindicate political goals. Yet, criminalising violence against women did not emerge from her work as a method either. Rendón and other feminists within this strand organised around demands for the state to better protect children. In the broader context, Latin American maternalist movements were prominent, particularly since 1916, with the inauguration of the Pan-American Child Congresses. These fora addressed issues such as child abandonment, adoption, education, and criminality, often depicting the state as liable for protecting mothers and children. Maternalist feminists linked women's status to children and the family, arguing that law reform on child custody, adoption and mothers' rights, was necessary for mothers to be able to raise their children (Guy, 2000).

In Ecuador, some feminists employed maternalist approaches to emphasise women's role in child rearing as decisive to raising good citizens, coinciding with the citizen's optimisation rhetoric I examined in Chapter 1. However, maternalist feminists also used the concept of child protection to demand women's access to education, paid labour, property, votes, citizenship, and public life. Some women's organisations at the turn of the 20th century focused on reforming laws to obtain *patria potestad* (parental authority) over their children. Zoila Rendón wrote on the connections between women's rights, the home, and the nation and, while agreeing that women's most patriotic duty was motherhood, she also argued that to achieve such goal women should be allowed to access education, not only in matters related to housekeeping and child rearing, but in broader aspects of knowledge, to nurture the leaders and workers of the future (Rendón, 1948/2006). Thus, "conforming" femininities were used to negotiate some advancements in women's participation in public life. However, this feminist strand did not interrogate the colonial state and its family-oriented discourse, which continued to inform the laws that were intended to protect women. Surely, laws criminalising "deviant" women (sex workers, adulterous wives, unmarried mothers, racialised women, etc.) coexisted with legislation granting rights to "good" women.

Although some authors have affirmed that criminal law was not as decisive as civil law to normalise femininity in Latin America (Zaffaroni, 2009), examining Ecuador's legal history together with feminist demands of the time, reveals that some women were constructed as subjects of criminal law when they deviated from their assigned roles. With this background, in 1948, Zoila Rendón presented a thesis at the first International Congress of Mothers in Argentina, addressing, amongst other topics, women's status in the Ecuadorian Penal Code. She had delivered a petition to the Constituent Assembly of 1928–1929, which included a demand for "legal equality in criminal law, with identical sanctions [for men and women] for common criminal offences" (Rendón, 1948/2006, p. 104).

The first injustice Rendón denounced was the status of adultery as a criminal offence. Since the enactment of the first Ecuadorian Penal Code, adultery was an offence that only women could commit (see Table 1.1 in Chapter 1). There was no equivalent offence for men, although in 1938 a husband's prolonged cohabitation with a mistress (known as *amancebamiento*) was criminalised. However, a single event of sexual intercourse outside of marriage constituted adultery for women, while, for men, only *continued* cohabitation with a mistress qualified as a crime. Women's sexual lives were thus scrutinised at all times, while men's sexual behaviour was penalised only if it disrupted stable family life. Deviance and criminality were, as explained in Chapter 1, understood as threats to women's modesty and the value of family integrity. In the same way, a spouse who caught the other during sexual intercourse outside marriage, and then killed her and/or her accomplice, was not criminally liable (see Table 2.1, 1906, Art. 24).[2] Given that only women could perpetrate adultery, the article in practice authorised killing unfaithful wives.[3]

2 Article 22 of the Ecuadorian Penal code was reformed in 2005 following a proposal presented by the National Women's Council (CONAMU) with the cooperation of women's NGOs and feminist lawyers.

3 In practice, the provision was inapplicable due to the difficulty to obtain evidence. There is no binding jurisprudence (case law) in historical legal databases regarding the criminal prosecution of adultery. Adultery was decriminalised in 1983 following the suggestions of (male) liberal scholars of the time, who considered the law to be archaic (Albán, 2012; Chico Peñaherrera, 2004). Adultery remains a legal grounds for divorce according to the Civil Code presently in force.

Table 2.1 Historical law reform of adultery in Ecuador (1906–2005)

1906	*1938*	*1983*	*2005*
Article 378.- The woman convicted for adultery, will be condemned to prison of three to five years. The husband may suspend the effect of this sentence by consenting to take his woman back.	Art. 479.- The following persons shall be punished with imprisonment from six months to two years: 1. The woman who commits adultery; 2. The partner of an adulterous woman; 3. The husband if he keeps a mistress within or without the conjugal home; and 4. The mistress of the husband.	Repealed	
Art. 380.- Prosecution or sentencing for adultery may take place only at the request of the husband, who cannot request it in the following cases: 1. If he has consented to the unlawful treatment between his wife and the adulterer; and 2. If he has voluntary and arbitrarily separated his wife from his side or abandoned her.	Art. 480. No action may be proposed by the husband against his wife if he has consented to the unlawful treatment of her and the adulterer; or if he has voluntarily or arbitrarily estranged himself from his wife, or has abandoned her.	Repealed	
Art. 24.- There is no infraction either when one spouse kills, injures, or hits the other, or their accomplice, at the moment of catching them in the act of adultery; or when a woman commits the same acts, in defence of her seriously threatened modesty.	Unchanged	Unchanged	Repealed

Table designed and produced by the author. Source(s): Lexis Finder database.

Unlike her earlier maternalist writings, Rendón's thesis on reforming the Penal Code moved away from child protection, to a critique that centred women's suffering, albeit not challenging the dominant familial ideologies. In her thesis, Zoila Rendón did not dispute the criminal offence of adultery, which would have been at odds with her own maternalist stance on the duties of women. Instead, she denounced men's *impunity*. She based her critique on the liberal notion of legal equality, which, she reasoned, meant that men should be punished for behaviours akin to those women were criminalised for. She resorted to the same logic to address other criminal offences: referring to prostitution-procuring, she argued that the men who requested sexual services from an underaged woman should be criminally punished. She addressed abortion and the fact that although women were criminalised for this conduct, there was no established punishment for the men who impregnated women and then facilitated abortion:

> Abortion is another frequent offence by women, a crime that, when proven, has its sanction. But, abortion, many times is advised by its very author, who seeks to evade his responsibility as a father, and kills the child he has engendered and, frequently, also the mother, who has been made his victim, through his seduction. And yet, only the woman bears the punishment and not the one who is directly the author.
>
> (Rendón, 1948/2006, p. 105)

Rendón made an analogous argument regarding infanticide: some women killed their young children moved by economic precariousness and despair, yet women alone were liable for the crime, even though the men who fathered those children and abandoned the mother had really caused the outcome.

As we see, the concept of formal equality guided Rendón's critique of criminal law, which allowed her to expose women's "legal inferiority" (Rendón, 1948/2006, p. 105). Being equal before the law, in Rendón's view, entailed recognising that the men who harm women and facilitate the conditions under which they offend, were infractors as much as women themselves. As a result, men deserved punishment for causing women to "fall from grace". Hence, Rendón exposed inequality before the law – not oppression through law, as the Marxist and indigenous women had. At the same time, there is no evidence in her work of any intention to use criminalisation to *protect* women.

The influence of Catholic values and colonial discourses about the family are visible in Rendón's acceptance of an essentialist approach to sexual difference; however, she rejected legal inequality also based on sexual difference. The fairness and legitimacy of penal punishment remained unquestioned, but a demand to create new criminal offences to protect women was never part of Rendón's argument. Rather, she demanded punishment for all the parties involved in the perpetration of an offence. Rendón stressed that many of women's reprehensible behaviours were the consequence of equally outrageous actions by men, and this was the core of her critique.

A closer look at these arguments reveals what Rendón was really denouncing: the vulnerable situation of women that resulted from the exercise of masculine power. In another text, Rendón (1923/2006) referred to the "seduction" of unmarried women by men, and the shame, abandonment, and public ridicule to which they were subjected when they "lost their virtue". She demanded that the Ecuadorian state intervene to protect unmarried mothers in the same way it protected married ones. This demand challenged the convention that only "virtuous" (married) women deserved the state's help. There was a drive, in Rendón's work, to make women's suffering visible, attributing it to the dominant (male) understanding of justice, which prevented women's needs from being addressed by state policy. Expounding the ills of criminal law, Rendón denounced women's misfortune. Her work stands out because it sought to overcome labelling women as evil or deviant, to make men equally liable, and to obtain welfare and assistance for women in hardship.

Emerging State offices, NGOs, and popular sectors: the first women's movements

From the 1970s onwards, feminist organisations proliferated across Latin America. These began to discuss issues besides suffrage, labour, and motherhood, and framed women's subordination as a pervasive pattern, which would lead them to identify VAW as a systemic problem.

Also during the 1970s, some fields of study connected the status of women with economic growth, especially Women and Development studies (Boserup, 1970). International development organisations disseminated the idea that modernising nations required a revision of the laws that undermined the status of women in "underdeveloped" countries. For instance, married women's economic and legal dependency on their husbands was deemed an obstacle for their inclusion in development. Yet, feminists did not regard creating criminal offences as a suitable response to VAW. Many framed VAW as a problem closely related to poverty and deficient social services.

The Latin American and Caribbean Feminist *Encuentros* (meetings) were inaugurated in 1981 and continue to this day. The *Encuentros* adopted a framing of patriarchy as a large-scale system of domination that included militarism, authoritarianism, compulsory heterosexuality, homophobia, and violence against women. During the first *Encuentros*, there were no discussions of law reform to recognise women's human rights, nor appeals to criminalise VAW. Feminists discussed the social services required to assist women in their everyday struggles against poverty and discrimination (Navarro, 1982). These framings were developed further in subsequent meetings, emphasising the complicity of the state in various forms of VAW beyond interpersonal abuse. During the *Encuentros*, November 25 was declared the International Day of Non-Violence Against Women, in memory of the Mirabal sisters, killed in the 1960s during Trujillo's dictatorship in the Dominican Republic.[4] Again, VAW was not

4 This date was later taken up by the UN as an international commemorative date.

presented as a target of law reform, it was rather regarded as a type of political violence connected to issues of social redistribution and state coercion.[5]

In Ecuador, organised feminist participation in political life developed from 1975 onwards, when the rejection of the military regime led to increased civil society mobilisation and protest (UNESCO, 1984). University-based student unions cooperated with trade unions and served as the first spaces where feminists met and organised. Many leaders who are considered *históricas* (historical characters), began their political activities at student unions (feminist historical leader, personal communication, April 13, 2015). During this period, Ecuadorian women attained the repeal of various penal provisions that authorised violence against women, such as those in Table 2.1.

Ecuador had subscribed to the World Plan of Action that emerged during the 1975 United Nations World Conference on Women, which contained specific recommendations pertaining to law reform, aimed at facilitating women's incorporation into development. Through the 1970s, legal changes took place regarding women's status within civil law. These included reforms to preserve the legal capacity of married women and to allow them to perform legal transactions without the need of an authorisation from their husbands. Economic development discourse leveraged many of these adjustments: the administration of the communal property within the conjugal society, which had been an exclusive right of husbands, was now by default to be shared by both spouses. These reforms were not connected to demands of women's movements; rather, they were boosted by the requirements of international organisations and the intervention of some liberal jurists (Htun, 2003; UNESCO, 1984).[6] The reforms constituted inaugural civil law changes that expanded women's individual rights.

Ecuador was the first Latin American country to return to democracy after the dictatorship era, with the election of Jaime Roldós Aguilera as president in 1979.[7] Redemocratisation gave Ecuadorian feminists an opportunity to enter

5 These framings have been constant at the *Encuentros*. During the 2010s, for instance, a central topic was feminicide, understood as the genocide of women, facilitated by state negligence and violence. The documents of the *Encuentros* are careful to acknowledge women's popular organisations, diversity in sexual orientation, and various forms of sexual dissidence. More recently, decolonial frameworks have been used to express a rejection of advanced capitalism. The *Encuentros* have also officially opposed UN processes, such as Beijing 1995, which was criticised for having little participation from autonomous feminist collectives.

6 The paradox of liberal law reform in Latin America during military dictatorships, (which are generally regarded as conservative in matters of women's rights), has been addressed by Htun (2003), whose main argument is that it was the existence of "expert issue networks" paired with the ability of elite reformers, which created possibilities of legal change. I would add that the influence of international cooperation was crucial as well.

7 Jaime Roldós Aguilera was a young politician with no affiliation with the traditional right-wing or the Marxist-left parties. He was also a promoter of human rights at a time of authoritarian rule in the Southern Cone. The circumstances of his death in a plane accident have never been thoroughly clarified.

mainstream politics by working at ministries, secretariats, and other state offices. The new First Lady, Martha Bucaram – a lawyer who promoted women's rights – activated the first state office dedicated to improving women's status: the Women's National Bureau (*Oficina Nacional de la Mujer*, OFNAMU). This had existed "on paper" since 1970 by request of the Organization of American States (OAS) (UNESCO, 1984), but only became operative under the new government. This process mirrored the rise of women's offices in other Latin American countries (Chant & Craske, 2003), often with the support of international development programmes. According to feminist lawyer and activist Marena Briones: "the 1980s were the awakening of women's movements, of women's organizations. That is, it was a permanent [mobilisation], it was [a] daily thing. We were always there doing something, thinking about something" (personal communication, October 22, 2020).

At least four strands of women's movements existed at this point: the working-class/poor women; the bureaucrats, based in state offices; the *damas* (upper-class ladies) who worked in charity and philanthropy; and NGO staff (Lind, 2005). The strands that would engage the most in campaigns denouncing VAW were the bureaucrats and the NGOs.

The Ecuadorian Centre for the Promotion and Action of Women (*Centro ecuatoriano para la promoción y acción de la mujer*, CEPAM), founded in Quito in 1983, was one of the first NGOs to offer services for women who suffered domestic abuse. It operated with the support of the Swedish Agency for Development Cooperation, and delivered capacity-building programmes for women in low-income neighbourhoods in the south of Quito. The organisation offered medical advice, psychological counselling, and legal aid on issues such as divorce and child support (CEPAM, 2019). CEPAM is still active today.

According to the documents of CEPAM and other NGOs working in low-income neighbourhoods, criminal justice was not a mechanism considered suitable to counteract VAW. Also, Ecuadorian women in lower-income sectors did not see law reform as a tool they could use to be protected from domestic abuse. For instance, a 1984 report to UNESCO covers meetings of women's trade unions and neighbourhood associations convened by CEPAM in Quito. These meetings addressed workers' rights, social benefits, and women's daily struggles for survival. Women from these poorer neighbourhoods lacked access to basic services, education, and training to get better jobs; they also demanded better transportation links, and more medical centres. The report shows that women discussed domestic violence in one meeting. Survivors were concerned that there was "no one to turn to for help" (UNESCO, 1984, p. 35). They demanded that an entity be created to assist them when they suffered abuse, but their predicament was not connected to the absence of legislation; it was rather posited as one of many hardships that women endure because of social marginalisation. While the researchers who wrote up the report presented the problem as "lack of insertion into the productive process" (UNESCO, 1984, p. 44), neither researchers nor neighbourhood leaders alluded to criminal justice as the answer.

The first meetings to demand the reform of the Penal Code

The 1980s marked an important turn for Ecuadorian feminism in terms of law reform achievements. In 1980, Ecuador signed the United Nations Convention on the Elimination of All Forms of Discrimination against Women (CEDAW), which had been adopted in 1979 by the UN's General Assembly. With this backdrop, the first joint efforts to defeat sexist laws bore fruit in the early 1980s. In 1982, a workshop to discuss "Women in the Ecuadorian Legislation" took place in Guayaquil (Valdez, 1982). This resulted in a set of documents proposing reforms such as eliminating the "carnal act excuse" from the Penal Code (which justified killing a wife who was found committing adultery), and equally punishing adultery by men and women. However, despite being delivered to representatives of the legislature, the proposals did not result in any legal change.

Nevertheless, these initiatives set in motion feminist advocacy groups, including the seminal "Action for the Women's Movement" (*Acción por el Movimiento de Mujeres,* AMM), created in 1986. The same year, another iconic feminist network was founded: the Azuay Network of Women (*Red de Mujeres del Azuay*), grouping left-wing feminists from the South of Ecuador. These are examples of the first spaces where women's demands directed at the state were systematically articulated.

A later set of law reform proposals by feminist networks came to be known as "the green portfolio" (former AMM member, personal communication, March 16, 2015). The portfolio proposed creating a Parliamentary Commission for Matters of Women, Children, and the Family, which crystallised in 1988 and which the feminist press called "the first public achievement of the women's movement" (Ayala Marín, 1988). The Commission was integrated by the only three congresswomen of the time,[8] who were not militants of women's organisations, nor identified as feminists. However, they became key allies of the AMM. For instance, they mediated a reform to the Civil Code that had

8 By 1986, Cecilia Calderón was the only woman at the Congress. In 1988 there were three congresswomen, including Calderón. They arrived at the legislature through their political parties, not the women's movement. By 1990 there were five congresswomen – less than 7% of the total of representatives (Ayala Marín, 1990). Analyses suggest that during the 1990s and early 2000s most parliamentary women were included in electoral lists due to quota laws (Mosquera Andrade, 2006). Once in office, they would frequently be appointed to "women and family issues" commissions, due to their alleged lack of knowledge in legal and economic matters.

been proposed by the AMM in 1989, broadening married women's rights to conjugal property and facilitating divorce.[9]

In 1988, the Commission, together with various women's organisations, convened the first national meetings on "Criminal Law and Women" to study potential reforms to the Penal Code. For the first time, feminists publicly discussed the Penal Code's discriminatory provisions. Around 200 representatives of women's organisations from across the country attended. The resulting call was to reform 23 articles of the Penal Code in order to "erase [its] patriarchal traits" and tackle "day to day acts that affect women and minors of both sexes". The CEDAW was cited to ground the reform of "laws that are still sexist" (Ayala Marín, 1989, p. 3).[10] This is one of the first instances when feminists invoked an international instrument to press the state to reform domestic legislation. Although controversial topics such as the decriminalisation of homosexuality and abortion – which had been addressed in internal discussions – were not foregrounded, the event was celebrated as a feminist accomplishment.

In 1989, Article 27 of the Penal Code, which had excused the murder of women who were caught committing an "illegitimate carnal act", was declared unconstitutional due to a lawsuit signed by Anunziatta Valdez and Mercedes Jiménez, two feminist lawyers who presented the petition before the Tribunal of Constitutional Guarantees (see Table 2.2).[11] The news was received with joy; for instance, a press release by Mujer/Fempress, a transnational feminist newsletter, affirmed that the defeated article had been a legal authorisation for men to kill women; therefore, its abolition should be celebrated (Cuvi et al., 2006).[12]

9 The reforms were not unopposed: prominent jurists of the time, such as priest Juan Larrea Holguín, famously opposed them arguing that they constituted an aggression against the family institution (Larrea Holguín, 1989), while businessmen asserted that women's economic autonomy disrupted the dynamics of commercial companies and obstructed trade (Briones, 1989b).

10 The CEDAW does not impose sanctions on countries that do not comply with its mandates, but the CEDAW Committee has an international prestige that allows it to expose lack of compliance through the publication of comments and reports that account for state policy measures oriented at eliminating discrimination. One aspect of the CEDAW monitoring process is that it provides spaces not only for government commissions, but also for NGOS to present their views through "shadow reports", which are analysed in the next chapter.

11 As shown in Table 2.2, the article had previously been reformed in 1938. The excuse originally targeted *any* "carnal act" and it deemed women who were found engaging in sexual relations, "delinquents". In the 1938 code, the active subject of the offense changed from "one" to "a person", and the carnal act was now to be "illegitimate" – presumably to prevent the possibility of a father killing his own son-in-law if found engaging in sexual relations with his daughter. The woman was now called "guilty" rather than delinquent. The changes had been inspired by the Italian code of 1930 and the Argentinian code of 1922 (Albán, 2012). But the words "daughter", "granddaughter", and "sister" preserved their feminine form in Spanish, therefore hardly entailing any significant difference, as killing sons, grandsons, and brothers was never excused.

12 Although this representation was not fully accurate, in the Ecuadorian system an "excuse" functioned as an incomplete exclusion of criminal liability which resulted in a reduced sanction for the defendant.

Table 2.2 Reform of the "carnal act excuse" (1906–1989)

1906	*1938*	*1989*
Art. 30.- The infraction that *one* commits when catching one's daughter, granddaughter or sister during a carnal act, is also excusable, whether one kills, injures or beats up the delinquent, or the man who lies with her.	Art. 27.- Likewise, the infraction committed by a person who catches their daughter, granddaughter or sister during an illegitimate carnal act, is excusable, whether the person kills, injures or beats up the guilty woman or the man who lies with her.	Declared unconstitutional

Table designed and produced by the author. Source(s): Lexis Finder database and the Constitutional Court of Ecuador's website.

Marena Briones: law plays a role in our oppression

Other strands of feminist thought articulated radical critiques of law during the 1980s. Rather than demand law reform, some feminists denounced law as an expression of the dominant morals, which prioritised "men's honour and women's modesty" (Ayala Marín, 1989), resulting in women's systemic discrimination. Here, I highlight the work of Marena Briones, a feminist lawyer from Guayaquil, who authored many articles during the decade. I have interviewed her on various occasions due to the uniqueness of her work in the context of the time.

Briones was a posthumous child, brought up by her mother, grandmother, and aunt. She attributes her interest in women's struggles to this upbringing and her reading of texts by women. From the mid-1980s Briones became involved with women's advocacy groups in Quito and Guayaquil, which led her to write and publish on women's status in the country. Briones' work broadly highlights the discriminatory discourses underlying law, which she considers a defining characteristic of legal frameworks.

In several texts, Briones expressed her concern that the law was more an obstacle than a means for social change, as it is limited by its bourgeois and sexist biases, which subject women to the "patriarchal scheme of the father/husband/employer" (Briones, 1988b). An enthusiasm regarding feminist-led legal change was already on the rise, and law reform strategies were being discussed at international fora where law was posited as a tool for women's liberation (Briones, 1989c). Conversely, Briones was (and still is) dubious about the legislation as an emancipatory instrument. She stressed that law, as a cultural and social product, cannot be regarded as neutral, objective, or apolitical (Briones, 1989a).

Marena Briones' articles were published in magazines dedicated to women's issues and also in more general publications that circulated as supplements of national newspapers. Such is the case of *Matapalo*, a periodical that often printed feminist opinion pieces. Some of Briones' critical perspectives on law were thus disseminated at a large scale. A 1988 *Matapalo* magazine article by Briones focused on statutory rape, which would only be reformed in 2005, and until then was defined as follows: "Art. 509.- Statutory rape is the intercourse with an *honest woman*, by resorting to seduction or deception to achieve her consent" (*Código Penal*, 1971 emphasis added). Briones emphasised that only "honest" women could be victims of statutory rape, which excluded other "deviant" women (such as sex workers) from the law's scope of protection, since they could not be considered "honest". Briones claimed that these laws made clear that women were second-class citizens, discriminated against by the Penal Code (Briones, 1988a). She denounced the moralistic underpinnings of the criminalisation of women's sexuality, which protected values such as chastity and virginity. Briones framed the family as the "origin of women's oppression, because it has been until today a patriarchal institution that has glorified the reproduction of the species, and law has consolidated these inequalities" (Briones, 1988a, p. 4). In a later text, she argued: "women have one more challenge: to discover our marginality within [law] and strive to defeat it" (Briones, 1989a, p. 8).

As of today, Briones' stance regarding law reform continues to be cautious. In a 2015 personal interview, she said:

> There is something that I am perhaps going to say at this time: although the law and legal norms in particular can be an instrument to obtain some achievements or social changes, they are not a sufficient instrument, nor are they the only instrument. [...] I am very critical, in that sense, of how rules have been conceived in that way.

Moreover, Marena Briones' views, then and now, point at how the law may mask the persistence of ingrained patriarchal subordination. In the same interview, she said:

> So, it's like we suddenly think: 'Ah, the category of femicide is already in the Penal Code, so now there is nothing more to do, or what can be done is very little'. What we know [of women's lives] is minimal compared to what really happens. And that is not resolved with the law.
>
> (personal communication, May 8, 2015)

Using words that resonated with her texts from the 1980s, referring in particular to criminal law, Briones declared:

> I do not think that everything has to be criminalised. [...] I also believe that great care must be taken not to make criminal law a kind of moralistic instrument. That worries me, it worries me to turn criminal law into a flag to conquer everything that seems wrong to us.

In a 2020 interview, Briones again declared: "It is a kind of blindness to maintain that modifying a legal provision or reaching the enactment of a legal provision that we believe may be optimal is going to be the only thing we need" (personal communication, October 22, 2020). When asked about her view of current feminist approaches to law reform, she added:

> law is essential, but every relationship implies a social relationship. It is essential, but we have to rethink law, we have to continue questioning and interrogating that object with which we work and that we want to know, and that we call law. Because, ultimately, if one begins to reexamine [social problems], they not only have to do with legal practice such as judgments, jurisprudence, doctrine; but also with the very theory of law and the philosophy of law, we are going to find that almost all, if not all aspects of law are controversial and problematic.
>
> (personal communication, October 22, 2020)

Overall, the stances that denounced the role of law in producing or worsening the subordination of women, translated into demands to *defeat* the law, that is, in reform proposals aimed at repealing rather than enacting legal provisions. A more heterodox sector of feminism, here represented by Marena Briones, advocated recognising that law marginalises women due to its very episteme, beyond the amendments that reform can achieve. However, these perspectives would later be displaced by the feminist drive to propose the creation of new criminal laws, which stepped away from these earlier depictions of law as a political and ideological apparatus.

Conclusion

This chapter presented an outline of feminist strands that stood out in Ecuador during the 20th century, until the 1990s. Feminist stances were diverse, ranging from indigenous women's strong scepticism regarding the state's law, to maternalist feminists who strategically invoked motherhood to demand better living conditions for women. For their part, middle-class NGO-based feminists implemented community projects and were able to obtain some legal change. One thing that these different feminist strands had in common was the absence of investment in new legislation; certainly, they were not proposing the use of criminal law to punish VAW. Instead, law reform efforts were oriented at defeating legal provisions that were considered violent and discriminatory. At the same time, VAW was framed as a form of social injustice aggravated by a lack of social services, rather than seen exclusively as interpersonal violence. The thought of Marena Briones illustrates critiques of women's "deviancy" as a legal construction that undermined their status as citizens. Her work expressed scepticism regarding the benefits of law reform, as she considered law as a potential reproducer of violence and insufficient as a mechanism to address women's systemic oppression.

Along the line, this chapter has shown that during this "pre-penal" period, some feminist approaches had more resonance than others, as was the case of the equality-based discourses, present in Zoila Rendón's critique and, later, in the 1980s' repeals. This strand of feminism prevailed over other approaches to women's struggles, such as the Marxist stances, the indigenous perspective, the Latin American *Encuentros* critiques, or popular sectors' demands for more social services. Understanding this scenario facilitates the identification of the "turn to criminal law" and the subsequent proposals to criminalise various forms of VAW, which I address in the next chapter.

References

Albán, E. (2012). *Manual de derecho penal ecuatoriano*. Ediciones Legales.

Ayala Marín, A. (1988, November). El primer logro público del movimiento de mujeres. *Mujer/Fempress., 86*, 3.

Ayala Marín, A. (1989, February). Crónica macabra y una esperanza. *Mujer/Fempress, 89*, 3–4.

Ayala Marín, A. (1990, September). Son tantas y tan pocas cinco diputadas. *Mujer/Fempress, 107*, 8.

Boserup, E. (1970). *Woman's role in economic development*. Earthscan.

Briones, M. (1988a, March). Ciudadanas de segunda clase. *Matapalo, 12.*

Briones, M. (1988b, May). Derecho y feminismo. *Matapalo, 23.*

Briones, M. (1989a). Descubriendo nuestra marginalidad de mujeres. In *Guía legal de los derechos de la mujer* (pp. 7–8). CAM.

Briones, M. (1989b, November). ¿Son negativas las reformas al Código Civil? *Tiempo Libre, 52*, 37–38.

Briones, M. (1988c, December). ¿Un instrumento de lucha para la emancipación de las mujeres? *La Mujer, 17.*

CEPAM. (2019). *Nuestra historia*. CEPAM. http://cepam.org.ec/nosotras/

Chant, S., & Craske, N. (2003). *Gender in Latin America*. Latin American Bureau (Research and Action).

Chico Peñaherrera, R. (2004). *Estudios de derecho penal*. Fundación Chico Peñaherrera.

Chinchilla, N.S. (1991). Marxism, feminism, and the struggle for democracy in Latin America. *Gender and Society, 5*(3, Special: Marxist Feminist Theory), 291–310.

Código Penal, Comisión Jurídica (1971) (testimony of Suplemento Registro Oficial 147).

Connell, R. (2015). Meeting at the edge of fear: Theory on a world scale. *Feminist Theory, 16*(1), 49–66.

Cuvi, M., Buitrón, L., Cuvi, M., & Buitrón, L. (eds.). (2006). *Pensamiento feminista y escritos de mujeres en el Ecuador: 1980–1990. Bibliografía anotada*. UNIFEM-UNICEF.

El Día. (2006/1938). Se reunió ayer la Asamblea de Mujeres Ecuatorianas (AFE). In A.M. Goetschel (ed.), *Orígenes del feminismo en el Ecuador. Antología* (p. 181). CONAMU.

El Mundo. (2009, May 12). *Tránsito Amaguaña, centenaria líder indígena de Ecuador*. El Mundo. https://www.elmundo.es/elmundo/2009/05/12/obituarios/1242095375.html

Gargallo, F. (2010). *Una metodología para detectar lo que de hegemónico ha recogido el feminismo académico latinoamericano y caribeño* (N. Blazquez Graf, F. Flores Palacios, & M. Ríos Everardo (eds.); p. 155). Centro Regional de Investigaciones Multidisciplinarias, UNAM.

Goetschel, A.M. (2006). Estudio introductorio. In A.M. Goetschel (ed.), *Orígenes del Feminismo en el Ecuador. Antología* (p. 93). CONAMU, FLACSO Sede Ecuador, Comisión de género y equidad social del MDMQ, UNIFEM.

Guy, D.J. (2000). *White slavery and mothers alive and dead: The troubled meeting of sex, gender, public health, and progress in Latin America* (Vol. 5). University of Nebraska Press.

Htun, M. (2003). *Sex and the state: Abortion, divorce, and the family under Latin American dictatorships and democracies*. Cambridge University Press.

Larrea Holguín, J. (1989). *Las últimas reformas al código civil - Ley #88*. Revista Jurídica Online. http://www.revistajuridicaonline.com/wp-content/uploads/1991/02/03_Ultimas_Reformas_Codigo_Civil.pdf

Lind, A. (2005). *Gendered paradoxes. Women's movements, state restructuring and global development in Ecuador*. Pennsylvania State University Press.

Martínez, M.E. (2006/1933). El problema feminista en el Ecuador. In A.M. Goetschel (ed.), *Orígenes del feminismo en el Ecuador* (p. 115). CONAMU, FLACSO Sede Ecuador, Comisión de género y equidad social del MDMQ, UNIFEM.

Mendoza, B. (2002). Transnational feminisms in question. *Feminist Theory*, *3*(3), 295–314.

Merry, S.E. (2003). Rights talk and the experience of law: Implementing women's human rights to protection from violence. *Human Rights Quarterly*, *25*(2), 343–381.

Molyneux, M. (2003). *Women's movements in international perspective: Latin America and beyond*. Institute of Latin American Studies.

Mosquera Andrade, V. (2006). *Mujeres congresistas. Estereotipos sexistas e identidades estratégicas. Ecuador 2003–2005*. Ediciones Abya-Yala/FLACSO.

Navarro, M. (1982). First feminist meeting of Latin America and the Caribbean. *Signs*, *8*(1), 154–159.

Prieto, M. (1978). *Condicionamientos de la movilización campesina: el caso de las haciendas Olmedo. Ecuador (1926–1948)* [Bachelor of Arts in Anthropology]. Pontificia Universidad Católica del Ecuador.

Rendón, Z. (1923/2006). Estado jurídico de la mujer casada. Seducción a las solteras, sus consecuencias. In A.M. Goetschel (ed.), *Orígenes del feminismo en el Ecuador* (p. 97). CONAMU, FLACSO Sede Ecuador, Comisión de género y equidad social del MDMQ, UNIFEM.

Rendón, Z. (1948/2006). La mujer en los diversos organismos humanos. In A.M. Goetschel (ed.), *Orígenes del feminismo en el Ecuador* (p. 93). CONAMU, FLACSO Sede Ecuador, Comisión de género y equidad social del MDMQ, UNIFEM.

UNESCO. (1984). *Problems that concern women and their consideration in development planning*. UNESCO. http://unesdoc.unesco.org/images/0006/000632/063207eb.pdf

Valdez, A. (1982). El primer taller de la mujer en la legislación ecuatoriana. *Nueva Mujer*, *4*, 40–41

Yánez del Pozo, J. (2006). Dolores Cacuango. In A.M. Goetschel & A.M. Goetschel (eds.), *Orígenes del feminismo en el Ecuador. Antología* (p. 189). CONAMU, FLACSO Sede Ecuador, Comisión de género y equidad social del MDMQ, UNIFEM.

Yashar, D.J. (2005). *Contesting citizenship in Latin America: The rise of indigenous movements and the postliberal challenge*. Cambridge University Press.

Zaffaroni, E.R. (2009). *El discurso feminista y el poder punitivo* (R. Avila, J. Salgado, & L. Valladares (eds.); 1st ed., pp. 321–334). Ministerio de justicia y derechos humanos.

Chapter 3

Violence against women, human rights, and the turn to criminal law

Introduction

In Chapter 2, I showed how the diverse strands of the early Ecuadorian women's movement engaged with criminal law. Some were sceptical of the state as a site to articulate their demands; others promoted reform to defeat discriminatory legal provisions. Overall, neither of these trends prioritised criminalisation as a mechanism to counteract violence against women (VAW). Instead, criminal law was interrogated as an institution that conveyed and reproduced women's subordination in Ecuadorian society.

This chapter covers the turn to criminal law, in a context whereby various international agencies posited VAW as an obstacle for economic development, a public health threat, and a human rights violation. Through the 1990s, feminists at an international and local level increasingly appealed to criminal law reform, based on the idea that rights are duly recognised and enforced when their violation is categorised as a crime. Fields of study such as public health, psychology, and women in development, also contributed to presenting VAW as a problem that requires a legal response. However, these framings did not challenge the colonial surveillance of women's bodies.

The first half of this chapter is based on content analysis of documents and international instruments from the United Nations (UN) and the Organization of American States (OAS). I show the role of these agencies in positing law reform and criminal justice as the best strategies to tackle VAW. The second half of the chapter focuses on Ecuador, and traces the establishment of the first commissariats for women and the family, and the passing of Act 103, the first specialised VAW law. At that point, I incorporate the testimonies of feminists who participated in those processes. The interviews were oriented towards understanding how feminists justified the use of criminal law in the 1990s, with a focus on domestic violence. I supplement interview data with a close reading of the parliamentary records that contain the debates on Act 103.

My analysis reveals that feminist demands, informed by human rights, development, and public health, were reframed and modulated by the National Congress. There was a compatibility between preexisting familial ideologies, and the 1990s demand to penalise domestic violence, a convergence that would

DOI: 10.4324/9781003098799-4

be decisive for women's movements' proposals to be accepted. A broader lesson can be learned from this finding: "carceral feminism" may be, in many cases, not only a product of feminist antiviolence campaigns, but also of non-feminist legislative and political reframings of violence as a broader social problem that is already inscribed in the realm of criminal law. Moreover, protecting the family was prioritised by the Ecuadorian legislature in the 1990s, suggesting the reincorporation of what feminist historians have called a "non-violent patriarchy" (see Chapter 2).

This chapter contributes to nuancing current accounts of the ascension of carceral feminism and its role in expanding penality. By showing that the framing of VAW as a criminal law issue was largely a result of the National Congress' intervention, and that feminist movements had a less punitive project in mind, I suggest that "mistranslation" and "mishearing" by the state should not be downplayed when it comes to critiquing feminist proposals. In Ecuador, rather than adopting the model proposed by the feminist lawyers, which contained non-penal elements and addressed child support and reparations, the legislature imposed the use of the ordinary penal system. The resort to the penal apparatus, the continuity of postcolonial family-protection discourses, and the reframing of feminist demands by the legislature, are recurring patterns that would remerge after the 1990s.

Violence against women: from social injustice to law reform issue

As shown in Chapter 2, VAW has not always been framed as a problem to be tackled mainly through law reform. Until the mid-1980s, it was broadly considered a manifestation of social inequality that required better access to resources and services for women. For instance, the Copenhagen 1980 report, which is one of the first instances where domestic VAW is addressed in a publicly available UN document, refers to "battered women and violence in the family" as "a problem of serious social consequences" requiring the intervention of states to provide women with assistance, through shelters, rehabilitation, child care, employment, healthcare, and housing (United Nations, 1980). Similarly, the emerging field of gender and development had started to refer to VAW as a developmental concern, but it did not overall see the rule of law or criminal law enforcement as central mechanisms to achieve development. There was a "before" the current global consensus about law reform as a tool to address maldevelopment and its causes (Bedford, 2020; Boserup, 1970).

However, through the 1990s we see law reform gradually take a central position in the agendas of international development agencies, including their prescribed strategies to address VAW. These years also marked a period of professionalisation of women's movements in Latin America, together with their incorporation into international organisations and transnational NGOs, which prompted a reconfiguration of feminist identities (Alvarez, 1999, 2000;

Rodas Morales, 2007). NGOs in particular constituted bridges between local activism and transnational approaches to women's rights. As feminist networks discussed the best strategies to tackle domestic violence, the knowledge provided by emerging fields of expertise, especially public health, gender and development, and human rights, informed the work conducted by mainstream women's organisations. These interrelated discourses expedited the turn to law reform as a priority in international and local efforts to combat VAW.

Domestic violence as a public health issue

From the 1970s onwards, VAW became a topic of interest within disciplines such as public health and development, which posited domestic violence as an issue that required the intervention of government agencies to create or enforce relevant laws. This is clear in the materials produced by development agencies such as the World Bank, which identified male violence against women as a "gender-related development issue" associated with public health challenges (Cole & Phillips, 2008; The World Bank, 2000). Unlike feminist work, however, these accounts did not posit VAW as an effect of deep-rooted patriarchal structures, but did emphasise how it hindered development.

Health agencies, like the Panamerican Health Organisation (PAHO), identified domestic violence as a risk factor for women during their reproductive cycle and as a maternal health complication (CEPAR, 2001; Cuvi, 1999). The expression "health with a gender perspective" became common in institutional documents that endeavoured to teach healthcare professionals how to identify domestic abuse. These presented violence as a threat to the family's health and well-being. Domestic violence was also deemed a risk factor for mental health problems. Psychology provided models that are still widely used in Latin America, including Lenore Walker's (2000) "cycle of abuse" (see Figure 3.1), and her account of "battered women's syndrome" and "learned helplessness". By this paradigm, VAW is cyclical and repetitive mainly due to the existence of a "honeymoon" phase whereby women forgive the aggressor and resume their relationship. This model and some feminist ideas stemming from the Anglo-American battered women's movement were mutually influential in creating a new narrative around VAW (Merry, 2006; Schneider, 2000).

On the basis of the cycle of abuse, a 1990s report on VAW sponsored by the PAHO (Cuvi, 1999) shows that NGO staff described domestic violence as the result of an "affective dependence" that confined women to a dead-end. The cycle of abuse illustrations are ubiquitous in printed materials on VAW in Latin America from the 1980s onwards. I have also identified the cycle as central to current lawyers' representations of VAW (see Chapter 6). In this model, women's "refusal" to leave their abuser is portrayed as a psychological disorder, a form of learned helplessness that facilitates a vicious violence circle whereby women forgive and forget and become victimised again and again.

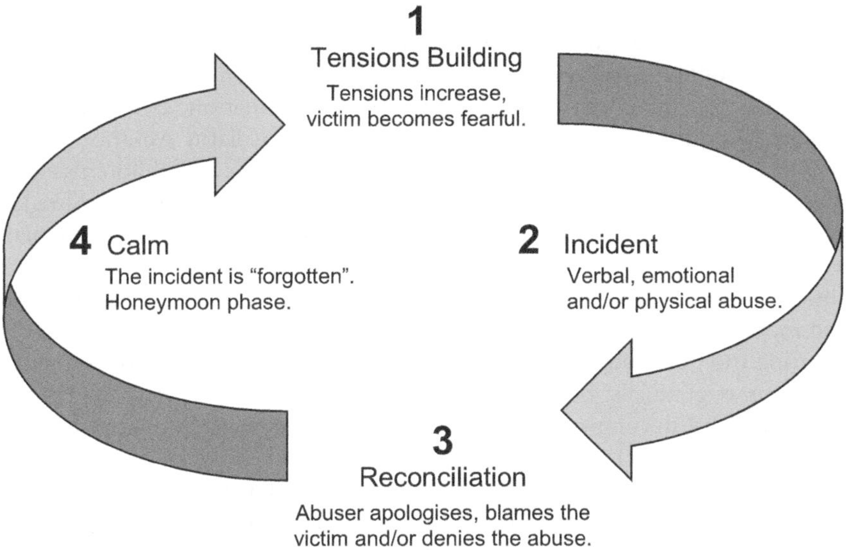

Figure 3.1 Cycle of Abuse. Source: designed and produced by the author.

Although these framings contributed to making VAW visible, presenting it as a mental health problem or an obstacle for economic development did not challenge dominant gender norms at their colonial roots. In fact, the concerns of feminists in previous decades (see Chapter 2), were not a primary issue of discussion in these newer materials. Yet, positing domestic violence in technical/scientific terms, together with the compatibility between fighting domestic abuse and protecting the family, rendered the problem less controversial than other feminist demands, such as those pertaining to sexual and reproductive rights. As a result, domestic violence was more amenable to legislators and policymakers to take up. These approaches introduced definitions of VAW from outside feminism, which validated the problem as a "non-ideological" and "objective" issue, facilitating state support for law and policy reform on battered women (Cole & Phillips, 2008). The technical framing of VAW thus constituted a condition of acceptability (Foucault, 1997) of law reform on VAW. In sum, domestic violence was portrayed as a threat to families, an obstacle to economic development, and a mental and physical health ailment. Gradually, VAW was established as a policy problem that needed to be managed to ensure a citizen's wellbeing and the nation's progress.

VAW as a development and human rights concern

From the 1970s, Women in Development studies identified gender-based inequalities in working conditions and access to resources as key development concerns. Studies linking gender inequality to development were gradually included in NGO programmes directed at women in low-income sectors across Latin America.[1] Importantly, early accounts of women's role in economic development, such as Ester Boserup's (1970) seminal work, did not propose law reform as a solution for women's discrimination (Bedford, 2020). Similarly, the pioneering work of Caroline Moser on Latin America framed VAW as a development concern, foregrounding women's and children's experiences of intra-family abuse (McIlwaine & Moser, 2001; Moser & Shrader, 1999). Still, criminalisation was not central to Moser's work, because the people most affected by it did not see crime control or police intervention as a solution. Indeed, Moser's analysis of violence perceptions in Guatemala featured more discussion of poverty than crime (Bedford & Tapia Tapia, 2021).

During the post-Washington Consensus era, proposing law reform to facilitate business gradually became commonplace. The rule of law emerged as central to global development efforts to secure democracy, human rights, and markets (Bedford & Tapia Tapia, 2021). In the post-1989 context, collaboration between international, national, and regional movements burgeoned (Cole & Phillips, 2008). With the end of the Cold War, redefinitions of security within the UN facilitated the displacement of militarism, and a focus on individual rights became fundamental. NGOs obtained access to the UN's processes, gaining consultative status and negotiation power. One such NGO is the US-based Center for Women's Global Leadership (CWGL).

In 1991, the CWGL published a book containing two essays (Bunch & Carrillo, 1991). The first, by Charlotte Bunch, focused on the failure of the international human rights movement to consider women's rights as human rights. The second, sponsored by UNIFEM and written by Roxanna Carrillo, focused on VAW as an obstacle to development. Bunch advocated for a feminist transformation of human rights to break down the barriers between public and private violence, making states liable for not preventing and punishing domestic abuse. She strongly expressed a "refusal to wait for permission from some authority to determine what is or is not a human rights issue" (Bunch & Carrillo, 1991, p. 14). She also argued that domestic VAW is often accepted and tolerated because some forms of VAW, such as domestic abuse, "are not

1 These included communal childcare facilities for underprivileged neighbourhoods, run by community mothers. The programmes had the purpose of assisting women in their incorporation to paid labour and public life. In Ecuador, many of these facilities were established during the presidency of Rodrigo Borja (1988–1992) and were introduced as a way to overcome paternalistic approaches to social welfare. Critics have observed that the communal facilities operated on the assumption that women could absorb the costs of services by providing unlimited amounts of their time for little or no pay, thus becoming the bearers of the state's welfare responsibilities are an example of how the formulation of traditional gender roles has served to institutionalise women's struggles (Bedford, 2009; Lind, 2005). The daycare centres were dismantled during the government of Sixto Durán-Ballén.

crimes in law" (Bunch & Carrillo, 1991, p. 11). Bunch claimed that governments dismissed domestic abuse and refused to recognise it as a violation of human rights for which they should be accountable. This "women's rights are human rights" framing helped reshape the international law and policy responses to VAW, influencing the UN's subsequent understanding of state responsibility to prevent and punish gender-based violence.

Although the argument that criminal law should be enforced to protect individual liberties was already common in the 19th century (Christie, 2007), between the 1980s and the 1990s, the idea that VAW constituted a violation of human rights repositioned criminal justice as a protagonist in the fight against gender-based violence. To an extent, this resulted in the relegation of some regional and local accounts that regarded law as a producer of gender subordination, such as the Latin American feminist *Encuentros* (see Chapter 2).

Delving into UN materials, I found that the first endorsements of criminal justice as a tool to counteract VAW appeared between 1985 and 1993; first, during the Seventh UN Congress on the Prevention of Crime and Treatment of Offenders and, later, in the first World Conference on Human Rights in Vienna. The 1985 Congress, based on a recommendation of the Commission on the Status of Women, urged the UN General Assembly to adopt a resolution inviting member states to introduce "civil and criminal legislation in order to deal with particular problems of domestic violence, and to enact and enforce such laws in order to protect battered family members and punish the offender" (DESA, 1986, p. 51). In 1986, the Economic and Social Council (ECOSOC) convened an Expert Group Meeting on violence in the family with special emphasis on women. Technical studies and statistics were presented to show that VAW crossed cultures, ethnicities, and social classes. Experts included law reform recommendations which, in contrast to previous welfare-oriented approaches, called for the use of the criminal justice apparatus. The report appealed to the symbolic power of criminal law, stressing that legislation, in naming and penalising VAW, could communicate that domestic violence is unacceptable. Criminal law would thus fulfil the purpose of deterring the perpetrator, as well as making him personally responsible for his actions (United Nations Branch for the Advancement of Women, 1987). This approach would thereafter dominate the mainstream global discourse on VAW.

Although the Convention on the Elimination of all Forms of Discrimination Against Women CEDAW (1979) did not originally address VAW, its ratification influenced the creation of laws in many countries (Hallward-Driemeier et al., 2013). In 1992, the CEDAW Committee introduced General Recommendation No. 19, which states that "Gender-based violence is a form of discrimination that seriously inhibits women's ability to enjoy rights and freedoms on a basis of equality with men". For the first time, VAW was formally framed as a manifestation of inequality, a hindrance to women's individual freedoms, and a violation of human rights. Only one year later, the campaigns carried out by Bunch's CWGL and other NGOs paid off, when the 1993 Vienna Conference finally declared that "women's rights are human rights". During the Conference, the Global Tribunal on Violations of Women's Rights, formed by representatives of organisations and shelters for battered women, including from Latin America, denounced that there were no explicit legal provisions penalising domestic violence in their countries and, as a result, the police and the judiciary would not take complaints seriously when they were filed by women (Bunch & Reilly, 1994).

After Vienna, the UN General Assembly adopted the Declaration on the Elimination of Violence Against Women, drafted by another Expert Group in 1991. While non-binding, the Declaration recommends that states "develop penal, civil, labour, and administrative sanctions in domestic legislation to punish and redress the wrongs caused to women who are subject to violence" (Article 4.d). We now see a solid association between protecting women's human rights and categorising VAW as a criminal offence.

The 1995 Fourth World Conference on Women, in Beijing, also adopted this approach. The resulting Platform for Action identified VAW as a "critical area of concern" exacerbated by "the *lack of laws* that prohibit violence against women; *failure to reform* existing laws; inadequate efforts by public authorities to promote awareness of and *enforce existing laws*" (paragraph 118l, emphasis added). The Beijing processes have been particularly influential in Latin America: the 1995 Platform for Action prompted the creation of new legislation in virtually every country in the region (Macaulay, 2006). However, it is important to highlight that non-mainstream feminist strands, such as the Latin American and Caribbean Feminist *Encuentros* (EFLAC), did not endorse the UN agenda uncritically (Stephen, 1997). The EFLAC pointed at the UN's centralisation, hierarchies, and unilateralism regarding the debate streams. UN instruments, which are based on consensus amongst states, have been noted to often represent the lowest common denominator of protection for women. These sites of resistance should always be recognised as key elements in the development of Latin American Feminisms.

Having outlined the discourses that leveraged the global turn to criminal law as a tool to counteract VAW, I will now address the regional scenario, namely, the Inter-American Human Rights System. Analysing this system is important to understand the broader use of criminal justice as a response to human rights violations across the world: many legal systems have been largely informed by the Inter-American processes and case law (Mavronicola & Lavrysen, 2020).

The Organization of American States and the Belém do Pará Convention

Through the 1990s, NGOs specialising in women's issues multiplied in Latin America. "NGOization" (Alvarez, 1998, 1999) has played a fundamental role in articulating mainstream feminist movements in the region, and in shaping feminist knowledge (Herrera, 2001). Staff professionalisation sped up during the decade, producing experts in mediating women's demands before international and domestic governance institutions (Gargallo, 2006). By 1994, the Organization of American States (OAS) appointed its first Special Rapporteur on Women's Rights. The same year, the OAS adopted the first VAW international treaty in the world: the Interamerican Convention on the Prevention, Punishment, and Eradication of Violence Against Women, known as the "Convention of Belém do Pará" after the Brazilian city where it was signed. The Convention has been ratified by all the OAS states (except for the United States and Canada). Its approval was the outcome of the work that the Inter-American Commission on Women (*Comisión Interamericana de Mujeres*, CIM) had been carrying out for decades.

The CIM is an autonomous technical body whose objectives are to ensure that state policies comply with human rights standards. It was established in 1928 as a result of the mobilisation of suffragists (Organization of American States, 2019), and it played an active role in various UN processes thereafter. In fact, it has been regarded as the "mother" of the UN Commission on the Status of Women (CSW), because its members pressed for the creation of the CSW and many were founding members of both commissions (Meyer, 1999). In 1988, the CIM's Executive Committee identified the absence of international laws addressing domestic violence as a pressing impediment to tackling the problem in the American states. The Committee also detected a void in the CEDAW, which at the time did not consider VAW as a form of discrimination against women. A special Meeting of Consultation was held in 1990 to address these matters and, as a consequence, member states were asked to submit reports on their existing legislation and statistics on VAW. The Meeting concluded that VAW surpassed the realm of the private, and affirmed that institutions, including the state, were responsible for its prevalence.

Two years prior to the CEDAW's Recommendation 19, the CIM had already stated that VAW constitutes a serious case of discrimination against women and a violation of human rights. It was thus agreed that an Inter-American convention on VAW was needed, and a team of ten women jurists with experience in women's rights and human rights law prepared a first draft. The Committee met again in 1993 to polish the text, and the final version was submitted to the General Assembly in 1994, after the member states had been asked to submit their comments. Ecuador reported the results of a national meeting where NGOs and state representatives, including the Parliamentary Commission for women and the family, expressed their support of the project (Comisión Interamericana de Mujeres, 1994).

The Belém do Pará Convention considers VAW a human rights violation, defined as "any act or conduct, based on gender, which causes death or physical, sexual or psychological harm or suffering to women, whether in the public or the private sphere" (Art. 1). Article 7, which establishes the duties that member states acquire under the Convention, focuses substantially on law reform. Seven out of eight items refer to the adoption of legal measures, including penal sanctions for gender-based violence (see Table 3.1). State accountability takes the form of commitments to reform the law and to make a judicial pathway available for the prosecution of VAW. Some non-penal mechanisms are mentioned as well, but they are presented as programmatic goals to gradually produce sociocultural change, while law reform remedies are presented as immediate courses of action. Economic measures and improving women's access to resources and services, such as those commonly found in seminal accounts of Gender and Development studies, are not mentioned anywhere in the Convention.

The Inter-American human rights system comprises two primary institutions: the Inter-American Commission on Human Rights (IACHR) and the Inter-American Court of Human Rights (IACtHR). Their recommendations and decisions make up the Inter-American case law (*jurisprudencia interamericana*). These entities have developed two fundamental concepts that most states have incorporated into their national laws on VAW: women's rights to a life's project, and women's right to a life free of violence and discrimination.

Table 3.1 Law reform duties of member states under Belém do Pará (Art. 7)

Not oriented to law reform	A.	refrain from engaging in any act or practice of violence against women and to ensure that their authorities, officials, personnel, agents, and institutions act in conformity with this obligation;
Oriented to law reform	B.	apply due diligence to prevent, investigate and **impose penalties** for violence against women;
	C.	**include in their domestic legislation penal, civil, administrative, and any other type of provisions** that may be needed to prevent, punish, and eradicate violence against women and to adopt appropriate administrative measures where necessary;
	D.	**adopt legal measures** to require the perpetrator to refrain from harassing, intimidating, or threatening the woman or using any method that harms or endangers her life or integrity, or damages her property;
	E.	take all appropriate measures, including **legislative measures**, to amend or repeal existing laws and regulations or to modify legal or customary practices which sustain the persistence and tolerance of violence against women;
	F.	establish fair and effective **legal procedures** for women who have been subjected to violence which include, among others, protective measures, a timely hearing, and effective access to such procedures;
	G.	Establish the necessary **legal and administrative mechanisms** to ensure that women subjected to violence have effective access to restitution, reparations, or other just and effective remedies; and
	H.	adopt such **legislative** or other measures as may be necessary to give effect to this Convention.

Table designed and produced by the author. Source: OAS website and the author's field notes.

The Belém do Pará Convention was applied for the first time by the Inter-American Commission in Maria da Penha Maia Fernandes v. Brazil (2001). The Commission's Report indicates that the State failed to fulfil its obligation to exercise due diligence to prevent, punish, and eradicate domestic violence, *by failing to convict and punish* the perpetrator for 15 years, despite the timely complaints by the survivor. The Commission concluded that Brazil was responsible for the violation of the rights that are protected by the American Convention on Human Rights, and that the State had violated Article 7 of the Belém do Pará Convention. This case is almost always cited in local and international discourses addressing VAW as a human rights violation.

Another prominent case is Gonzáles et al. (Cotton Field) v. Mexico (2009). Here, the Inter-American Court remarked on the recklessness of Mexican police in investigating the connected murders of numerous women in Ciudad Juarez. Many of the victims' bodies were found in a cotton field with evidence of serious physical assault and sexual violence. The Court noted that most cases remained unsolved, with the homicides that presented sexual violence being the ones with the highest levels of *impunity*. The Court thus affirmed that Mexico had violated the human rights protected under the Inter-American instruments, and stressed that impunity sends the message that VAW is tolerated, which favours its perpetuation and social acceptance of the phenomenon.[2]

In Ecuador, Inter-American instruments and case law have been highly influential and have at times operated in place of feminist critique, enhancing an approach that increasingly relied on law reform and litigation. The next section will show how these internationally developed frameworks docked in Ecuadorian feminist initiatives regarding VAW.

Ecuador's first laws on VAW: the encounter of feminism and familialism

After 1981, Ecuador entered a period sometimes called the "long neoliberal night".[3] Presidents Oswaldo Hurtado (1981–1984), Leon Febres-Cordero (1984–1988), Rodrigo Borja (1988–1992),[4] and Sixto Durán-Ballén (1992–1996) enforced the prescriptions of the Washington Consensus. Discourses of "state modernisation" proliferated during these years, as governments used a large proportion of the national budget to pay off foreign debt, to the detriment of social welfare (CLADEM, 2006). In this context, a major indigenous uprising in 1990 forced the government to negotiate with the Confederation of Indigenous Nationalities of Ecuador (*Confederación de Nacionalidades Indígenas*

2 For further detail on the Inter-American human rights jurisprudence on VAW see Tojo (2011).

3 The expression was coined by former Ecuadorian President Rafael Correa (2011).

4 While President Borja represented a left of centre party and identified as a social democrat, he did not fundamentally disrupt the agenda deployed by the other presidents.

del Ecuador, CONAIE), which has since gained international notoriety as a crucial political actor (Yashar, 2005). Sectors of the women's movement, particularly popular organisations, also protested against the economic adjustments, although their stance on neoliberal restructuring has not been homogeneous (Lind, 2005).

Scholars and activists have referred to this period as the "golden age" of the women's movement, given that alliances and collectives strengthened, while NGOs multiplied.[5] The funding provided by international development organisations opened up opportunities for local NGOs to put together projects to influence policy-making. As development agencies required local NGOs to incorporate a "gender approach", the demand for "gender experts" increased. Because the need for expertise was pressing, training programmes often took the form of short workshops designed for the trainees to use the tools right away, rather than to reflect on feminist theories and debates (Cuvi, 1999). In other words, gender was disseminated and incorporated through channels that were largely technocratic. According to some critics, this contributed to a depoliticisation of women's action and a lack of deeper theoretical reflection in Ecuadorian mainstream feminism (Rodas Morales, 2007; Vega Ugalde, 2004). Yet, critical voices promoting specifically feminist approaches to VAW were still audible, as shown next.

Following Beijing 1995, Ecuador had committed to strengthen DINAMU, the women's state department established during Jaime Roldós' presidency. The Women's National Council (*Consejo Nacional de la Mujer*, CONAMU) was created to oversee public policy involving "women's affairs". The office mostly hosted groups of middle-class feminist professionals. Although the Ecuadorian women's movement includes collectives from diverse origins – including popular sectors, indigenous and rural organisations, women's NGOs, and state officials – the strand that most actively engaged with law reform during the 1990s corresponds to what Htun (2003) has termed "feminist issue networks".

On the ground, child-development and micro-credit programmes were the key channels through which NGO staff came in contact with women from low-income sectors. One activist who worked in a community childcare programme and later participated in anti-VAW campaigns, told me that her work in low-income neighbourhoods, witnessing first hand how women were harmed every day, allowed her to discover the magnitude of men's violence against women (personal communication, April 13, 2015). Likewise, a former staff member of an influential NGO stressed that her work initially comprised

5 Some of the most prominent women's collectives created in Ecuador between the 1980s and 1990s include: the Ecuadorian Women's Permanent Forum (1994), the Ecuadorian Women's Political Coordinator (1995), the National Movement of Women from Popular Sectors (1989), the National Council of Indigenous Women, and the Black Women's National Coordinator (1997) (Rodas Morales, 2007). NGOs created between the 1980s and 1990s include: CEPAM in Quito and later in Guayaquil, Fundación María Guare in Guayaquil, and Corporación Mujer a Mujer and SENDAS in Cuenca. These NGOs are still active and have had some opportunities to influence VAW policy.

economic projects to provide microcredit for women in popular sectors, which let her become aware that domestic violence was rampant (personal communication, April 22, 2015). Because these projects allowed specialists to identify domestic abuse as a worrying issue, some NGOs started to design programmes to assist violence survivors, and established the first shelters for battered women in the early 1990s.[6] These often operated alongside legal aid departments offering advice in areas like divorce, child custody, and child support. After some time, according to a former staff member of a pioneering NGO, the reality of domestic violence had become crudely apparent, suggesting that they needed to expand their services. Staff began to think about the law reform that was needed to address domestic abuse and prompt state intervention (personal communication, April 13, 2015).

While advising domestic violence survivors, NGO lawyers encountered a series of difficulties. In principle, any form of physical violence could be prosecuted using the existing Penal Code and its criminal offences and misdemeanours. However, Article 28 of the 1983 Code of Criminal Procedure mandated:

> Art 28.- No accusation shall be admitted from descendants against ancestors and vice versa, nor from a spouse against the other, nor a sibling against a sibling. Once the complaint is presented, the Judge will require the complainant, under oath, to state whether he or she is included in any of the prohibitions of the previous paragraph. If so, [the judge] will reject the complaint.

This meant that, in practice, women could not report aggressions from close family members or spouses. While the Code allowed public prosecutors to act *ex officio* if they came to hear about domestic abuse, the concealed nature of these cases made that almost impossible. Feminist activists then figured that to abide by Art. 28, if a woman wanted to report her husband, a third party would have to file the complaint.[7] In this way, for some time, the NGOs' modus operandi consisted of staff listening to women, and then reporting the violence as a third party. A former staff-member of Fundación María Guare reminisced

6 Casa de Refugio Matilde was the first shelter for battered women in Ecuador, and one of the first in Latin America (Casa de Refugio Matilde, 2017). It was created in Quito in 1990 with the sponsorship of CEPAM, an NGO. It implemented assistance guidelines that were standardised and involved aspects such as social work, medical care, psychological counselling, and legal advice. It is in operation to this day with sponsors that include United Nations Agencies.

7 This situation persisted until after the first year of operations of the specialised commissariats for VAW established in 1994. Although a 1989 note from Fempress mentions that the AMM had requested the revision of the article to the Parliamentary Commission for Matters of Women and the Family, it was only the enactment of Act 103 as a specialised law in 1995, that allowed women to report violence of their own accord. The article from the Code of Criminal Procedure itself would only be repealed when a new Code was enacted in 2000.

that there were long queues of women waiting to file complaints of abuse through the NGO every day. She recalled:

> since it was not possible to report [domestic violence] we had to come up with a strategy: the woman, with us taking the risks as attorneys, would inform us, would tell us, would narrate what was happening and we, as we did not have a kinship relation with the aggressor, filed the complaint against him. We operated that way for almost a year but we realised that this was not sustainable [...]. I then started to investigate [...] and noticed that in other countries there were police stations for women.
>
> (personal communication, April 13, 2015)

In a publication of the time, feminist lawyer Anunziatta Valdez (1988) denounced the lack of an expedited and dedicated procedure to access justice in cases of domestic violence. The demand for a specialised and rapid process would become emblematic of the women's movement from then on. In Valdez's view, a specialised process would help women overcome what NGO staff perceived as a fear of reporting their abusive partners: they had noted that complainants were treated with disdain and their situation was minimised when they turned to police stations (Gómez, 1989). Therefore, NGO staff figured that a specialised law, penalising domestic violence against women specifically, would force police and judges to take complaints seriously.

Meanwhile, feminist magazines were disseminating information on women being abused by their partners due to jealousy or because they did not fulfil their "domestic responsibilities". One article estimated that as many as 95 out of every 100 women in Guayaquil suffered physical, sexual, and psychological violence inflicted by their husbands (Ayala Marín, 1989). At the time, there were no official statistics on VAW; therefore, feminists often relied on information that indirectly allowed them to assess the scale of the problem.

The Demographic Survey of Maternal and Infant Health (*Encuesta Demográfica de Salud Materna e Infantil*, ENDEMAIN), sponsored by the United States Agency for International Development (USAID), was carried out in Ecuador every five years from 1987 to 2004. This was the first and, until 2012, the only source of quantitative data on the incidence of domestic violence, extrapolated from reports of maternal health complications. Women's organisations used this data as evidence that domestic violence was generalised and required state action. An emerging discussion related to the possibility of establishing specialised police stations equipped with an interdisciplinary team that could respond to women's needs. These are the immediate antecedents of the commissariats for women and the family in Ecuador.

The commissariats for women and the family

In 1985, São Paulo was the first Latin American city to have a specialised police station to assist women who experienced domestic violence. This started a regional trend: in Ecuador, Fundación María Guare sent one of their associate lawyers to Lima, where specialised commissariats had been recently established, to figure out how they operated and propose a similar model for Ecuador (former staff member, personal communication, April 13, 2015). Drawing from the information gathered in Peru, as well as from international guidelines and their own experience, a team of Ecuadorian feminist lawyers prepared a proposal to create specialised commissariats, which was taken to the President of the Republic's legal adviser.

Several interviewees agreed that the relationship between some NGO leaders and the Ministry of Government, was key to success: in 1994, new units known as *Comisarías de la mujer y la familia* (Commissariats for women and the family) were established. One activist, who worked at a counterpart NGO during this phase, told me that the expression "and the family" had been added at the request of the Ministry. While the offices in Peru and other countries were actual police stations, in Ecuador, the commissariats were hybrid entities, ascribed to the Ministry of Government, but with some judicial attributions. The pilot commissariats opened in Guayaquil, Quito, Portoviejo, and Cuenca.[8] Each commissariat worked with a counterpart NGO whose staff provided gender expertise. This hybrid public/private co-governance model illustrates the influence that NGOs have had on gender policy. The first counterpart NGOs were Fundación María Guare in Guayaquil, CEPAM in Quito, and Corporación Mujer a Mujer in Cuenca. While becoming a counterpart NGO required signing an agreement with the Ministry of Government, NGO staff did not have any contractual relationship with the state. As the number of commissariats across the country increased over the years, due to growing demand, it became difficult to find an associated NGO for each commissariat, given that these did not always exist in the smaller districts. Some ad hoc NGOs were created to support commissariats but, eventually, the requirement of a counterpart NGO ceased to be mandatory in 1997.

The commissariats first applied the existing laws, whereby misdemeanours (*contravenciones*) were prosecuted outside the ordinary criminal courts. However, the commissariats did not fulfil all the functions that feminists had envisioned: in their 1980s meetings, some NGOs had devised them as offices that would deal not only with offences against women, but also with minor infractions committed *by* women. Commissariats had thereby been expected to provide an alternative to the ordinary penal apparatus. Instead, in the actual commissariats, the degree of specialisation was compromised, for instance, by their competence to hear child abuse cases and complaints presented by men against women.

8 For smaller towns and villages, local police stations would be made competent to hear domestic violence complaints.

According to the Ministerial Agreement, the commissariats were created based on the premise that the family, whose most vulnerable members are women and children, required special protection to prevent domestic abuse and its devastating consequences for public health and development. This document oddly resonates with the early 20th century policies on child development and family protection. For instance, the introduction stated that "violence against women and minors" was a social problem that demanded resources to be "technically managed", which the existing police offices at the time did not have (Ministerio de Gobierno y Policía, 1994). At the same time, anyone, including husbands, siblings, in-laws, etc., could file a complaint against any other close family member. Although not a large volume, the commissariats did receive complaints presented by men, often as a response to a previous complaint filed by a woman (Jácome Villalba, 2003).

Regarding procedural rules, the commissariats attempted to apply the General Code of Criminal Proceedings; however, their day-to-day operations were affected by uncertainty regarding the mechanisms that could grant women swift and effective protection and halt the aggravation of violence. The Penal Code did not contemplate many protective measures, and there were discordances in the ways each commissariat handled cases.[9] In view of all these limitations, activists felt that a dedicated law was required. The commissariats were the precedent to the creation of Act 103, the first law against violence toward women and the family.

The first specialised law for violence against women

Act 103 passed in 1995, in the midst of a regional trend whereby specialised national laws were created in almost every country in Latin America. It is a landmark in Ecuador, as it was the first piece of legislation that answered specific demands from women's movements. It was "made by us, legitimate" (historical feminist leader, personal communication, April 16, 2015). However, the proposal did not make it unaltered after transiting the national legislature. Although facilitating the prosecution of domestic violence was a goal of the women's movements, the actual link between VAW and criminal law was established by the National Congress, when it reframed the feminist proposal using the existing penal framework.

Act 103 had two chief artificers: Anunziatta Valdez and María Leonor Jiménez, who acted as spokespersons of the women's movement. Valdez and Jiménez did not have formal political affiliations, but they were close to some

9 Even after the enactment of Act 103 in 1995, which clarified the competences of the commissariats, and an executive decree that created rules of procedure in 2004, the discordances persisted to the point that the Ministry of Interior issued a manual of procedure in 2010 to homogenise the procedures.

influential groups – Valdez had connections with the Bar Association and a centre-right party, whilst Jiménez had links with the Marxist left. DINAMU, several NGOs, the Parliamentary Commission for Women, Children, and the Family, and some international organisations backed the proposal. They submitted the draft to the Legislative Commission for Civil and Penal Matters, which entrusted José Cordero Acosta, an academic and militant of the Popular Democratic Party (aligned with the international Christian Democracy), with a preliminary study of the project (Congreso Nacional del Ecuador, 1995).

Even though the draft bill included concepts taken from human rights instruments such as the CEDAW and the Belém do Pará Convention, the parliamentary records show that family protection was the main *ratio legis* animating Act 103. In fact, human rights were not incompatible with this family-first approach. Some feminists who promoted the new law told me that the draft bill was originally entitled "Law against violence toward women", whereas "and the family" was added after the preliminary negotiations, allegedly because a law to protect families was more likely to be accepted by all members of the Congress. In this way, VAW was again conflated with family protection and the regulation of domesticity.

During the first parliamentary debate, Cordero introduced modifications to the proposal on behalf of the Legislative Commission. Amongst these was a redefinition of the "nuclear family". In Cordero's opinion, the concept should not include unmarried partners and former partners as the original draft had intended. There was a preoccupation with legal coherence in relation to the Civil Code, which then limited family ties to marriage and kinship. In addition, other legislators stressed family union as the central good to be protected: Santiago Bucaram, for instance, asked the Commission for Civil and Penal Matters to present "a project for the State to take care of the situation of the family, because it is not only a matter of dividing the family but also of *defending* the family" (Congreso Nacional del Ecuador, 1995, p. 78 emphasis added).

The reinscription of family protection is evident in other sections of the parliamentary debates: for instance, during the second meeting to discuss the draft bill, Bucaram objected to the expression "sexual freedom" as a target of protection. He insisted that "sexual integrity" was a more adequate expression. His reasoning was that "nowhere [in Ecuadorian law], can we find a definition that tells us what kind of sexual freedom [the draft bill] is referring to (Congreso Nacional del Ecuador, 1995, p. 10). He added that protecting sexual freedom could open a programmatic door to legitimise activities like prostitution. Another congressional representative then requested to preserve the original draft bill as a tribute to "these beautiful women" (presumably referring to the activists that were present in the session), to "save" them after "two thousand years of Christian existence" (Congreso Nacional del Ecuador, 1995, p. 10).

These examples illustrate how difficult it was for feminists to break the long-standing association between women and the family without losing the opportunity to pass the law. The objections posited by legislators revealed a concern with giving women "too much freedom", or protecting spheres of their lives that did not correspond to "proper" family values. By contrast, the intention of feminists had been to expose and prevent everyday gender-based violence in intimate relationships. For instance, Article 4 of the original draft bill referred to sexual violence in this terms:

> Notwithstanding cases of rape and other crimes against sexual freedom, sexual violence is *any* maltreatment that constitutes an *imposition* in the exercise of a person's sexuality, forcing them to have intercourse or other sexual practices with the aggressor or a third party, using physical force, intimidation, threats or any other coercive means.
>
> (Congreso Nacional del Ecuador, 1995, emphasis added)

Since the Code of Criminal Proceedings prohibited complaints against spouses, marital rape or sexual violence within marriage were difficult to prosecute. Feminists thus aimed at enabling the prosecution of sexual violence within marriage and the family, but this proposal did not make it to the final text. The legislative commission considered that sexual violence was already prosecutable and did not require any further laws. This example illustrates two competing paradigms: the feminist plan to address VAW with specialised legal provisions, and the Congress' response to rely on existing rules as much as possible.

In the end, the new law only preserved the elements of the feminist proposal that were compatible with the idea of family integrity. For example, congressman Bucaram succeeded in modifying Article 13. The expression "sexual freedom of women" was replaced by "sexual freedom *of the family*" (emphasis added). Bucaram insisted that singling out women was dangerous, because it authorised behaviours that were immoral, such as sexual promiscuity. Again, women were deemed worthy of legal protection only as long as they conformed to the dominant parameters of morality. The coloniality of gender remained undisrupted by a proposal that was originally based on women's organisations' knowledge of human rights and gender. The partial acceptance of the proposal can be understood under the notion of "non-violent patriarchy" described in Chapter 1; that is, a model that moderates excessive male violence against women, aiming at preserving the family, not at emancipating women.

Another interesting element of the original draft was that, although it highlighted the aggressors' accountability, it also suggested alternatives to imprisonment, such as fines or community work, especially if the aggressor did not have sufficient economic resources. Fundamentally, whether it was because women's organisations did not think that proposing more carceral penalties would be successful, or because their experience with violence survivors had taught them otherwise, their proposal did not really revolve around incarceration. Expectedly, the alternative sanctions did not make it into the final text (see Table 3.2).

Table 3.2 shows some of the changes that the Legislative Commission and other members of Congress made to the original project presented by women's

Table 3.2 Act 103: from draft bill to law

Women's organisations draft	*National Congress proposal*	*Final text*
Violence against women	Violence against women *and the family*	Violence against women and the family
The family includes unmarried partners	The nuclear family *does not* include unmarried partners	The nuclear family does not include unmarried partners
Sexual freedom	Sexual integrity	Sexual freedom of the family
Temporary child support as urgent measure	Not to include temporary child support	No temporary child support included
Alternatives to imprisonment	No such alternatives are found in existing penal laws	No alternatives to imprisonment are established

Table designed and produced by the author. Source: the Archive of the National Assembly of Ecuador.

organisations. Ultimately, the legislature reassessed the project and used existing criminal laws to "fill in the gaps" they had found in the original project. The new legal provisions would apply to those forms of VAW that were not already categorised as misdemeanours or criminal offences in the general Penal Code.[10] Congressman Cordero argued that any given infraction constitutes at least a misdemeanour, and anything outside these penal categories was "inconceivable". Thus, all forms of aggression should fit into an available penal category (Congreso Nacional del Ecuador, 1995).

In other words, to Cordero, the Penal Code already covered all forms of interpersonal violence, and what the new law would do was situate the abuse in the family context to be handled by the commissariats. Battery, for instance, was adapted using the existing misdemeanour of physical injury, and was assigned the same procedural rules. By contrast, women's organisations had intended to establish special procedural rules to tackle the forms of intimate partner violence that affect women disproportionately, such as battering, verbal abuse, humiliation, sexual coercion, hostility, emotional abuse, and physical injuries that do not leave bodily marks. Their aim was not simply to affirm that existing criminal offences can take place in the family context. Therefore, the adjustments made by the Congress invite us to think about the challenges, for feminists, to escape existing legal categories whenever we attempt to use law to achieve an emancipatory goal. Even more so in the context of unequal power relations vis-à-vis the legislature. This reflection is not pertinent only when a deliberate will to use criminal law is present: as we see, the focus of the women's movements was not ensuring carceral punishment, but rather creating specialised legal alternatives.

10 In the Ecuadorian system, penal infractions are classified as either criminal offences or misdemeanours (*delitos y contravenciones*), according to their severity. Physical injuries can qualify as either, depending on whether or not an injury causes inability to work for more then three days; when the inability exceeds three days, it is considered a criminal offence (*delito*).

Ultimately, the resulting law mandated that commissariats prosecute existing misdemeanours such as verbal abuse, property damage, and minor physical injuries, utilising the existing procedural rules. The only form of abuse that made it to the final text as feminists originally intended, that is, with a specialised procedure, was "psychological violence", because it did not have any parallel in the existing legislation. Psychological violence was thus assigned a *sui generis* non-penal proceeding, meant to be rapid and simple. This process was oral (at a time when the dominant model was written) and based on negotiation and settlement: only when an agreement was not reached was the commissioner to enable the litigation to start. Later, however, negotiations in matters of VAW would be prohibited.

If the new legal configuration seems hard to understand, the reader is not alone: for several years after the passing of Act 103, each commissioner still interpreted the law differently. Sometimes they used the general procedural rules for all VAW infractions, at other times they used the specialised process for psychological violence. This chaos was solved only between 2004 and 2006, when the General Rules and the Manual of Procedures for Act 103 were approved. Table 3.3 outlines what rules applied to what offences and with what sanctions.

As we see, the law that feminists envisioned ended up relying on ordinary criminal law to become functional. Moreover, Act 103 led to an atypical combination of rules: most infractions were to be judged using criminal law procedures, while psychological violence implemented a non-penal, specialised process. In this way, Act 103 turned out to be civil and penal at the same time. If a commissariat came to identify an infraction that qualified as a criminal offence, it was obliged to redirect it to the Public Prosecutor. Staff from counterpart NGOs knew that bringing cases to the ordinary criminal courts would not be of much benefit for complainants. One former staff member of an NGO said:

> I remember that, at the women's commissariat, sometimes we preferred that the person, even if the injuries granted more than three days [of disability]… sometimes we preferred to process it as a misdemeanour rather than as a criminal offence, because [violence against women] was not recognised as a crime, so it had to be framed as a different criminal offence and, therefore, it would have to follow a longer process […]. The lady would have to pay for a lawyer and all that. So sometimes, in injuries that were more serious than three days […] the commissioner preferred to treat it as a misdemeanour, so [the claimant] would be able to access the protection measures and everything else.
>
> (personal communication, February 20, 2015)

At this point, we see that the complexity of ordinary criminal justice was acknowledged by feminists and considered disadvantageous for women. A

Table 3.3 Act 103: Infractions, procedures, and sanctions

Infraction	*Procedure*	*Jurisdiction*	*Sanction*
Psychological violence/ Sexual violence not resulting in physical injury and not categorised as crime in the Penal Code	Special (non-penal) procedure created by Act 103	Specialised Commissioner	Payment of compensations, from one to fifteen minimum wages.
Attacks on property	General penal procedure for misdemeanours	Specialised Commissioner	Payment of a fine from seven to 14 US Dollars and imprisonment of two to four days.
Non-defamatory insults	General penal procedure for misdemeanours	Specialised Commissioner	Payment of a fine from seven to 14 US Dollars and imprisonment of two to four days.
Physical injury that does not cause inability to work	General penal procedure for misdemeanours	Specialised Commissioner	Payment of a fine from 14 to 28 US Dollars and imprisonment of five to 30 days.
Physical injury causing inability to work for up to three days	General penal procedure for misdemeanours	Specialised Commissioner	Payment of a fine from 14 to 28 US Dollars and imprisonment of five to 30 days.
Physical injury causing inability for work for more than three days	General penal procedure for criminal offences	Criminal Court	Varied according to severity. From 15 days to five years of imprisonment.
Sexual criminal offences	General procedure for criminal offences	Criminal Court	Varied according to the severity of the offence. From three months to 25 years of imprisonment.

Table designed and produced by the author. Source: Penal Code of Ecuador and the author's field notes.

close examination of the process by which Act 103 came to be, offers a more nuanced picture of feminists' drive to criminalise, revealing that not all efforts to obtain specialised legislation were uncritical of the shortcomings of criminal law. Indeed, most interviewees recognised that the merits of Act 103 were at the level of its protective measures. Feminists also understood that domestic violence involves a continued exposure to abuse, which is difficult to prove in a court because it occurs "behind closed doors". This is why they insisted on making Act 103's protective measures immediate, meaning that the claimant's testimony was presumed truthful before any evidence was submitted and before the litigation formally started.

In the experience of many practitioners and researchers, protection/restraining orders are pivotal in VAW processes (Tamayo, 1998; Tapia Tapia, 2020; Valdivieso & Armas, 2008). Violating restraining orders constitutes an offence itself, which can result in one to six months of imprisonment. Although there is no evidence suggesting that incarceration for violating restraining orders is a common occurrence, these instruments are requested every day, in high numbers, until today. Most protective measures in Table 3.4 still apply via the 2014 Penal Code and the 2018 Comprehensive Law for VAW, which replaced Act 103.

As mentioned above, Act 103 is a landmark for Ecuadorian feminists. Some activists told me that the law was successful, inasmuch as it became ingrained in the community's legal consciousness. It is widely agreed that for many women, Act 103 offered unprecedented tools to feel safer and enfranchised. They often regarded protection orders as a sort of "shield", even if limited, to protect themselves from abuse (Camacho & Hernández, 2011; Friederic, 2013). However, through the years, some feminists came to see Act 103 as insufficient and ineffective. The workload was increasing at the commissariats year after year, while attrition rates were high: most VAW lawsuits did not conclude with a verdict, guilty or otherwise (Tamayo, 1998). According to different estimates, only

Table 3.4 Protection measures in Act 103

Art. 13. The authorities referred to in Article 8, when in any way come to know of a case of domestic violence, shall immediately impose one or more of the following measures of protection in favour of the assaulted person:

1. Grant the necessary restraining orders to women or other members of the family;
2. Order the aggressor to leave the home if cohabitation involves a risk to the physical or mental safety or the sexual freedom of the family;
3. Impose a ban on the aggressor impeding them from approaching the assaulted person at their place of work or study;
4. Prohibit or restrict the attacker's access to the abused person;
5. Prevent the aggressor from performing acts of persecution or intimidation of a victim or a member of their family, be it on his own or through third parties;
6. Reintegrate the assaulted person to their home, ordering the simultaneous departure of the aggressor in case of common housing, preventing them from withdrawing the goods of family use;
7. Grant the custody of the child victim or legally incapable individuals to an adequate person following the provisions of Article No. 107 (108), rule 6th of the Civil Code and the provisions of the Code of Minors; and,
8. Define the therapy that is needed by the parts and their underaged children if it be the case.

Table designed and produced by the author. Source: Lexis Finder database.

between 4% and 11% of complaints received a resolution (Jácome Villalba, 2003; Jubb, 2008). In most cases, procedures were dropped after issuing the protection order. In fact, most women did not advance the lawsuit any further, because they did not always want the aggressor to be incarcerated (Camacho & Hernández, 2011).

Paradoxically, despite a general recognition that most complainants do not usually pursue punishment, many feminists began to argue that VAW should be treated as a criminal offence in full. The fact that Act 103's sanctions were not severe "enough" was linked to the prevalence of VAW (CLADEM, 2006). Feminists insisted that specialised procedural rules were required, stressing that they should be accessible and simple. In 1998, VAW was foregrounded again as Ecuador prepared to approve a new Constitution. The promise of a new legal framework, one that would be *truly* specialised and frame VAW as a serious criminal offence at the same time, encouraged women's organisations to draft a women's human rights plan of action for the forthcoming Constitutional Assembly.

Conclusion

In this chapter, I have shown that during the last decades of the 20th century, emerging framings of VAW as a hindrance to economic development, a public health concern and a violation of human rights, facilitated its incorporation into international instruments that would encourage states to criminalise VAW. This brought about a "turn to criminal law" in the domain of gender-based violence, which had previously been addressed mainly as an issue related to poverty and other forms of social inequality. Thus, criminalising violence and recognising women's rights were construed as inseparable projects, and VAW shifted from being regarded as a problem that required better access to services and resources, to a penal issue that required criminalisation and prosecution.

These international shifts landed in Ecuador successfully and, while contested by some, were taken up by many feminist advocacy groups. Unlike the 1970s and 1980s feminists who denounced criminal law as an artefact of patriarchal oppression, NGO staff in the 1990s started to see criminal justice as a tool that could be used to counteract VAW. That said, Ecuadorian feminists did have a distinctive law reform agenda, which, notably, contained non-penal elements to address VAW via fines, community work, and therapy, as well as an emphasis on specialised rules and authorities. Many of these initiatives were ultimately excluded by the national legislature in favour of a more traditional criminal law approach. Hence the importance of careful empirical research that gives a voice to feminist experiences of interacting with the state. Coloniality, human rights, and criminal law formed an assemblage that complicates the common narrative pointing at the "co-optation" of feminism.

Even though the 1990s were a period when feminist governance capacity increased, this chapter has revealed the limitations faced by women's organisations.

Human rights did not suffice to disrupt the family-protection rationales that the National Congress promoted. What we can observe, instead, is an endorsement, by Ecuador's legislature, of "non-violent patriarchy" (see Chapter 1) as a key *ratio legis* for the passing of the first VAW law. The Congress did not challenge the surveillance of women's sexuality nor fully incorporate the feminist proposal to create specialised legal procedures. The state's preoccupation with protecting the family and regulating domestic life was renewed and reaffirmed with the support of the language provided by public health, development, and human rights. While feminists were focused not only on prosecuting and punishing, but also on providing women with rapid procedures and protective tools, the legislature's intervention did focus on prosecution and punishment.

Act 103 established the first formal connections between criminal law and VAW in Ecuador. The National Congress' decision was to rely on the existing penal categories and proceedings, rather than employing the specialised rules proposed by feminists. In practice, the coexistence of two sets of procedural rules caused confusion and irregularities in the operation of the commissariats and their handling of VAW. In addition, the research that was produced at the time shows that women increasingly used the tools of Act 103, but VAW did not diminish, nor were many guilty verdicts passed.

An important broader lesson to learn here is that feminist self-critique should not only include our own projects and actions, but also take into account how they are reshaped when we resort to law reform as a strategy. Surely, a critique of "carceral feminism" should not avoid paying attention to the role of non-feminist lawmakers in producing carcerality beyond and outside anti-violence women's movements.

References

Alvarez, S.E. (1998). *Latin American feminisms "go global": Trends of the 1990s and challenges for the new millennium* (S.E. Alvarez, E. Dagnino, & A. Escobar (eds.); p. 293). Westview Press.

Alvarez, S.E. (1999). Advocating feminism: The Latin American Feminist NGO "Boom." *International Feminist Journal of Politics, 1*(2), 181–209.

Alvarez, S.E. (2000). Translating the global effects of transnational organizing on local feminist discourses and practices in Latin America. *Meridians, 1*(1), 29–67.

Ayala Marín, A. (1989, February). Crónica macabra y una esperanza. *Mujer/Fempress, 89*, 3–4.

Bedford, K. (2009). *Developing partnerships: Gender, sexuality, and the reformed World Bank.* University of Minnesota Press.

Bedford, K. (2020). Law, gender, and development: Potent hauntings. *Law and Development Review, 13*(1), 229–264. https://doi.org/10.1515/ldr-2019-0066

Bedford, K., & Tapia Tapia, S. (2021). Specialised (in)security: Violence against women, criminal courts, and the gendered presence of the state in Ecuador. *Latin American Law Review, 7*, 21–42.

Boserup, E. (1970). *Woman's role in economic development.* Earthscan.

Bunch, C., & Carrillo, R. (1991). *Gender violence: A development and human rights issue.* Center for Women's Global Leadership.

Bunch, C., & Reilly, N. (1994). *Demanding accountability. The global campaign and Vienna tribunal for women's human rights*. Centre for Women's Global Leadership.
Camacho, G., & Hernández, K. (2011). *Comisarías de la mujer y acceso a la justicia en Cuenca* (L. Pásara (ed.); pp. 229–282). Ministerio de Justicia y Derechos Humanos, Naciones Unidas.
Casa de Refugio Matilde. (2017). *Acerca de*. Fundación Casa de Refugio Matilde. https://fundacionmatilde.org/acerca-de/
CEPAR. (2001). *Ecuador Reproductive Health Survey 1999*. Centers for Disease Control and Prevention. https://microdata.worldbank.org/index.php/catalog/997/get-microdata
Christie, N. (2007). *Limits to pain: The role of punishment in penal policy*. Wipf & Stock Publishers.
CLADEM. (2006). *Informe sombra: una mirada alternativa a la situación de discriminación de la mujer en el Ecuador. Período 1990–1998*. CLADEM.
Cole, S., & Phillips, L. (2008). The violence against women campaigns in Latin America: New feminist alliances. *Feminist Criminology*, *3*(2), 145–168.
Comisión Interamericana de Mujeres. (1994). *Resumen del proceso de preparación del proyecto de convención interamericana para prevenir, sancionar y erradicar la violencia contra la mujer* (No. CIM/doc.5/94). Organization of American States.
Congreso Nacional del Ecuador. (1995). *Acta no. siete* (Vol. 7). Congreso Nacional del Ecuador
Correa, R. (2011). *Conferencia magistral del economista Rafael Correa Delgado en la Universidad de Buenos Aires*.
Cuvi, M. (1999). *Violencia contra las mujeres. La ruta crítica en el Ecuador*. Organización Panamericana de la Salud.
DESA. (1986). *Seventh United Nations Congress on the prevention of crime and treatment of offenders* (A/CONF. 121/22/Rev.1). United Nations.
Foucault, M. (1997). *What is critique?* (p. 41). Semiotext(e).
Friederic, K. (2013). Violence against women and the contradictions of rights-in-practice in rural Ecuador. *Latin American Perspectives*, *41*(1), 19–38.
Gargallo, F. (2006). *Ideas Feministas Latinoamericanas*. Universidad Autónoma de la Ciudad de México.
Gómez, R. (1989, February). Comisarías de y para mujeres. *La Mujer*, *18*.
González et al. ("Cotton Field") v. Mexico, Series C No. 205 (Inter-American Court of Human Rights November 16, 2009). https://www.corteidh.or.cr/docs/casos/articulos/seriec_205_ing.pdf
Hallward-Driemeier, M., Hasan, T., & Rusu, A. (2013). *Women's legal rights over 50 years. Progress, stagnation or regression?* The World Bank Development Research Group
Herrera, G. (2001). *Los estudios de género en el Ecuador: entre el conocimiento y el reconocimiento* (G. Herrera (ed.); p. 9). FLACSO Ecuador.
Htun, M. (2003). *Sex and the state: Abortion, divorce, and the family under Latin American dictatorships and democracies*. Cambridge University Press.
Jácome Villalba, N. (2003). *Estudio cultural de la práctica jurídica en las comisarías de la mujer y la familia* [MSc]. Facultad Latinoamericana de Ciencias Sociales.
Jubb, N. (2008). *Mapeo regional de las comisarías de la mujer en América Latina*. CEPLAES.
Lind, A. (2005). *Gendered paradoxes. Women's movements, state restructuring and global development in Ecuador*. Pennsylvania State University Press.
Macaulay, F. (2006). Judicialising and (de) criminalising domestic violence in Latin America. *Social Policy Report / Society for Research in Child Development*, *5*(1), 103.
Maria da Penha Maia Fernandes v. Brazil (Inter-American Commission on Human Rights April 16, 2001). http://cidh.org/annualrep/2000eng/ChapterIII/Merits/Brazil12.051.htm

Mavronicola, N., & Lavrysen, L. (2020). Coercive human rights: Introducing the sharp edge of the European Convention on Human Rights. In *Coercive human rights: Positive duties to mobilise the criminal law under the ECHR* (pp. 1–26). Hart.

McIlwaine, C., & Moser, C. (2001). Violence and social capital in urban poor communities: Perspectives from Colombia and Guatemala. *Journal of International Development, 13*(7), 965.

Merry, S.E. (2006). *Human rights and gender violence: Translating international law into local justice*. University of Chicago Press.

Meyer, M. (1999). *Negotiating international norms: The inter-American commission of women and the convention on violence against women* (M. Meyer & E. Prugl (eds.); p. 58). Rowman & Littlefield Lanham.

Ministerio de Gobierno y Policía. (1994). *Disposiciones organizativas para el funcionamiento de las comisarías de la mujer y la familia*. Registro Oficial No. 410. Ministerio de Gobierno y Policía.

Moser, C., & Shrader, E. (1999). *A conceptual framework for violence reduction*. World Bank, Latin America and Caribbean Region.

Organization of American States. (2019). *OAS: CIM: Brief history*. OAS. https://oas.org/en/cim/history.asp

Rodas Morales, R. (2007). Estudio introductorio. In R. Rodas Morales (ed.), *Las propias y los ajenos. Miradas críticas sobre los discursos del movimiento de mujeres del Ecuador*. (p. 9). FIG, ACDI, CONAMU, Abya-Yala.

Schneider, E.M. (2000). *Battered women and feminist lawmaking*. Yale University Press

Stephen, L. (1997). *Women and social movements in Latin America: Power from below*. University of Texas Press.

Tamayo, C. (1998). *Entre la sombra y la esperanza: investigación de impacto de las comisarías de la mujer y la familia*. CEPAM.

Tapia Tapia, S. (2020). Beyond carceral expansion: Survivors' experiences of using specialised courts for violence against women in ecuador. *Social & Legal Studies*, 0964663920973747.

The World Bank. (2000). *Ecuador gender review. Issues and recommendations*. The World Bank.

Tojo, L. (ed.). (2011). *Sumarios de lurisprudencia. Violencia de género* (2nd ed.). Centre for Justice and International Law.

United Nations. (1980). *Report of the World Conference of the United Nations decade for women: Equality, development and peace, Copenhagen, July 1980* (U.N. Doc A/CONF.94/35 (80. IV.30)). United Nations.

United Nations Branch for the Advancement of Women. (1987). *Report of the expert group meeting on violence in the family with special emphasis on its effects on women: Vienna, 8–12 Dec. 1986*. United Nations.

Valdez, A. (1988, June). Mayor viabilidad en el proceso penal. *Matapalo, 26*, 4.

Valdivieso, C., & Armas, A. (2008). *La situación de las mujeres ecuatorianas: una mirada desde los derechos humanos*. Ministerio de Coordinación de Desarrollo Social.

Vega Ugalde, S. (2004). Movimiento de mujeres. ¿Cuál es el nuevo momento? *La Tendencia. Revista de Análisis Político, 1*, 70–77.

Walker, L. (2000). *The battered woman syndrome*. Springer Publishing Company.

Yashar, D.J. (2005). *Contesting citizenship in Latin America: The rise of indigenous movements and the postliberal challenge*. Cambridge University Press.

Chapter 4

From neoliberal to post-neoliberal

The constitutional journey of rights-based penality

Introduction

This chapter presents the concept of "rights-based penality", which augments current discussions of carceral feminism, as well as critical approaches to human rights that do not always speak to the carceral dimension of human rights discourse. Firstly, the idea of a rights-based penality highlights that the notion of rights underlies many justifications of criminal justice. Penal expansion thrives not only through "tough on crime" conservative policies, but also through liberal legal discourses, which have come to be regarded as "neutral". Endorsements of rights-based frameworks that justify the use of criminal law are posited by actors all across the political spectrum, including leftist feminists. Secondly, identifying a rights-based penality lets us reveal that contemporary penal expansion is closely linked to the belief that there can be a minimal, constitutional criminal law that is sympathetic to human rights. This approach is present in Ecuador's both "neoliberal" and "post-neoliberal" constitutions.

In the next chapter, I will address how feminists specifically utilised rights-based penality; here, I preemptively analyse the legal discourses that create the conditions of intelligibility for a "progressive" criminalisation project. Thereby, I pose a cardinal question: what is enabling so many political actors, including leftist feminists, to advocate for strategies that centre criminal justice? It would be condescending to simply assume that they do so uncritically; therefore, what can constitutional reform tell us about progressive actors' "reconciliation" with penality? The case of Ecuador allows us to nuance the debate, given that many feminists who secured governance roles at the time of the Citizen's Revolution were invested in the government's social redistribution initiatives. Is feminists' increased reliance on criminal law a deliberately regressive stance, a consequence of co-option based on the oblivion of our radical origins, or a genuine belief, shared by many others, that criminal law can become a progressive force? Perhaps so-called carceral feminism is more a manifestation of liberal legality than feminist governance.

Naomi Murakawa (2014) has suggested, in the context of the US, that liberalism has played a role in the growth of the carceral state. Here, via an

DOI: 10.4324/9781003098799-5

account from the South, I also emphasise the penal elements of liberalism, but I centre my analysis on the coloniality of power. My review of a judgment by the Constitutional Court of Ecuador on the applicability of indigenous justice, frames the ubiquity of the penal response as a manifestation of legal coloniality, a phenomenon that is older, deeper, and broader than carceral feminism, with effects that surpass the realm of gender-based violence. Essentially, I want to turn our gaze back to law itself, and to liberal criminal law in particular, to consider how multiple "benign" criminalisation discourses are part of mainstream human rights frameworks today. Human rights are invoked by progressive actors who genuinely advocate for the protection of dignity.

Of course, the chapter also disputes the liberal idea that criminal law can be constitutionalised and subsequently become unproblematic. The theory of "constitutional criminal law", as I show, has fuelled penality in various domains, enhancing the appeal to criminalisation including during a period when social redistribution and decolonisation were emphasised. The idea of a minimal penal intervention that is respectful of human rights, in practice relegitimises criminal justice as inherent to democracy and the defence of individual liberties. Rights-based penality is thus harnessed to justify the displacement and subordination of non-Western and non-carceral approaches to justice, letting progressive actors justify the resort to criminal law and overcome the paradox of demanding harsher punishments while also promoting emancipatory agendas.

In Chapter 3, I showed how the turn to criminal law in the domain of violence against women (VAW) docked in Ecuador, via the synergy between human rights, development, public health, and other emerging fields of expertise. The said framings did not really challenge the colonial narratives on family protection described in Chapter 1, which resonated with the National Congress' discourse on protecting women, in the 1990s. This chapter resumes this historical analysis, first addressing the 1998 Constitution, whereby penality solidified as a fundamental framework to counteract VAW. Next, I cover the advent of the left-leaning Citizens' Revolution, which brought about the Constitution of 2008. Although the new regime was successful in reverting some policies crafted during the "long neoliberal night", and the new Constitution embraced elements of Andean cosmology, it did not challenge the coloniality of human rights, including its penal approach to VAW. Andean principles could have disrupted the dominant discourse; instead, a rights-based penality prevailed.

Penality and violence against women in the Constitution of 1998

The late 1990s were turbulent in Ecuador. After the presidency of Sixto Durán-Ballén (1992–1996), who performed privatisation, labour flexibilisation, and deregulation of markets and financial institutions, Abdalá Bucaram Ortiz

(1996–1997) was elected. He was in office for less than six months, as corruption scandals within his cabinet elicited massive public protests. Amidst dubious political manoeuvres, the National Congress deposed Bucaram and appointed Fabián Alarcón Rivera (1997–1998) as "interim" president. During Alarcón's mandate, *Dirección Nacional de las Mujeres* (DINAMU), the state's secretariat for women's affairs, became *Consejo Nacional de las Mujeres* (CONAMU), the National Council of Women. This widened the sphere of influence of women's organisations over some areas of policy. However, there are feminists who consider that this period marked the loss of the women's movement's subversive character (Rodas Morales, 2007). A former CONAMU director said:

> This is a period, as I say, a very high "peak" [term originally in English] for the feminist movement and the women's movements, with important achievements, which are also regarded critically by some of us now, because it is said, or we say, that this was when we let ourselves be co-opted by a state apparatus, by an institutional feminism that subtracted force from the movement. Well, this is very debatable, it is an entire discussion.
>
> (personal communication, March 16, 2015)

Partly because the National Congress needed to legitimise the dismissal of Bucaram, a Constituent Assembly was summoned in 1998. Today, many see the Constituent Assembly as emblematic of neoliberal politics (Quintero López, 2008). Critics have also argued that the 1998 Constitution failed to transform institutional structures and establish effective mechanisms to materialise the rights that it proclaimed (Grijalva, 2009). Nonetheless, some progressive sectors welcomed it, as it was the first body of law to proclaim Ecuador as a "multicultural"[1] country, recognise the collective rights of indigenous peoples, and also the right to personal integrity, which included a mention of violence against women. Further, for the first time, the Constitution included an anti-discrimination clause for sexual orientation.

Some women's collectives did secure alliances with assembly members who were not necessarily supporters of feminist movements, but helped them introduce some reform proposals. Rural, indigenous, and Afro-descendant women, for their part, were not widely represented at the Assembly, although some indigenous women channelled their demands through the umbrella organisation *Confederación de Nacionalidades Indígenas del Ecuador* (CONAIE). Ultimately, feminist organisations attained 34 items of their agenda, which

1 The term "multicultural" has since been questioned by decolonial and indigenous thinkers as a liberal acknowledgement of diversity that does not recognise the historical subordination of indigenous peoples, aiming more at assimilation than to establish effective mechanisms for intercultural dialogue and legal pluralism (Bowen, 2011; Estermann, 2014; Sieder & Sierra, 2011).

included provisions on political parity (quotas), affirmative action, the recognition of unwaged domestic labour, and the protection of (some) sexual and reproductive rights:

> In the constituent process of 1998, which was marked by the hegemony of sectors that were close to the neoliberal project, we obtained the integration of new individual and collective rights to the constitution, through a tireless work of proposing, mobilising, lobbying and forming alliances with other social movements.
>
> (Nosotras en la Constituyente, 2008, p. 1)

Still, the influence of the conservative lobbies was decisive; again, there were debates and disputes regarding "threats" to family integrity. For instance, in front of feminist proposals regarding the definition of the family, some assembly members expressed their concerns that expanding it outside the traditional heterosexual two-parent model would promote same-sex unions (Valladares, 2003).

At the same time, while Act 103 had introduced some elements from international human rights instruments, the Constitution of 1998 went further, and declared them part of the national legal system. This move has been read as an enshrinement of the fundamental principles of protection and promotion of human rights (United Nations Committee on the Elimination of Discrimination against Women, 2002). Women's organisations have stated that "the Political Constitution [of 1998] constitutes a fundamental progress in the legal-formal field of human rights and women's rights in particular" (CLADEM, 2006, p. 7). Importantly, the 1998 Constitution's framework to address VAW would define the legal treatment of gender-based violence in the long term.

New feminist stances on violence against women: toward full criminalisation

As mentioned above, the Constitution of 1998 consecrated the human right to personal integrity, mentioning in particular violence against women, children, adolescents, and elderly people (see Table 4.1). This was the first formal acknowledgement that VAW is a human rights violation requiring criminal law reform (Camacho & Hernández, 2011; Valdez, 2006). Indeed, Article 23, No. 2, introduced the state's duty to *punish* VAW. Protecting the right to personal integrity and forcing the state to *prosecute* and punish its violation were thus conflated, signalling a more solid penality/rights assemblage.

As shown in Table 4.1, Article 24 authorised criminal complaints against family members, abolishing the prohibition to report close relatives from the Code of Criminal Proceedings. The impediment had been partially overcome by Act 103, but was now integrally repealed, which suggests an enhanced

Table 4.1 1998 constitutional framework for VAW

Recognition of the human right to personal integrity	Art. 23.- Notwithstanding the rights established in this Constitution and the international instruments in force, the state will recognise and guarantee the following: 2. Personal integrity. It is prohibited to apply cruel penalties, torture; all procedures that are inhumane, degrading or involving physical, psychological, sexual, or moral violence, and the application and unlawful utilisation of human genetic material are forbidden. **The state will adopt the necessary measures to avoid, prevent, eliminate and sanction violence especially against children, adolescents, women and the elderly.**
Authorisation to prosecute family members	Art. 24.- 9. Nobody shall be forced to declare in a trial against their spouse or family members up to the fourth degree of consanguinity or second of affinity, or forced to declare against oneself, in matters that can result in criminal liability. The voluntary declarations of those who turn out to be victims of a crime or those of their family members, will be admissible independently of the degree of kinship. These persons, additionally, will be able to present and pursue the corresponding criminal prosecution.
Legal defence in family violence lawsuits	Art. 24.- 10. Nobody shall be deprived of the right to legal defence in any stage or degree of the corresponding process. The state will designate public attorneys for the legal sponsorship of indigenous communities, workers, women, and minors who have been abandoned or are victims of family violence or sexual violence, as well as every person who does not have economic means available.
Vulnerable groups	Art. 47.- In the public and private sphere, children, and adolescents, pregnant women, disabled people, people with highly complex catastrophic illnesses, and seniors, will receive priority, preferential and specialised attention. Persons in situations of risk and victims of domestic violence, child maltreatment, natural, or anthropogenic disasters, will be cared for in the same way.

Table designed and produced by the author. Source: Lexis Finder database.

drive to criminally prosecute family violence. The Constitution added that the state would provide public attorneys to those lacking funds to pay for a private lawyer in family violence cases (Article 24). The measure was intended to facilitate litigation, which confirms that the juridification of VAW was solidifying.

Yet, this framework is not distinctively feminist in a way that departs from the insights of the liberal legal tradition. For instance, the provisions on personal integrity posited violence as a matter of interpersonal conflict rather than systemic discrimination. Some women's organisations acknowledged this; however, they still considered that criminalisation could be a means to achieve the visibility of VAW. According to the Shadow Report[2] to the CEDAW for 1990–1998:

> The Penal Code does not categorise family violence specifically as a crime, however, kinship is an aggravating factor for punishing infractions such as injuries, rape, etc. One consequence of the inexistence of a specific categorisation is the dismissal of family violence as a severe violation of women's rights.
>
> (CLADEM, 2006, p. 7)

The fragment above reiterates a narrative that equates non-criminalisation to non-recognition and, therefore, non-protection of women's human rights. The same report denounced that Act 103 treated domestic violence "only" as a misdemeanour, that is, an "inferior" category compared to a criminal offence. The situation was presented as evidence of the state's lingering indifference towards VAW. Similar arguments surfaced in the 1998–2006 Shadow Report, which affirmed that not criminalising domestic violence restricts access to justice because it "reinforces the justice officials' conception that family violence is a problem of little importance" (Universidad Andina Simón Bolívar, 2006, p. 12). Impunity was also brought forward as a major obstacle in the struggle against domestic violence. While the Report did mention the absence of state-funded shelters for women and children, and recognised that this void stemmed from reductions in social investment, the main demand was for coherence between the human rights instruments that require states to criminalise VAW, and national laws. "Updating the legal framework that sanctions gender violence on the basis of international standards" was declared a priority (Universidad Andina Simón Bolívar, 2006, p. 10). The Penal Code would, from then on, become a major target of reform.

With these precedents, the next section addresses the paradigm shift brought about by the 2008 Constitution, and the extent to which it did and did not challenge the approach to VAW introduced in 1998.

The "post-neoliberal" Constitution of 2008

Between 2007 and 2017, Ecuador navigated a period that many call "post-neoliberal", because the government endorsed the "socialism of the 21st century" (Dieterich, 2009; Santos, 2010a), and proclaimed the end of the "long and sad neoliberal night" (Correa, 2011). The measures taken for the bailout of the

2 A Shadow Report is a formal review of the state's report to the CEDAW, prepared by civil society organisations. Shadow reporting has been an important tool for Women's NGOs as it allows them to submit alternative information and highlight issues that have not been raised in the state's official report. The shadow report then becomes part of the CEDAW's Committee official record.

collapsed banking system during the presidency of Jamil Mahuad (1998–2000) had exacerbated popular discontent. An indigenous uprising, supported by civil society, ousted Mahuad. Later on, Rafael Correa, an academic who was not linked to traditional partisan politics, secured the support of left-leaning movements and intellectuals, including Pachakutik, the electoral wing of the indigenous movement. The resulting coalition became known as the "Fatherland Alliance" (*Alianza País,* AP). In 2007, when Correa won the presidency, he dubbed his programme the "Citizens' Revolution" (*Revolución Ciudadana*).

Commentators have recognised that the Citizens' Revolution performed a turn to the left, away from neoliberal orthodoxy – at least in some economic aspects and approaches to development (Ospina, 2009; Radcliffe, 2012). Certainly, during Correa's government, public expenditure increased, involving budgetary allocations for education, health, housing, and social benefits (Albuja et al., 2017). Poverty and inequality were overall reduced (Grupo Banco Mundial, 2020; Ordóñez et al., 2015). This positioned Ecuador as part of the "Pink Tide" or "New Left" in Latin American (Ewig, 2012; Kampwirth, 2011).

In 2007, Correa summoned a Constituent Assembly. Ample spaces were opened for civil society collectives to voice their demands during the process: indigenous organisations, environmentalist activists, LGBTIQ+ collectives, and women's advocacy groups participated in legislative *mesas* (commissions) to develop various aspects of the draft bill. The new Constitution was approved via national referendum in 2008.

In Latin America, new constitutions often stand for a refoundational moment, such that the term "aspirational constitutionalism" (García Villegas, 2012) has been coined to convey how these changes symbolise the people's aspirations for a new order. In fact, the 2008 Constitution of Ecuador has been considered a prominent example of legal innovation (Santos, 2010a, 2010b), and archetypical of the trends known as "New Latin American Constitutionalism"[3] and "New Andean Constitutionalism". The latter specifically refers to the integration of Andean philosophy (in Bolivia and Ecuador) into national constitutions, which challenges neoliberal development models (Noguera Fernández, 2011). Indeed, the 2008 Constitution recognised indigenous justice and proclaimed a plurinational state (Art. 1), which were both central demands of the indigenous movement. In addition, the Constitution recognised the rights of *Pacha Mama* (Mother Nature) and adopted *Sumak Kawsay* (the Andean paradigm of a good life) as a guiding principle for the nation. In parallel, the Constitution

3 The denomination usually includes the Colombian Constitution of 1991, the Venezuelan Constitution of 1999, the Ecuadorian Constitution of 2008, and the Bolivian Constitution of 2009 (Pastor & Dalmau, 2011; Uprimny, 2011). Some authors have disputed the extent to which New Constitutionalism has distinctive characters. In Gargarella's view, for instance, Latin American constitutions are consolidated structures with over two centuries upon their backs, which have incorporated few changes in recent times upon a basis that remains the same (Gargarella, 2015).

proclaimed the protection of human rights as one of the state's fundamental purposes (Art. 3), again connecting it to the obligation to criminally prosecute human rights violations. Given these competing approaches, it is pertinent to ask what changes could have operated as a result of the new constitutional model in the realm of VAW, considering that Andean cosmovision and indigenous justice comprise non-carceral aspects, which I examine below.

The radical potential of Andean philosophy: a non-penal approach to gender justice

As mentioned above, in 2008, *Sumak Kawsay* became a constitutional principle. The concept has its roots in pre-Columbian thought, but its contemporary rendition dates back to the 1970s and 1980s. To rebuild the paradigm, indigenous intellectuals have drawn from oral histories, the work of chroniclers like Guamán Poma de Ayala, Pachacuti Yamqui Salcamaygua, and archaeological evidence. *Sumak Kawsay* roughly translates as "good living" or "good coexistence". It is a term that conveys a non-anthropocentric, non-individualistic model of social life, in harmony with nature and the entire cosmos. In Andean cosmovision, a single life force animates the universe: Andean ontology is a form of robust monism whereby reality is composed of deeply interconnected beings (Trownsell, 2013). As a consequence, human existence is not above or at the centre of nature, but thrives in reciprocal interdependence with its elements[4]. *Sumak Kawsay*, *Pacha Mama*, and anti-colonialism appear in the Constitution from its very preamble:

> We, women and men, the sovereign people of Ecuador;
>
> Recognizing our millennial roots, forged by women and men from different peoples,
>
> Celebrating nature, Mother Earth (Pacha Mama), of which we are a part and which is vital to our existence,
>
> Invoking the name of God and recognizing our diverse forms of religion and spirituality,
>
> Calling upon the wisdom of all the cultures which enrich us as a society,
>
> As heirs to the liberation struggles against all forms of domination and colonialism;
>
> And with a profound commitment to the present and the future,
>
> Decide to build:

4 It is fair to note that there are some disagreements regarding *Sumak Kawsay* at a conceptual level: indigenous intellectuals have disputed the common Spanish translation, *buen vivir* (good living), as they consider it does not convey the deeper meaning of *Sumak Kawsay*, which only makes sense if reality is understood as a relational space. "Good living" has been considered a Westernised translation that alludes to what is beneficial or desirable, disregarding the significance of community life (Macas, 2011)

> A new way to live together as citizens, in diversity and in harmony with nature, to realize the good way of living, the Sumak Kawsay;
>
> A society that respects the dignity of individuals and groups in all their dimensions;
>
> A democratic country, committed to Latin American integration – the dream of Bolívar and Alfaro – peace and solidarity with all peoples of the Earth;
>
> In the exercise of our sovereignty, in Ciudad Alfaro, Montecristi, Province of Manabí, we adopt the following:
>
> Constitution of the Republic of Ecuador.

Indigenous assembly members had strived to define Ecuador as a "plurinational" state during the Constituent Assembly. The recognition of legal pluralism and indigenous jurisdiction, based on ancestral legal systems, appeared to break up with classic liberal legalism, as indigenous justice was incorporated at the same level as the state's law. Moreover, given that *Sumak Kawsay* was consecrated as a fundamental constitutional principle, there was a legitimate expectation that many aspects of justice administration could be transformed to reflect it, including in the realm of gender.

Notably, Andean thought on gender largely differs from binary Western conceptions. While the duality of feminine and masculine forces is central to Andean cosmovision, this duality is not based on the *contrast* of opposites (light/dark, heat/cold, life/death, mind/body, male/female), but in the continuity between them. Beings are female and also male; "the body is not the opposite of the soul, but its continuation" (Gargallo, 2014, p. 204). In this way, the Andean figuration of *Chacha-Warmi*, which is man and woman at once, represents the father/mother of all beings. *Chacha-Warmi* has been described as a parallel unity of complementary opposites: the feminine and the masculine are always moving and producing balance, without antagonism or hierarchies (Lugones, 2009). Rather, contrast is relative, situated, and negotiable, such that "third" genders can emerge and be embraced (Benavides, 2008; Dean, 2001). Since Andean opposites do not exclude or contradict one another, but interrelate, they produce a third "potentiality" that is always accepted and included (Medina, 2011).

That said, the idea of complementarity is not unproblematic for a feminist politics of emancipation: for instance, indigenous leader Norma Mayo has affirmed that "in practice, complementarity hides the true inequalities that exist between men and women [within indigenous communities]" (Mayo, 2009, p. 139). In response, scholars like Francesca Gargallo (2014) have argued that the coloniality of gender imposed a "sexual hierarchy" upon Andean complementarity; that is, outside the Andean ontology of interconnectedness, complementarity can result in fixed, hierarchical gender roles. Since Andean gender does not produce hierarchies, complementarity should result in "correspondence" rather than separation (Sobrevilla, 2008). Thus, there would be no dichotomy between "maleness" and "femaleness" (Burman, 2011). An epistemic decolonisation that challenges the dualistic hierarchies of Western ontology should bring forward the gender fluidity of *Chacha-Warmi*. This representation could then open up possibilities for women to recreate themselves within a colonial world but outside colonial hierarchies, including those that persist within indigenous communities.

Insights like these suggest possibilities to decolonise gender justice by negotiating and reconfiguring the roles and identities that have become narrow and rigid through colonial and postcolonial power arrangements. The idea of a third potentiality, for instance, can inform queer approaches to sexuality and rights.[5] In the field of VAW, while Western human rights centre criminal law responses, an Andean lens could entail something else. Notably, a strict carcerality is not compatible with an Andean cosmovision, because justice is generally understood as relational. Given that relationality – not the individual – is the fundamental category of Andean ontology, technologies like the prison, based on isolation and exclusion, are often considered a destiny worse than death. Consequently, Andean justice could temper the punitive elements of Western rights-based approaches.

Admittedly, the debate on indigenous justice as an alternative justice model is complex and multifaceted. Certain elements of indigenous rituals, such as using stinging nettle and ice cold water to purify the offenders, could be considered punitive from a Western perspective. Assumptions that indigenous practices are opposed to human rights are not uncommon. Of course, the indigenous rituals of today are themselves mediated by contemporary Western legality and applied in contexts of social violence that affect the country as a whole. Thus, I do not intend to romanticise indigenous proceedings, especially considering that indigenous women and feminists have posited legitimate concerns about a gender justice based on indigenous customs. For example, some empirical research has shown that indigenous responses to domestic violence can result in the dismissal of the problem as an issue that does not affect the entire community and, therefore, should not be solved by the communal authority (Barrera Vivero, 2015). In some cases, when indigenous communities have intervened, the conciliatory nature of the solution has been read by critics as inadequate, because the negotiations often exclude the opinion of indigenous women (Pequeño, 2009; Vintimilla, 2009).

That said, there are also experiences of indigenous women constructing their own concepts of justice and redress, including in the domain of sexual violence, based on non-carceral indigenous models whose patriarchal elements have been questioned to produce a new paradigm (Fulchiron, 2016, 2017). Therefore, some scholars still think that Andean justice could offer alternatives to the pervasiveness of carcerality, given that imprisonment/isolation is not the

5 For a decolonial queer study of Andean culture see, for instance, Horswell (2005).

fundamental mechanism within indigenous conceptions of conflict resolution (Ávila, 2012, 2013). Indigenous justice usually prioritises reparations and the reinsertion of the offenders into the community: "balance is achieved through the inclusion (social reintegration) of the offender and the satisfaction of the victim, which also strengthens community ties" (Ávila, 2013, p. 198). Along these lines, during the 2007–2008 Constituent Assembly, indigenous assembly member Margarita Morocho explained:

> In our culture, punishment, as it is applied today, was not known: physical, emotional destruction, the destruction of man by man, the European and North American cultural inheritance [...]. In our culture, we use human values for human cohabitation between men and women [...] The forms of punishment were not death, prison, or physical and psychological punishment. The mechanisms to correct and help the offenders [were proportional to] the seriousness of the offences. [The offenders] had to work, because that is how man builds himself for the survival of his family, of the community, and of the state.
>
> (*Asamblea Constituyente Acta 036*, 2008, p. 146)

Similarly, indigenous leader and politician Lourdes Tibán has noted:

> The *ama killa* is our fundamental principle, to not be lazy. Incarceration, instead, teaches us to be lazy and imposes fifteen years of sitting down to play cards, eating for free on the state's account. That cosmovision is not part of indigenous justice.
>
> (Tibán, 2009, p. 72)

I do believe that Andean justice does contain interesting elements that can inform a decolonial approach to social violence, for example, by thinking about violence as a breach in the continuous balance of *Sumak Kawsay*. This is different from the Western conception of inter-personal violence as a matter that only concerns the parties involved. Addressing violence, from an Andean perspective, would entail acknowledging our complete interdependence and striving to restore a harmonious coexistence. The injuries that are produced by a disruption in relational balance cannot heal by marginalising or eliminating any element that is part of the continuum; damage and injury cannot be posited only in terms of individual interest or bipersonal conflict, but should be situated within the all-encompassing equilibrium of *Sumak Kawsay*. If opportunities exist to rethink criminal justice and gender on the basis of Andean thought, even if "only" at a philosophical and conceptual level, it is pertinent to ask whether contemporary legal and judicial practices have unpacked any of the decolonial elements of the 2008 Constitution to produce transformational legal frameworks. In the next section, I address these questions focusing on VAW.

A non-Andean framework for VAW?

Despite the radical potential of Andean cosmovision, there is no evidence that feminist advocacy groups have considered utilising these insights to address VAW. Initially, women's organisations were suspicious of the 2007–2008 constituent process, as they "thought that several of the things that we had conquered in 1998 would be put at risk" (former CONAMU officer, personal communication, March 16, 2015). When the constitutional reform had become inexorable, various organisations held a "Pre-Constituent Assembly", which resulted in a Women's Agenda. The consensus there was to *defend* the achievements of 1998 at all costs (Rosero, 2007). Feminists proposed few innovations in the realm of VAW, except for the specialised criminal proceedings described below. Overall, rather than attempting to reimagine gender–state relations or proposing alternative approaches to gender justice, the Women's Agenda reintroduced the achievements of the recent past.

This is not to say that the women's movement did not acknowledge other novel elements proposed by the Citizen's Revolution: for instance, the Women's Agenda did support the "social and solidary" economic model that the government advocated. To this, the Agenda added that the economy should be "caring, non-discriminatory, communal, equitative, democratise the means of production, redistribute wealth amongst individuals, collectives and regions, with social, economic and environmental justice" (Nosotras en la Constituyente, 2008, p. 8). While women's organisations endorsed the post-neoliberal proposal in regards to the economy, at the same time they adhered to the liberal human rights model that had been constitutionalised in 1998. Rather than resorting to *Sumak Kawsay* or other indigenous concepts, the women's movements focused on the "pre-eminence of human rights" and "universal and non-discriminatory inclusiveness" (Nosotras en la Constituyente, 2008, p. 8) as the foundations of a democratic state. In this way, women's organisations situated themselves outside the currents that were endorsing alternative justice models based on Andean cosmovision.

Regarding VAW, the Women's Agenda referred to penal sanctions as cardinal mechanisms to counteract discriminatory practices: "it is necessary to identify material and symbolic forms [of discrimination], both visible and subtle, and act upon them through concrete measures for sanction and non-impunity" (Nosotras en la Constituyente, 2008, p. 3). An emphasis on penality was also evident when the Agenda proposed the elimination of statutory limitations and all possible alternatives to incarceration in the domain of gender-based violence: "these crimes are not susceptible of pardon or amnesty and they are not susceptible of an alternative sanction" (Nosotras en la Constituyente, 2008, p. 10). Criminal prosecution was inextricably linked to human rights protection, and any other framing was regarded as downplaying VAW.

Ultimately, the Constitution of 2008 declared that human rights instruments are directly applicable by all national judges (Art 11.3), which reflects a stronger rights-based framework compared to 1998, when human rights treaties were considered inferior to the Constitution. Article 77 mentions "gender" violence for the first time in an Ecuadorian constitution, while Art. 77.-8 enables women to criminally report family members and declare in criminal trials prosecuting VAW. These provisions, as was the case in 1998, are based on the individual right to personal integrity (Art. 66).

Table 4.2 outlines the 2008 constitutional framework for VAW, which is remarkably similar to that of 1998. Additions include the mandate to adopt specialised criminal proceedings for offences against "priority attention groups" (equivalent to the former "vulnerable groups"), and to create specialised courts for family, children, and adolescents. The new right to a specialised penal process (Art. 81), on one hand, conveys the drive to ensure that priority groups receive adequate treatment, reducing re-victimisation. On the other hand, however, the idea that the protection of rights requires penalisation and incarceration was reaffirmed. Little emphasis was put on preventive mechanisms and economic redistribution to counteract VAW.

Although some indigenous women participated in the women's Pre-Constituent Assembly, their demands were not centred in the resulting Agenda. Indigenous leader Cristina Cucurí (2009), who would lead campaigns on indigenous women's political participation, noted: "in [the Constituent Assembly] we saw that our proposals had fallen off along the way: the topic of indigenous women did not exist anymore in the proposal of the general women's movement" (p. 134).

Again, although the Constitution of 1998 had been deemed a neoliberal legacy, its human rights elements crossed over into the 2008 Constitution nearly without interrogation. In fact, human rights allowed feminists to present their arguments as more "objective". For instance, a former staff member of a prominent NGO referred to the neutrality and broadness of international human rights:

> The issue of violence has already crossed beyond the haven of feminism… the international treaties defined what we are saying when we talk about violence against women. […] these terms, as I said, have overpassed the feminist stronghold and are instead being used in diverse fields, in scholarship, laws, the Constitution itself.
>
> (personal communication, March 12, 2015)

As we see, human rights are portrayed as non-ideological devices to reach equality. This framing expectedly led to recentring the criminal justice apparatus to protect women's rights. Great significance is attributed to criminal law and the threat of punishment. For instance, Paola Pabón, a militant of the Citizen's Revolution who would later lead the Parliamentary Group for Women's Rights, considered that "the penal field in this case, with these great achievements that we have made, can become an instrument to defend the lives of women, because when we talk about violence we are talking about life" (cited in Tapia Tapia, 2018, p. 296).

Table 4.2 Constitutional framework for VAW (2008)

Right to personal integrity and to a life free of violence	Art. 66.- The following rights of persons are recognised and guaranteed: 3. The right to personal integrity which includes: a) Bodily, psychological, moral, and sexual integrity. b) A life free of violence in the public and private sectors. The State shall adopt the measures needed to prevent, eliminate, and punish all forms of violence, especially violence against women, children and adolescents, elderly persons, persons with disabilities, and against all persons at a disadvantage or in a vulnerable situation; identical measures shall be taken against violence, slavery, and sexual exploitation. c) Prohibition of torture, forced disappearance and cruel, inhuman, or degrading treatments and punishments. d) Prohibition of the use of genetic material and scientific experimentation that undermines human rights.
Obligation to declare in cases of gender violence	Art. 77.- 8. No one can be required to make a statement in a criminal trial against one's spouse, life partner or relatives up to the fourth degree of consanguinity or second degree of affinity, except in cases of family, sexual, and gender violence. The voluntary statements made by the victims of a crime or by the relatives of these victims, regardless of the degree of kinship, shall be admissible. These persons can file and pursue the corresponding criminal proceedings.
Priority attention groups	Art. 35.- Senior adults, girls, boys and adolescents, pregnant women, disabled persons, those deprived of their liberty and those who suffer catastrophic or highly complex illnesses, will receive specialised priority attention in the public and private sphere. The same priority attention will be received by persons in risky situations, victims of domestic and sexual violence, of child maltreatment, natural or anthropogenic disasters. The state will provide special protection to persons in condition of double vulnerability.
Specialised procedures to prosecute gender violence	Art. 81.- The law shall establish special and expeditious procedures for prosecuting and punishing the crimes of family violence, sexual offences, hate crimes and crimes perpetrated against children, adolescents, young people, persons with disabilities, elderly persons and persons who, due to their specific characteristics, require greater protection. Specialised public prosecutors and defence attorneys shall be appointed for the treatment of these cases, in accordance with the law.
Specialised courts for the family	Art. 186 [...] In each canton, there shall be at least one judge specializing in the family, children, and adolescents and one judge specializing in adolescent offenders, in accordance with the needs of the population.

Table designed and produced by the author. Source: Lexis Finder database.

Similarly, officialist assembly member Rosana Alvarado stated:

> Right now we are expanding criminal law. [...] Everything that refers to discrimination, to hate crimes, to crimes against humanity, starts to be integrated in the national legislation, even though it used to be only a matter of international agreements and treaties [...]. Therefore, this is a criminal law that has grown, that is growing, and from that point of view, I would say, feminism also has to use that criminal law.
>
> (cited in Tapia Tapia, 2018, p. 296)

Alvarado's comments point at larger trends that surpass feminist concerns: her view was that Ecuador was undergoing a process of human rights "nationalisation", by which past positions that regarded international instruments as merely programmatic and non-applicable by national judges, could be overcome.

Along these lines, a judge at a specialised court for violence against women and the family also referred to criminal law as a legal instrument to defend human rights:

> When [a right] is violated within a context of family violence, a context of gender violence with the exercise of power, we are talking about human rights. It is not like a crime against property, it is not like a crime against state security. Here we are speaking about legal goods that are protected as human rights. And penal prosecution is [thereby] absolutely necessary.
>
> (personal communication, April 16, 2015)

Although the women's movement contributed to the adoption of a human rights-based approach to VAW, there were reversals during the constituent process, often related to sexuality and reproductive rights: for instance, the demands to allow same-sex marriage and legal abortion were obstructed by Catholic lobbies and other conservative sectors.[6] In reality, VAW was the least controversial issue on the table. A leader who worked for decades with women's collectives in the south of the country said:

> I remember that violence was not too complex an issue to manage in the Constituent [Assembly], it was one of the [topics] that better fitted the discourses of the assembly members [...]. Very rarely an assembly member would say that [violence against women] should not constitute a criminal offence and that it should continue to be treated the way it was in Act 103.
>
> (personal communication, May 15, 2015)

In other words, it was easy to incorporate VAW as a question of human rights into the Constitution. As it happened in 1995 and 1998, positing VAW as a

6 In 2019, Ecuador's Constitutional Court ruled to recognise same-sex marriage, overhauling the Constitution's prohibition.

criminal infraction was not met with any significant resistance; not even from the conservatives who generally oppose the women's movement's agenda.

Having demonstrated that human rights framings of VAW travelled all the way from a neoliberal to a post-neoliberal constitution, despite the decolonial "disruption" performed in 2008, I shall now bring the reader's attention to the ways in which indigenous justice, as a non-carceral approach, was largely excluded from Ecuador's legal system in the name of human rights, even though it had been constitutionally recognised. Key in this process was the articulation of what I term "rights-based penality", explained in detail below.

Rights-based penality: the shield that enabled the sword

Critical criminologist Nils Christie (2007) famously noted that the imposition of punishment always entails the deliberate infliction of pain. Because inflicting pain is at odds with moral values like kindness and forgiveness, legal theories of punishment usually endeavour to hide the harmful character of incarceration by rationalising its justifications. In this section, I describe an influential theoretical framework used in Ecuador to justify the infliction of pain under the rule of law, which I term "rights-based penality", that is, a modern and rational penal apparatus contained by constitutional principles and suited to defend human rights.

In his analysis of the paradoxical relationship between criminal law and human rights, Tulkens (2011) notes that the latter have both a defensive and an offensive role, that is, they neutralise and trigger criminal justice, functioning as "shield and sword". The shield, I contend, is in reality what enables the sword. The shield *is* the sword. In Ecuador, a human rights-based justification of punishment has not only allowed penality to travel from a neoliberal to a post-neoliberal constitution; it has also resulted in the expulsion of non-penal and non-carceral possibilities from the realm of genuine justice. Some scholars have made a distinction between two periods of the Citizen's Revolution: the first (2007–2010), *Garantista*, was focused on protecting human rights, and the second (2010–2017), *Punitivista* (Aguirre Salas et al., 2020), was focused on punishment. I contend that the first period is what facilitated the second. Hardening carceral punishment is only possible when carcerality per se has been legitimised. Once inflicting pain is legally and morally justified, it is easy to overlook that it is still pain.

Although indigenous and non-indigenous intellectuals have affirmed that the 2008 Constitution promised "a utopia of our own, pre-hispanic and which becomes anti-capitalist" (Ávila, 2013, p. 186), I contend that its internal tensions have resolved in favour of liberal legality. Scholars like Boaventura de Sousa Santos (2007) have envisioned an "ecology of knowledges", by which the wealth of diverse worldviews may be redeemed and harmonised; however, other scholars have been less optimistic, noting that, when dissimilar ontological and epistemological presuppositions encounter each other, the hegemonic perspective tends to suppress the other (Estermann, 2014; Walsh, 2009). I will show, in the following sections, that the penal and coercive dimensions of human rights have prevailed in Ecuador and precluded the integration of indigenous justice and, more broadly, of a non-penal approach to conflict resolution.

A truncated pact: the reinscription of rights-based penality

> The effect of the claim that punitive power, without major social changes, only by virtue of punctual reforms to the existing laws, can become an ally of anti-discrimination struggles, is that punitive power receives a partial critique that does not greatly bruise it, because society is habituated to these type of critiques; but, at the same time – and as an excessive compensation – [punitive power] benefits of a formidable legitimation resulting from the reaffirmations of its usefulness.
>
> (Zaffaroni, 2009, p. 333)

> What type of law do we need in the [criminal justice] field that is in line with the new vision that *Buen Vivir* represents? How does such vision fit in the context of an alternative conception of society?
>
> (feminist leader, personal interview, May 2015)

Despite the radical potential of Andean cosmovision, indigenous justice has been virtually displaced by liberal legalism in Ecuador. In this section, I describe the doctrines that underlie the 2008 Constitution's approach to criminal justice. I argue that a rights-based framework reconciles penal coercion and human rights, re-legitimising penality, and facilitating the dismissal of non-penal alternatives. In this way, criminal justice emerges as the only legitimate response to human rights violations.

Let us start by considering Article 424 of the Constitution. As noted before, human rights instruments are at the highest levels of the legal system:

> The Constitution and the international human rights treaties that are ratified by the State, which recognise rights that are more favourable than those enshrined in the Constitution, shall prevail over any other legal regulatory system or action by public power.

In parallel, a close reading of the Constitution reveals that the recognition of indigenous justice was ambiguous from the outset:

> Article 171.- The authorities of the indigenous communities, peoples, and nations shall perform jurisdictional duties, on the basis of their ancestral traditions and their own system of law, within their own territories, with a guarantee for the participation of, and decision-making by women. The authorities shall apply their own standards and procedures for the settlement

> of internal disputes, *as long as they are not contrary to the Constitution and the human rights enshrined in international instruments*. The state shall guarantee that the decisions of indigenous jurisdiction are observed by public institutions and authorities. These decisions shall be subject to monitoring of their constitutionality. The statute shall establish the mechanisms for coordination and cooperation between indigenous jurisdiction and regular jurisdiction.
>
> (emphasis added)

As we see, although the recognition of indigenous justice has been seen as a sign of the state's acknowledgement of legal plurality, the Constitution itself limits its scope via human rights instruments. Oddly, indigenous justice is, a priori, suspect of being incompatible with human rights.

In fact, even though *Sumak Kawsay* appears in the very preamble of the Constitution, Andean cosmovision is left at the margins in most parts of the text. References to Andean principles only appear in the passages that are related to environmental rights, the recognition of communal property, and the introduction of social and environmental responsibility as limitations to private property. *Sumak Kawsay* is also mentioned in the sections about sustainable development. However, the Constitution does not invoke *Sumak Kawsay* in the chapters that address individual rights.[7] Various aspects of individual freedom, including personal integrity, were brought unmodified from the 1998 Constitution. As a consequence, the state's response to human rights violations was again conceived mainly as the obligation to criminally prosecute and punish.

Some critics have noted that recognising new rights often results in penal expansion: for instance, declaring that Pacha Mama (Mother Earth) has rights, rather than facilitating the treatment of nature as a *subject* of rights, has resulted in a response from criminal law in the form of new environmental crimes (Zaffaroni, 2011). In this regard, there are critiques of "human rights penality" that point to the dangers of aligning human rights protection with criminal law (Mavronicola, 2020). One such danger would be risking the integrity of the human rights edifice itself. For instance, if we consider a principle, such as the prohibition of inhuman and degrading punishment, a human rights penality could destabilise human rights' stance on the punitive machine, and on carcerality more broadly (Mavronicola, 2015). Also, penality tends to sideline the social and redistributive dimensions of human rights. Still, dominant

7 Contemporary constitutional scholars have pointed out that the change of paradigm in the Constitution of 2008 entails an elimination of the distinction between individual and collective rights that was defined in the Constitution of 1998. The new framework supposes that all human rights are fundamental rights, and that all fundamental rights have both an individual and a collective dimension (Ávila, 2008).

Table 4.3 Penal guarantees: ten axioms

1.	*Nulla poena sine crimine* (no punishment without a crime).
2.	*Nullum crimes sine lege* (no crime without a law).
3.	*Nulla lex poenalis sine necessitate* (no criminal law without necessity).
4.	*Nulla necessitas sine iniuria* (no necessity without injury).
5.	*Nulla iniuria sine actione* (no injury without an action).
6.	*Nulla actio sine culpa* (no action without guilt).
7.	*Nulla culpa sine iudicio* (no guilt without a trial).
8.	*Nullum iudicium sine accusatione* (no trial without accusation).
9.	*Nulla accusatio sine probatione* (no accusation without evidence).
10.	*Nulla probatio sine defensione* (no evidence without defence).

Table designed and produced by the author. Source: Ferrajoli (1995).

scholarship has proposed the *moderation* of criminal law as the way to make penality and human rights compatible.

In Ecuador and Latin America, the theoretical and doctrinal current known as *garantismo penal*[8] has had a high resonance in some liberal and progressive legal circles. This rights-based approach to criminal law revolves around the idea that punitive power can be limited by due process and legal rules (or guarantees) that restrain state coercion (Vallejo Jiménez, 2011). According to Italian jurist Luigi Ferrajoli,[9] law should act as a system of guarantees that ensure the "double subjection" of law to law, both in formal and material aspects. Ferrajoli proposes a "minimum" criminal law because penal power always contains some degree of brutality: punishment is a second violence that follows the violence of crime itself (Ferrajoli, 1995). To mitigate the violence of criminal law, Ferrajoli conveys ten axioms for a rational penal model in the modern democratic state (see Table 4.3).

Similarly, but within the Anglo-American tradition, Dubber (2004) has affirmed that "criminal law consists of the state's most potent and most intrusive means of interfering with those very [fundamental] rights" (p. 46). For this reason, he argues, not only procedural criminal law should be constitutionalised via due process; substantive criminal law must also incorporate constitutional principles that preserve human rights, particularly the principle of human dignity and autonomy. Because the foundation of *mens rea* and *actus reus* in Common Law has not stood in the way of practices like "the war on crime" and "the war on terrorism", says Dubber, it is necessary to "construct a

8 In Anglo-American contexts similar perspectives have been referred to as "constitutional criminal law" (Dubber, 2004).

9 Ferrajoli is amply cited by Ecuadorian and Latin American authors. Ferrajoli positions himself as a critic of "social projects that are disciplinary, correctionist, police-oriented or otherwise anti-liberal" (Ferrajoli, 1995, p. 213).

meaningful constitutional jurisprudence of criminal law within the framework of a system of human rights" (2004, p. 5).

In my view, the idea of "constitutionalising" criminal law is not a harmless enunciative restriction of coercive power. It doubles as a discourse that resolves the paradox of a violent penal apparatus and formally legitimises state coercion. This discursive manoeuvre excludes representing criminal law as a problem: a reasonable, moderate state violence is legitimate because it is controlled and measured. Ultimately, theories like *Garantismo Penal* and Constitutional Criminal Law "coat" the central concern of criminal law, that is, social control, and present it as the protection of rights. Criminal law thus appears to fulfil a new purpose: it is the guardian of the fundamental rights of victims and offenders. *Garantías penales* (due process and its safeguards) are deemed sufficient "dams against arbitrariness and error" (Ferrajoli, 1995, p. 210) that minimise inefficiency (impunity) and/or injustice (incarceration of innocents). *Garantías penales* are the *conditio sine qua non* to punish and, since incarceration can only emerge from a valid trial whereby human rights are protected, punishment is legitimate, lawful and reasonable.

Ecuadorian proponents of penal guarantees introduced this approach into scholarly and technical texts after the advent of the Citizen's Revolution. *Garantismo penal* has been widely featured in publications by the former Ministry of Justice and Human Rights. While some authors reflected on how the state could learn from indigenous justice as a non-carceral alternative (Ávila, 2012, 2013), a more widespread strand supported the reduction (and preservation) of a criminal law based on penal guarantees (Silva Portero, 2008). In addition, the 2008 Constitution waves at *garantismo penal* in various passages: for instance, it mandates that the state protects the human rights of victims, of the prosecuted, and of those deprived of their liberty (Art. 51). It also establishes an array of "procedural guarantees" (Art. 76) for administrative or judicial processes. These include the presumption of innocence, the principle of legality, *in dubio pro reo*, *non bis in idem*, amongst others. These are expected to "radiate" into the substantive and procedural legislation, ensuring the "constitutionalisation of criminal law" (Ávila, 2013).

Evidently, no element in the theory of penal guarantees disputes the legitimacy of carceral punishment. At the same time, very few commentators of the Constitution have considered that rights-based penality may reinstate and encourage carceral punishment. Moreover, in 2009, a preliminary draft for what was then called the "Code of Penal Guarantees" (*Anteproyecto de Código de Garantías Penales*) was devised by a team of scholars and lawyers on behalf of the Ministry of Justice and Human Rights. The project was introduced as "the penal code that a guarantee-based constitution demands" (Ávila, 2009, p. 21). One passage of the preface reads:

> Guarantee-based criminal law delivers a justification for the existence of criminal law, as it regulates and minimises punitive violence; it establishes the parameter of legitimation of the state when it uses its sanctioning

> power; it is adapted to a model of substantial democracy that is characteristic of a constitutional state of rights and justice.
>
> (Ávila, 2009, p. 23)

This fragment positions penal guarantees as a constitutive element of the democratic state. Due process not only limits the power of the state as it does in classical liberal legalism; now that it has evolved into penal guarantees, it sets out to transform coercive power into the very custodian of rights. If so-called penal guarantees are deemed essential for the existence of a democratic state, this presupposes the legitimacy of criminal law and coercive power. Penality, as a consequence, is indispensable to construct rights and justice within democracy. All appeals to criminalisation and punishment are constitutionalised a priori, that is, legitimised at the highest level of the legal system. The penal apparatus – the most violent structure that can be used by the state – is impregnated with the affirmation that coercion can be rational, legitimate, and just.

Of course, the constitutionalisation of criminal law does not imply that incarceration ceases to be the penal sanction *par excellence*. The Constitution consecrates penal guarantees, but it does not contain any principles that challenge carcerality as such: for example, preventive detention (the imprisonment of a legally innocent individual) is still legitimate. Although rights-based penality is presented as diametrically opposed to retributive criminal justice, given that carcerality is not displaced, imprisonment remains available, acceptable, and expandable. My contention is that carcerality stays uninterrogated (and the prison is unspokenly deemed unavoidable) not despite, but *because* of penal guarantees. As I demonstrate in the next section, state justice does not accommodate a response to human rights violations that does not take the form of criminal prosecution and carceral punishment.

Rights-based penality in practice: a Lesson from indigenous justice

The preceding sections have illustrated the tensions between indigenous justice – based on a monistic ontology and a cosmovision that centres interconnectedness – and the rights-based liberal framing that travelled from the "neoliberal" to the "post-neoliberal" constitution. In this section, I bring in case law from the Constitutional Court of Ecuador to show how these tensions were resolved in high-court practice: the encounter between liberal and non-liberal approaches to justice resulted in the silencing of the non-dominant perspective (Estermann, 2014; Merry, 1988, 2003; Walsh, 2009).

In La Cocha, a community of Panzaleo people,[10] a group of men had been found guilty of killing a man during a celebration. By order of the local

10 Panzaleo people, also known as Kichwa from Cotopaxi, reside in the southern region of the Cotopaxi province, in Ecuador's highlands. It is estimated that this nationality comprises between 45,000 and 76,000 persons, organised in 850 communities (CONAIE, 2014).

authority (the indigenous Communal Assembly), the accused were whipped with stinging nettle (a ritual plant), forced to undress and carry heavy rocks around the village, bathed with ice cold water,[11] compelled to apologise to the entire community, and forced to pay compensation to both the community and the mother of the deceased. Even though these measures have an important symbolic and ritualistic meaning common to various Andean communities, when the procedures reached the media, they were depicted as "torture" (El Universo, 2010).[12] A Public Prosecutor and police then entered the indigenous territory to "rescue" the offenders. A state court heard the case and considered that the defendants had been "kidnapped" by the indigenous authority and, since there was evidence that a murder had been committed, both the offenders and the indigenous authority were arrested.[13]

Facing these events, a community member presented an "extraordinary protection action" (*acción extraordinaria de protección*)[14] to the Constitutional Court of Ecuador, demanding a binding pronouncement on the application of indigenous justice. Amongst other queries, the petitioner asked the Court to determine whether the offenders were facing a second criminal trial, given that they had already been judged by the indigenous authority for the same offence. In 2014, the Constitutional Court issued a resolution. The arguments and conclusions presented by the majority of the judges[15] are illustrative of the role of human rights in enabling the state's punitive power.

One of the first steps taken by the Constitutional Court was to commission a forensic anthropological study to confirm the customary nature of the sanctions applied by the indigenous assembly, as well as the legitimacy of the indigenous authority, and the correspondence between the proceedings and indigenous cosmovision. According to the Court, the anthropological study would let them "take into account criteria and parameters that are characteristic of legal pluralism" (*Sentencia 113-14-SEP-CC*, 2014, p. 10). Despite taking this seemingly pluralistic step, the Court relied on Western doctrinal concepts thereafter. For instance, Austrian jurist Hans Kelsen was invoked to define the

11 According to research carried out in various provinces of the Ecuadorian highlands, physical punishment is an exceptional sanction amongst indigenous authorities' decisions. Most cases are solved through conciliation (Vintimilla, 2009).

12 Regarding the depiction of indigenous rituals as incompatible with human rights, indigenous leader Lourdes Tibán has formulated the following explanatory question: "sanctioning a person with a stinging nettle whiplash, or putting them in jail for 14 years, which violates human rights the most?" (Tibán, 2009, p. 70)

13 The community indigenous authorities were released through habeas corpus.

14 This action (Art. 94 of the Constitution) proceeds against sentences of definitive authority resolutions through which constitutionally recognised rights are presumed to have been violated.

15 In regards to this resolution, there was one dissenting vote from a judge who considered that the indigenous proceedings were legal and legitimate, and that any additional state trial would constitute a second judgment.

scope of the word "authority" and determine whether the indigenous assembly was legitimate. It is indeed perplexing that a paradigmatic representative of legal positivism was cited in an indigenous justice case, even though the legitimacy of the Communal Assembly was never questioned by any of the parties involved, including the offenders themselves. This is evidence of the privilege that Western legal knowledge has over that of indigenous communities (Hernández Castillo, 2017).

The Court then addressed the apparent tensions between the state's law and the indigenous custom, aiming at harmonising "the legal devices of the local constitutional system" with "the conventional and international juridical order of human rights" (*Sentencia 113-14-SEP-CC*, 2014, p. 13). Importantly, the Court framed homicide, first and foremost, as a violation of the human right to life. It pointed out that, from the standpoint of the community, the killing disrupted *Sumak Kawsay*. In that context, the indigenous authority had aimed at re-establishing community balance by repairing the damages and eventually inserting the offenders back into the community. However, according to the Court, the indigenous authority *did not* address the violation of the human right to life. The Court made a sharp distinction between what the indigenous community intended to preserve – *Sumak Kawsay* – and what the state protects – the human right to life. Based on this distinction, the Court decided that the indigenous judgment was not sufficient to respond to the violation of a human right, and that indigenous justice and state justice had different purposes. Each system protects different legal goods. The judges' reasoning revolved around the idea that a person's life is an end in itself, and it was implied that the indigenous representation of life as relational and interconnected is incompatible with the sanctity of life that is inherent to Western human rights. As a consequence, framing a killing as the rupture of communal balance does not speak to the intrinsic value of human life:

> What the community members who are vested with authority investigate is the degree to which the behaviour of the implicated [offenders] provokes damage to the collective community. This is evinced by assessing the sense and scope of the sanctions prescribed by the [Community] Assembly.
>
> (*Sentencia 113-14-SEP-CC*, 2014, p. 20)

The Court then cited a passage from one of the forensic reports:

> [For the indigenous community, life] is not a value in itself as a personal being or individual entity but to the extent to which it participates in the family (ayllu) or community [...], and what is meant to be protected is precisely this: life as a value of communal cohabitation, of social understanding and harmony with one's surroundings.
>
> (*Sentencia 113-14-SEP-CC*, 2014, p. 22)

In my view, the Court was not making a legal argument only; it also made an ethical, epistemic, and ontological distinction: the monistic conception of complete interconnectedness was dismissed as insufficient grounds for delivering justice, vis-à-vis life understood as an individual human right. The Court implied that indigenous justice does not regard life as a right, and insisted that the leitmotif underlying their judgment was to ensure the protection of human rights. The Court asked itself what the duty of the state is when human rights are violated, and answered that, since the Constitution and the Universal Declaration of Human Rights "determine that all individuals have a right to life, freedom and the safety of their own person", the public authorities are obliged to establish a system that protects life by sanctioning any attack against it. "It is necessary to activate all the national and international means and mechanisms for [the] effective protection [of the human right to life], including the obligation of all the states to effectively *prosecute* any behaviour that endangers this right, and attain the *sanction* of its authors, always with the aim to *prevent impunity* and avert and eliminate behaviours that are against the right to life" (*Sentencia 113-14-SEP-CC*, 2014, p. 27 emphasis added).

Because the Constitutional Court's judgments are binding case law, this sentence largely ruled out future possibilities of implementing indigenous justice when a conflict relates to human rights. The Court reaffirmed the duty to prosecute and sanction human rights violations as an exclusive prerogative of the state, which eclipses the constitutional recognition of indigenous justice. According to the Court: "ultimately, it is the duty of the state and its institutions, as a priority, to prevent crimes against life from going *unpunished*, ensuring that the corresponding sanction falls into the responsibility of whoever causes the death" (*Sentencia 113-14-SEP-CC*, 2014, p. 27 emphasis added). In short, only the state can prosecute and punish human rights violations through criminal justice:

> Since the inviolability of life is a right protected by the Constitution, by international human rights instruments and by the principles contained in the ius cogens, it is the duty of the state to grant this right in all its dimensions and ensure that facing any threat or violation, the behaviour as such is *judged and sanctioned*.
>
> (*Sentencia 113-14-SEP-CC*, 2014, p. 27)

The judgment, of course, did not allude to the significance and implications of incarceration for the indigenous community and its way of life. It did not reflect on the reparations that are central to indigenous justice, nor how dissimilar the time periods are for each type of process (an ordinary criminal trial can last several years). Not even the fact that the offended parties and the entire indigenous community, including the offenders themselves,[16] had

16 Initially, when the constitutional action was filed, the offenders demanded that the Court declare the indigenous procedures to be contrary to human rights, arguing that they had been treated

expressed their satisfaction with the decision of the indigenous authority, was considered.

This Constitutional Court judgment was the first binding precedent in matters of indigenous justice since the enactment of the 2008 Constitution. Hence, the highest court regarded indigenous justice as an obstacle of sorts for the integrity of the state system that "truly" guards human rights. Furthermore, this judgment confirmed that a rights-based penality results in criminal justice being posited as the only legitimate path to address the violation of human rights, averting alternative conceptions of justice.

Formally, the judgment did not invalidate the Indigenous Assembly decision. According to the Court, the ordinary criminal trial did not produce a "double judgment". From the perspective of the Court, indigenous justice centred community life, while the state dealt with the actual violation of human rights. Even though the Constitutional Court did not explicitly characterise indigenous justice as incompatible with human rights, the judgment in practice entails the impossibility that the indigenous paradigm be implemented as an alternative to incarceration, even within their own territories. The Court authorised indigenous justice, but only as a kind of ritual that is outside the sphere of "genuine" justice. According to indigenous leader Mónica Chuji:

> in fact, the Constitutional Court has basically disowned and ceased to recognise the indigenous justice system... That is, it has disallowed the communities from exercising indigenous justice. It disregards [indigenous justice] and assumes that the ordinary system is the only one that can judge.
> (personal communication, April 17, 2015)

The case of La Cocha lets us anticipate how difficult a non-penal approach to VAW would be. If *Sumak Kawsay* has not borne fruit in the realm of a constitutionally recognised indigenous justice, it is even less likely to be invoked to modify a domain that has long been mediated by human rights and penality. The impossibility to dislodge penality from human rights justice, together with the dissemination of the penal guarantees doctrine, results in fertile land for the expansion of punitive approaches, since these are justified and presented, not only as human rights-compliant, but as the *only* way to protect human rights. Penality has solidified as the foundation to legislate and uphold human rights, and therefore, to manage VAW.

inhumanely. However, by the time the first hearing took place, the offenders, who were still confronting the state criminal trial, stepped back and supported the petitioner's argument that the state procedure constituted double judgment and demanded that the Court declare the indigenous procedure valid, thus accepting all the community decisions.

Conclusion

This chapter has confirmed what some feminist critics have already remarked: not only conservative law-and-order politics produce and maintain the carceral state (Murakawa, 2014; Whalley & Hackett, 2017); there are broad progressive discourses that have been complicit in the normalisation of penality as a proxy for justice. My contribution here has consisted of delving deeper into the idea of a "constitutional criminal law" by comparing two constitutional reform processes, which have been deemed neoliberal and post-neoliberal, respectively. Why, I asked, can people coming from such different intellectual and political traditions have such similar faith in criminal justice? I will engage thoroughly with VAW in Chapter 5; here, I have shown how two apparently opposite constitutions framed VAW almost identically, as they both relied on human rights as their starting point. This rights-based penality was later used to displace indigenous justice as an alternative to conflict resolution in the domain of human rights.

My aim has been to uncover the mechanisms that facilitate the dissemination of penality through progressive law reform, even when this has questioned liberalism in several aspects, such as its economic dimension. I have argued that the liberal heart of dominant legality is still beating vigorously within left-leaning law reform and enabling the punitive state through its formal promise of a fair, almost innocuous criminal justice system. Despite the many interpellations that the 2008 Constitution posed to liberal legalism, its decolonial elements have not shaken the rights-based penality that was introduced during the neoliberal period. Human rights frameworks do not appear to have been suspicious for leftist feminists or other progressive groups, even though voices from indigeneous women did rise and disputed the inclusivity of the mainstream women's movement and its legal strategies.

I conclude that it is critical to interrogate liberal legality before moving onto a critique of how feminists use it specifically. Liberalism is the field of intelligibility that justifies the rights and wrongs of law, and we often let it go unquestioned when we look at law reform. As Carol Smart put it: "we must produce a deeper understanding of law in order to comprehend its resistance to and denial of women's concerns" (1989, p. 160). Smart also commented, in her pioneering work, that the language of rights is empowering in that rights can be claimed by everyone no matter what class or gender, and it is also limiting in that it constructs law as the centre of so many political campaigns. I have turned my gaze back to the limitations of liberal law itself and how it materialised in Ecuador's attempt to attain a constitution that intends to be decolonial and rights-based at the same time. In this way, I addressed how liberal legalism informs what we understand as justice and, more specifically, how the marriage between liberal criminal law and human rights has produced the broader model through which we enunciate what is fair.

The liberal conflation between protecting human rights and criminally punishing their violations, allowed many elements of the 1998 Constitution to land in the 2008 Constitution. Although the Constitution of 2008 introduced some aspects of Andean cosmovision on social relations, welfare, and wellbeing, when it came to human rights and VAW, it deployed the same framework of 1998. Then, the clash between the two conflicting paradigms resulted in a limited recognition of indigenous justice, which was, from the outset, hampered by liberal legality. The prevalence of human rights penality was confirmed in the "La Cocha" judgment, which disallowed the use of indigenous justice in matters of human rights, reducing indigenous procedures to ritualistic devices that do not deliver "real" justice.

In addition, *garantismo penal*, a rights-based approach to criminal law, has smoothed out the paradox that using penality can itself constitute a violation of human rights. However, in its pursuit to overcome the penal paradox, rights-based penality has reaffirmed state coercion via doctrinal principles that present criminal justice as human-rights-compliant. Because a human rights-based criminal justice is presented as an indispensable element of democracy, carcerality implicitly becomes a requisite for a democratic state. In this way, penality is tacitly deemed unavoidable: it has become constitutive of democratic representations of justice and required to protect human rights. As a result, criminal law is reconfigured to become not only a mechanism of social control but also a guardian of rights. The reinscribed legitimacy of penality leads to a deeper consolidation of criminal justice. In Ecuador, this has translated into the exclusion of the indigenous perspectives that the Constitution itself introduced. It is the constitutional authorisation of penal force as the main tool to protect rights that makes penality, available, inevitable, and therefore susceptible to expansion, including in the field of VAW.

References

Aguirre Salas, A., Léon, T., & Ribadeneira González, N.S. (2020). Sistema penitenciario y población penalizada durante la Revolución Ciudadana (2007–2017). *URVIO: Revista Latinoamericana de Estudios de Seguridad*, *27*, 94–110.

Albuja, S., Arias, M., Arroyo, M., Astudillo, M., & Bermúdez, K. (2017). *Informe de desarrollo social 2007–2017*. Ministerio Coordinador de Desarrollo Social.

Asamblea Constituyente 2007–2008. (2008). *Asamblea Constituyente Acta 036*. AC-07-08-033, Archivo de la Asamblea Nacional del Ecuador, Quito. http://archivo.asambleanacional.gob.ec/index.php/actas-2007-2029

Ávila, R. (2008). *Estado constitucional de derechos y justicia* (R. Ávila (ed.); pp. 19–38). Ministerio de justicia y derechos humanos.

Ávila, R. (ed.). (2009). *Anteproyecto de código de garantías penales*. Ministerio de justicia y derechos humanos.

Ávila, R. (2012). *¿Debe aprender el derecho penal estatal de la justicia indígena?* (B. de S. Santos & A. Grijalva (eds.); pp. 279–304). Abya Yala.

Ávila, R. (2013). *La (in)justicia penal en la democracia constitucional de derechos. Una mirada desde el garantismo penal*. Ediciones Legales.

Barrera Vivero, A. (2015). *Violence against women in legally plural settings. Experiences and lessons from the Andes*. Routledge.

Benavides, O.H. (2008). The representation of Guayaquil's sexual past: Historicizing the enchaquirados. *Journal of Latin American Anthropology*, 7(1), 68–103.

Bowen, J.D. (2011). Multicultural market democracy: Elites and indigenous movements in contemporary Ecuador. *Journal of Latin American Studies, 43*(3), 451–483.

Burman, A. (2011). Chachawarmi: Silence and rival voices on decolonisation and gender politics in Andean Bolivia. *Journal of Latin American Studies, 43*(1), 65–91.

Camacho, G., & Hernández, K. (2011). *Comisarías de la mujer y acceso a la justicia en Cuenca* (L. Pásara (ed.); pp. 229–282). Ministerio de Justicia y Derechos Humanos, Naciones Unidas.

Christie, N. (2007). *Limits to pain: The role of punishment in penal policy*. Wipf & Stock Publishers.

CLADEM. (2006). *Informe sombra: una mirada alternativa a la situación de discriminación de la mujer en el Ecuador. Período 1990–1998*. CLADEM.

CONAIE. (2014, July 19). *Panzaleo*. CONAIE. https://conaie.org/2014/07/19/panzaleo/

Correa, R. (2011, December 3). *Conferencia magistral del economista Rafael Correa Delgado en la Universidad de Buenos Aires*. https://www.presidencia.gob.ec/wp-content/uploads/downloads/2012/10/031210_Conferencia-Magistral-dictada-por-el-Presidente-en-la-UBA.pdf

Cucurí, C. (2009). *El acceso de las mujeres indígenas a la justicia en la nueva constitución del Ecuador* (M. Lang & A. Kucia (eds.); pp. 132–135). UNIFEM.

Dean, C. (2001). *Andean androgyny and the making of men* (C.F. Klein (ed.); pp. 143–177). Dumbarton Oaks Research Library and Collection.

Dieterich, H. (2009, March 11). *El gran salto adelante del Socialismo del Siglo XXI*. Rebelión. https://rebelion.org/el-gran-salto-adelante-del-socialismo-del-siglo-xxi/

Dubber, M.D. (2004). Toward a constitutional law of crime and punishment. *The Hastings Law Journal, 55*, 1–77.

El Universo. (2010, May 23). *Justicia indígena se dicta sin control por falta de ley*. El Universo. https://www.eluniverso.com/2010/05/23/1/1447/justicia-indigena-cuestionada-tema-derechos-humanos.html

Estermann, J. (2014). Colonialidad, descolonización e interculturalidad. Apuntes desde la filosofía intercultural. *Polis, Revista Latinoamericana, 13*(38), 347–368.

Ewig, C. (2012). Introduction. *Politics & Gender, 8*(2), 246–248.

Ferrajoli, L. (1995). *Derecho y razón. Teoría del garantismo penal* (Vol. 2). Editorial Trotta.

Fulchiron, A. (2016). La violencia sexual como genocidio. Memoria de las mujeres mayas sobrevivientes de violación sexual durante el conflicto armado en Guatemala. *Revista mexicana de ciencias politicas y sociales, 61*(228), 391–422.

Fulchiron, A. (2017). Actoras de Cambio en Guatemala: poner el cuerpo y la vida de las mujeres en el centro de la justicia. In I. M. Azkue, G. Guzmán Orellana, & I. Zirion Landaluze (Eds.), *Género y justicia transicional. Movimientos de mujeres contra la impunidad* (pp. 65–112). Universidad del País Vasco.

García Villegas, M. (2012). Constitucionalismo aspiracional: derecho, democracia y cambio social en América Latina. *Análisis Político, 25*(75), 89–110

Gargallo, F. (2014). *Feminismos desde Abya Yala. Ideas y proposiciones de las mujeres de 607 pueblos en Nuestra América*. Editorial Corte y Confección.

Gargarella, R. (2015). El "nuevo" constitucionalismo latinoamericano. *Estudios Sociales, 48*, 169–172.

Grijalva, A. (2009). El estado plurinacional e intercultural en la constitución ecuatoriana de 2008. In C. Espinosa & D. Caicedo (Eds.), *Derechos ancestrales. Justicia en contextos plurinacionales* (pp. 389–408). Ministerio de Justicia y Derechos Humanos

Grupo Banco Mundial. (2020, March). *Ecuador*. Banco Mundial. https://datos.bancomundial.org/pais/ecuador

Hernández Castillo, R.A. (2017). Activismo legal y talleres penitenciarios. Las paradojas de la antropología juridica feminista y del trabajo cultural en espacios de reclusión. In R.A. Hernández Castillo (ed.), *Resistencias penitenciarias. Investigación activista de espacios de reclusión* (pp. 51–82). Juan Pablos Editor.

Horswell, M.J. (2005). *Decolonizing the sodomite: Queer tropes of sexuality in colonial Andean culture*. University of Texas Press.

Kampwirth, K. (2011). *Latin America's new left and the politics of gender: Lessons from Nicaragua*. Springer.

Lugones, M. (2009). Hacia una lectura decolonial de Chacha-Warmi. *Reunión Anual de Etnología, II*, 153.

Mavronicola, N. (2015). Crime, punishment and article 3 ECHR: Puzzles and prospects of applying an absolute right in a penal context. *Human Rights Law Review, 15*(4), 721–743.

Mavronicola, N. (2020). The potential dangers of aligning human rights protection with criminal law (enforcement). In L. Lavrysen & N. Mavronicola (eds.), *Coercive human rights: Positive duties to mobilise the criminal law under the ECHR* (p. 184). Hart Publishing.

Mayo, N. (2009). *Políticas de la CONAIE a nivel nacional para fortalecer el acceso de la justicia de las mujeres indígenas* (M. Lang & A. Kucia (eds.); pp. 139–141). UNIFEM.

Medina, J. (2011). *Acerca del Suma Qamaña* (I. Farah & L. Vasapollo (eds.); p. 39). CIDES-UMSA.

Merry, S.E. (1988). Legal pluralism. *Law & Society Review, 22*(5), 869–896.

Merry, S.E. (2003). From law and colonialism to law and globalization. *Law & Social Inquiry: Journal of the American Bar Foundation, 28*(2), 569–590.

Murakawa, N. (2014). *The first civil right: How liberals built prison America*. Oxford University Press.

Noguera Fernández, A. (2011). El neoconstitucionalismo andino: ¿una superación de la contradicción entre democracia y justicia constitucional? *Revista Vasca de Administración Pública, 90*, 167–196.

Nosotras en la Constituyente – Movimiento de Mujeres del Ecuador. (2008). *Agenda de las mujeres para la nueva constitución ecuatoriana*. UNIFEM.

Ordóñez, A., Samman, E., Mariotti, C., & Borja Borja, I.M. (2015, October). *Sharing the fruits of progress:* Poverty *reduction in Ecuador*. Overseas Development Institute. https://www.odi.org/publications/9958-sharing-fruits-progress-poverty-reduction-ecuador

Ospina, P. (2009). *Historia de un desencuentro: Rafael Correa y los movimientos sociales en el Ecuador (2007–2008)* (R. Hoetmer (ed.); pp. 195–218). Universidad Nacional Mayor de San Marcos.

Pastor, V., & Dalmau, R.M. (2011). Fundamentos teóricos y prácticos del nuevo constitucionalismo latinoamericano. *Gaceta Constitucional, 48*, 309.

Pequeño, A. (2009). *Violencia de género y mecanismos de resolución comunitaria en comunidades indígenas de la sierra ecuatoriana* (M. Lang & A. Kucia (eds.); pp. 81–89). UNIFEM.

Quintero López, R. (2008). *La Constitución de 2008. Un análisis político*. Abya-Yala.

Radcliffe, S.A. (2012). Development for a postneoliberal era? Sumak kawsay, living well and the limits to decolonisation in Ecuador. *Geoforum, 43*(2), 240–249.

Rodas Morales, R. (2007). Estudio introductorio. In R. Rodas Morales (ed.), *Las propias y los ajenos. Miradas críticas sobre los discursos del movimiento de mujeres del Ecuador*. (p. 9). FIG, ACDI, CONAMU, Abya-Yala.

Rosero, R. (2007). Las mujeres ecuatorianas, la constituyente y la constitución. *La Tendencia, 5*, 109–113.

Santos, B. de S. (ed.). (2007). *Another knowledge is possible: Beyond northern epistemologies*. Verso.

Santos, B. de S. (2010a). Hablamos del socialismo del buen vivir. *América Latina En Movimiento, 452*, 4–13.

Santos, B. de S. (2010b). Para una democracia de alta intensidad. *Ecuador Debate, 80*, 63–76.

Sentencia 113–14-SEP-CC, CASO 0731–10-EP 1 (Corte Constitucional del Ecuador 2014). http://www.funcionjudicial.gob.ec/pdf/Caso%20Cocha%20C%20Const.pdf

Sieder, R., & Sierra, M.T. (2011). *Acceso a la justicia para las mujeres indígenas en América Latina* (WP 2011:2). Michelsen Institute.

Silva Portero, C. (ed.). (2008). *Ejecución penal y derechos humanos. Una mirada crítica a la privación de la libertad.* Ministerio de Justicia y Derechos Humanos.

Smart, C. (1989). *Feminism and the power of law.* Routledge.

Sobrevilla, D. (2008). La filosofía andina del P. Josef Estermann. *Solar, 4*(4), 231–247.

Tapia Tapia, S. (2018). Feminism and penal expansion: The role of rights-based criminal law in post-neoliberal Ecuador. *Feminist Legal Studies, 26*(3), 285–306.

Tibán, L. (2009). *Desafíos en la construcción de un estado plurinacional* (M. Lang & A. Kucia (eds.); pp. 67–72). UNIFEM.

Trownsell, T.A. (2013). *Robust relationality: Lessons from the ontology of complete interconnectedness for the field of international relations* [PhD]. American University.

Tulkens, F. (2011). The paradoxical relationship between criminal law and human rights. *Journal of International Criminal Justice, 9*(3), 577–595.

United Nations Committee on the Elimination of Discrimination against Women. (2002). *Consideration of reports submitted by States Parties under article 18 of the Convention on the Elimination of All Forms of Discrimination against Women. Combined fourth and fifth periodic reports of States parties. Ecuador* (No. CEDAW/C/ECU/4-5). United Nations.

Universidad Andina Simón Bolívar. (2006). *Informe alternativo ante el Comité para la eliminación de todas las formas de eliminación de discriminación contra la mujer.* CLADEM. http://hdl.handle.net/10644/471

Uprimny, R. (2011). Las transformaciones constitucionales recientes en América Latina: tendencias y desafíos. In C. Rodríguez-Garavito (ed.), *El derecho en América Latina* (pp. 109–136). Siglo XXI.

Valdez, A. (2006). *Constitución con equidad de género: experiencia ecuatoriana* (S. Montaño & V. Aranda (eds.); p. 287). CEPAL.

Valladares, L. (2003). Los derechos de las mujeres en la Constitución Política de la República del Ecuador de 1998. *Foro. Revista de Derecho, 2*, 55–103.

Vallejo Jiménez, G. (2011). En busca de otro derecho penal. *Opinión Jurídica, 10*(19), 141–154.

Vintimilla, J. (2009). *Las mujeres en la justicia comunitaria: víctimas, sujetos y actoras - un estudio comparativo entre Ecuador y Perú* (M. Lang & A. Kucia (eds.); pp. 73–80). UNIFEM.

Walsh, C. (2009). *Interculturalidad, estado, sociedad: luchas (de)coloniales de nuestra época.* Abya Yala.

Whalley, E., & Hackett, C. (2017). Carceral feminisms: The abolitionist project and undoing dominant feminisms. *Contemporary Justice Review, 20*(4), 456–473.

Zaffaroni, E.R. (2009). *El discurso feminista y el poder punitivo* (R. Avila, J. Salgado, & L. Valladares (eds.); 1st ed., pp. 321–334). Ministerio de justicia y derechos humanos.

Zaffaroni, E.R. (2011). *La naturaleza como persona: de la Pachamama a la Gaia* (C. Espinosa & C. Pérez (eds.); p. 3). Ministerio de Justicia, Derechos Humanos y Cultos.

Chapter 5

A new Penal Code

Criminalising violence against women using rights-based penality

Introduction

In Chapter 4, I demonstrated that rights-based penality is prevalent in Ecuador, despite the "left turn", the inclusion of Andean cosmovision in the Constitution and its adherence to a non-neoliberal development model. Rights-based penality informs not only the constitutional framework to address violence against women (VAW), but human rights violations more broadly. Coercive power, purportedly contained by constitutional guarantees, due process, and human rights, is indispensable to ensure a democratic state's response to human rights violations. With this backdrop, in 2014, state punishment was relegitimised by the Constitutional Court to the detriment of indigenous conceptions of justice.

This chapter shows how rights-based penality has efficiently docked in feminist approaches to violence against women (VAW) in Ecuador. Existing literature on carceral feminism has stated that feminists' entry into governance has taken place mainly through "punitive, carceral and tort-based reforms" and, as a consequence, it has become "harder to think distributively, from the Left", within governance feminism (Halley, 2018, p. 25). Yet, in this chapter we encounter many leftist feminists who were invested in social redistribution endorsing criminalisation, and attempting to introduce "feminicide" as a criminal offence that can be committed *by* the state. Based on the concept of rights-based penality developed in Chapter 4, I now ask if so-called carceral feminism is an effect of feminists' diluted oppositional stance toward the state (Kotiswaran, 2018), or more a symptom that liberal criminal law is regarded as a tool to resist the state? If so, is this only a question of feminist uncritical practice or, rather, an evidence of the fundamental pervasiveness of liberal legalism as a discourse?

This chapter is based on institutional documents from different state agencies and women's organisations, feminist publications, and feminist networks' documents. I also interviewed feminist activists, politicians, and public servers who were involved in discussing the 2014 Penal Code. Chronicling the making of the Penal Code enables an exploration of the dynamics of Ecuadorian feminism, considering the generational and ideological fragmentations that

DOI: 10.4324/9781003098799-6

surfaced during the post-neoliberal period. These illustrate that liberal legalism is rarely questioned by feminists, from left to right(s). I also show that prohibition and punishment are not so much the force that animates women's movements when they appeal to criminal law; instead, protecting women's rights and making wrongs visible (for instance, by enabling a statistical registry of crimes) arise as fundamental preoccupations.

Ultimately, penality *does* prosper through left-leaning governance. A rights-based penality can be asserted as compatible with progressive politics, because it has been rationalised through human rights and constitutional guarantees. Thus, pro-government feminists, who defended the Citizen's Revolution programme, supported the resort to criminal law. Moreover, there are other ways of reasoning, beyond feminist "punitive ambitions", which play a role in boosting penality: for example, the necessity of maintaining a coherent and systematic legal order, which is linked to the practicality and efficiency of agglutinating criminal offences in a single body of law. This hierarchical and logical ordering of rules is also distinctive of liberal legalism.

In the second half of this chapter, I return to the subject of legal coloniality, by analysing a different dimension of the 2014 Penal Code process: the attempts made by feminists to decriminalise abortion. I thereby use decolonial theories to look at the debates on carceral feminism: the chapter shows that the social construction of women and the family in the post-neoliberal context still resonated with earlier narratives on family protection. Feminists were able to succeed in criminalising various forms of VAW, because these offences do not challenge postcolonial representations of female bodies and social roles. By contrast, the decriminalisation of abortion failed. It was a continued coloniality, I argue, rather than the dominance of a right-wing agenda or a carceral feminist lens, that was most determinant of the scope, nature, and outcome of feminist law reform.

Rights-based penality as a framework for VAW

The portrayal of constitutional criminal law as a guardian of human rights, described in Chapter 4, has echoed powerfully in some contemporary feminist analyses of VAW. For instance Ecuadorian feminist Gayne Villagómez has recognised that law is "one of the main articulators of feminine subordination", and that Latin American penal codes are "permeated by archaic conceptions when it comes to women" (Villagómez, 2013, p. 56). At the same time, however, she affirms that New Constitutionalism is able to protect human rights, including women's rights, and their right to a life free of violence. Therefore, she presents constitutional criminal law reform as an "opportunity to substantially advance" women's rights (p. 57). This reflects an investment in constitutional guarantees and human rights to conceptually mitigate *both* the sexism of law and excessive state coercion. Put in a different way, criminal law *used to be* patriarchal, but its constitutionalised version can be at the service of feminism by mitigating discrimination and violence against women. While Villagómez acknowledges that penalising VAW may be problematic, she resolves the tension by resorting to rights-based penality. She also stresses that rights-based penality is not lenient toward criminals:

> Minimal or guarantee-based criminal law does not perceive offences as less serious, far from it, but it addresses them from the perspective of social and individual responsibility on the one hand, and on the other, it provides the victim with an active role to find the reparations to her life project.
>
> (Villagómez, 2013, p. 57)

Here, the author recaptures a pivotal feminist argument: criminal law has significant symbolical value. Through criminalisation, from this perspective, the state and the community manifest and condemn what is considered unacceptable. Simultaneously, constitutional criminal law does not produce an unreasonable inflation of the state's punitive power, because it is restricted by human rights and constitutional guarantees. Moreover, reparations are now linked to the criminal trial, although they had previously been understood exclusively as a civil law institution. Certainly, the 2014 Penal Code introduced principles that are fairly representative of rights-based penality and the justifications used by feminists:

> Art. 2.- General principles: In criminal matters all the principles emanating from the Constitution of the Republic, international human rights instruments and those developed in this Code shall be applied. In particular, the principles of effective judicial protection and due diligence shall be applied in order to guarantee integral reparation for the victims and the prevention of recidivism and impunity.

As we see, rights-based penality "overcomes" retaliatory criminal justice; women's rights violations can be vindicated, symbolically and materially, with minimal "side-effects" and encompassing reparations. In addition to symbolising the social rejection of gender-based violence, criminal law has now come to be a device that can remedy damages. Villagómez argued that the older Penal Code "respond[ed] to retributive justice, in contradiction with a guarantee-based conception of the Constitution, when [criminal law] should be in line with restorative justice" (2013, p. 57). In sum, this stance advocates for a criminal justice model that is not (too) punitive and includes reparations for survivors.

Rights-based penality was also present in the reasoning of many activists. In the run-up to the passing of the 2014 Penal Code, their narratives revealed trust in the ability of law to correct itself through the incorporation of human rights principles. A historical leader of the women's movement said:

> sometimes the great excuse [to not criminalise VAW] is that criminal law is not adequate for prevention... then we say, this is why it is about the integral protection of rights. Because criminal policy can effectively play a role if you have systems of integral protection of rights which are in charge of prevention, assistance to victims, at the rural level, with multiple services.
>
> (personal communication, March 16, 2015)

This interviewee presented an argument whereby social services should be somewhat connected to the criminal justice system – an idea that has not materialised in practice, as shown in Chapter 6. However, perhaps the most recurrent rationale amongst activists was that not criminalising VAW equates to leaving women unprotected. None of the interviewees considered that non-penal responses to VAW could be an option: doing without criminal law is very difficult to imagine, even for those who are critical of the state's coercive power. A feminist municipal officer stated: "in the logic of a penal state... a repressive state, [law] is understood as 'the more I care about a legal good, the more penalties I impose to the infractions against that legal good'". She then added: "[but] if there is no sanction...and I dislike the sanctions of criminal law...but if there is none, what message are we passing on to the aggressors? That nothing happens here" (personal communication, February 13, 2015).

María Paula Romo, a feminist assembly member who was not aligned with the government at the time, reminisced that she had proposed "rapid exits" for VAW criminal trials; that is, the possibility of an arrangement between the parties to end the criminal process early. This caused outrage amongst militants of the women's movement, as they adhered to the thesis that settlements only serve the purpose of perpetuating power imbalances (personal communication, April 22, 2015).

What perhaps was not well thought out by feminists, was that, even with a constitutionalised criminal law, establishing criminal responsibility remains the fundamental aim of criminal justice, even above providing protection, reparations, and the material resources that women require to overcome violence. These limitations would become apparent later, when the first drafts of the 2014 Penal Code were discussed.

The pathway to the 2014 Penal Code: feminists discuss penality

Once the 2008 Constitution passed, a central goal for the women's movement was to convert VAW misdemeanours into full criminal offences. This was also a pending international commitment for Ecuador: official documents, such as the country's 2010 Report for the Beijing +15 Review, acknowledged that VAW had not yet been fully criminalised, and that this issue should be urgently addressed (Gobierno de la República del Ecuador, 2009).

Counteracting gender-based violence was declared a national state policy in the 2007 National Plan for the Eradication of Gender Violence Toward Children, Adolescents, and Women (*Plan Nacional para la Erradicación de la Violencia de Género Hacia Niñez, Adolescencia y Mujeres*). This plan linked the state's obligation to prevent, eliminate, and sanction violence against young boys, girls, adolescents, and adult women, to the human right to personal integrity. Also, the National Plan for Living Well 2013–2017 (*Plan Nacional para el Buen Vivir*) featured the eradication of gender-based violence and discrimination as a primary development goal. Strategies to reach this objective included "dissemination, awareness, promotion and respect of human rights, with emphasis on the rights of boys and girls, adolescents, youths, older adults, women, LGBTI persons and disabled persons". The need to "prevent impunity in matters of violence" appears in several places of the plan (SENPLADES, 2013, p. 124). These approaches brought about, in 2013, the creation of 28 Specialised Judicial Units for Violence Against Women and the Family (*Unidades Judiciales Especializadas de Violencia contra la Mujer y Familia*), which replaced the Commissariats that operated since 1994.

With the Citizen's Revolution, feminists who had supported the electoral coalition and the Constituent Assembly joined the reformed state agencies, including the legislature. However, their efforts were limited to a large extent by extrinsic factors that included political negotiations and the prevalence of a family-oriented perspective in the legislature, as shown in the second part of this chapter. NGOs and grassroots activists, on their side, were not as influential as they had been in the 1990s. *Consejo Nacional de las Mujeres* (CONAMU), which used to be a bridge between civil society and the state, was dissolved by the new government and replaced by a transitory commission of lesser rank and attributions, presently called National Council for Gender Equality (*Consejo Nacional para la Igualdad de Género*). These new configurations were summarised by a feminist municipal officer who said: "The [central] government now has its own women's movement [...]. CONAMU used to be linked to the women's movement, but not anymore; now the regime has its own movement aligned with its own principles" (personal communication, March, 2015). Another way to explain the reconfiguration of the women's movement has been that some social movements were "institutionalised" when they entered the state administration:

> The peculiarity is that social movements, citizen's movements felt they had come to power with Correa's administration and, in fact, they became part of the institutions and functions of the State. But it seems to me that... we are not discussing this enough, that this institutionalization of social movements can be harmful. I am sad to say it but it is so. It is as if the social movements ended up being silenced. Suddenly they disappeared, the women's movement disappeared, the indigenous movement disappeared. Militancy or citizen actions disappeared [...]. It is as if, suddenly,

> certain people from the social movements occupied power but power was not occupied by social movements.
>
> (Marena Briones, personal communication, October 22, 2020)

Indeed, an increased tension between the government and the social movements during Correa's periods has been widely documented (Lind & Keating, 2013; Ramírez Gallegos, 2010). In addition, I did observe an estrangement amongst feminist militants of the Citizen' Revolution and those outside the government. From the interviews, it was apparent that this division correlated with a generational divide between feminist *históricas* (veteran militants of the women's movement), and the younger generations.

With this backdrop, women's advocacy groups discussed the draft bill with public servers and lawmakers and engaged in debates and dialogues with the National Assembly, especially the Parliamentary Group for Women's Rights (*Grupo Parlamentario por los Derechos de las Mujeres*). A 2012 National Assembly report records several meetings between assembly members and representatives of women's collectives and refuges, including CEPAM and Fundación María Guare. Here, the participants discussed domestic violence, femicide, abortion, patrimonial violence, and sexual violence (Asamblea Nacional de la República del Ecuador, 2013). Some disagreements were manifest from the beginning: pro-government assemblywomen, for instance, sometimes viewed the demands of women's organisations as somewhat inessential to social redistribution, which was in turn seen as the central aim of the Citizen's Revolution. When asked about their relationship with activists and advocacy groups outside the state, four out of six assembly members said their first commitment was with their constituency; therefore, they could not always attend to certain requests from the women's movement.

These assembly members recognised that a thorough dialogue between activists and lawmakers was not attained, but explained it as a failure of women's organisations to understand the commitments of the elected officers. According to Paola Pabón, a Citizen's Revolution militant and member of the Parliamentary Group for Women's Rights, when the Penal Code was debated, her role involved making decisions as a feminist, but also considering the broader goals of the political programme: "[there is] a confusion between roles, [...] and the [women's] movement does not understand our role as legislators" (personal communication, May 7, 2015). Gina Godoy, also militant of the Citizen's Revolution, affirmed:

> [our] relationship with the organised women sometimes did not flow in the way that... perhaps they or we as lawmakers wanted it to. Because it turns out that, as a legislator, I not only have to work on and look at a single topic, but at the entire legislative production [...]. I also have a responsibility as a political actor within the functions that I deploy as a legislator and also toward my constituency.
>
> (personal communication, April 22, 2015)

Rosana Alvarado, another representative of the governing coalition and Vice-President of the National Assembly, believed that the women's movement had become "mono-thematic"; that is, campaigners, in her view, sometimes failed to reckon the broader problems that affect Ecuadorian women:

> I believe that this has been an error of the feminist movement... of some feminist collectives, to think that feminism is only about sexual and reproductive rights. This is a significant and determinant part of feminism, of course, but it is not that alone. [Feminism] is [about] eradicating all the inequalities and all the violences, and one of the nastiest violences against women is poverty.
>
> (personal communication, April 21, 2015)

Diego Vintimilla, pro-government legislator and self-identified feminist, agreed:

> There are some inflexible stances. I do not mean that they are inflexible in their radicalism, but rather that they insulate themselves in the logic of vindicating women's rights because they are women. [It is] like [some feminist groups] are dissociated from the other components of social life, detached from [the fact] that in Ecuador other matters... of rich women, of poor women, of exploitation, operate. [...] I put a lot of emphasis on the economic aspect as one of the central factors that enable or perpetuate schemes of domination between men and women.
>
> (personal interview, April 19, 2015)

These feminist assembly members coincided in portraying some women's organisations as corporate groups. They did not dismiss the women's movement's vindications, but depicted them as relatively narrow, alleging that activists were failing to acknowledge economic inequality as a structural issue. Therefore, government supporters often described activist demands as a middle-class agenda – regardless of the fact that some activists and NGO staff were self-identified leftists.

One may think that the feminists who prioritised economic redistribution and fighting women's poverty would attempt to displace criminal law – if the latter was understood as part of a conservative law-and-order agenda. However, there was a broad consensus among all feminist sectors regarding the need to criminalise VAW. In fact, several interviewees, inside and outside the government, discussed "patrimonial violence" as a criminal offence to be included in the new Penal Code. This form of gender-based violence had been identified in a national survey as a distinctive type of abuse whereby a male aggressor restricts a woman's access to money and other vital resources (INEC, 2012). I had access to a communication that circulated amongst activists, sent by the Ecuadorian Centre for the Promotion and Action of Women (CEPAM). This working document, intended to reach the National Assembly, read: "[Patrimonial violence], not being categorised as a criminal offence, almost always goes undetected, which naturalises it and contributes to perpetuate it and maintain a historical unequal relationship between men and women" (CEPAM Guayaquil, personal communication, October 8, 2013). Patrimonial violence did not ultimately make it into the 2014 Penal Code for reasons that remain unclear to most interviewees (see Table 5.1); but the proposal demonstrates that criminal law had come to be seen as an instrument to combat gender-based economic inequalities.

When the time came to discuss the draft bill, some potential "side-effects" of inserting VAW in the Penal Code were brought forward. Because activists anticipated that procedural rules would become too complex, many demanded a specialised law for VAW, whether it was a reformed Act 103, or a new legal body. Instead, supporters of the government were keen to incorporate all forms of VAW into the general Penal Code. According to Gina Godoy, the demand that Act 103 be preserved became the bone of contention between the lawmakers and the advocacy groups. In her opinion, it was imperative to "leave behind that dispersion of the legal apparatus whereby we have thousands and thousands of laws [...]. All the behaviours that have a penal sanction [...] would have to be in [the new Penal Code]" (personal communication, April 22, 2015). Conversely, the organisations argued that protecting women's rights would become more difficult through "blanket" laws and policies that were

Table 5.1 Feminist interventions in the 2014 Penal Code

Issue	*Proposal by the parliamentary group for women's rights*	*Outcome*
Domestic violence against women and the nuclear family (psychological, physical, sexual, and patrimonial).	-Convert misdemeanours of domestic VAW (physical and emotional abuse) into full criminal offences. -Create a "patrimonial violence" offence.	-Successful implementation of two new criminal offences: physical and psychological violence. -Patrimonial violence was unsuccessful.
Abortion	-Decriminalise abortion in all cases when pregnancy results from rape.	-Unsuccessful.
Femicide and feminicide	-Create "femicide" and "feminicide" as criminal offences to tackle gender-based murders of women and obtain individual and state accountability.	-Successful introduction of "femicide" as the murder of a woman for being a woman. -"Feminicide" was unsuccessful.

Table designed and produced by the author. Source: interviews conducted by the author, the Archive of the National Assembly of Ecuador and the author's field notes.

not specialised. One activist who had worked at CONAMU stated: "from the present dogma [...] of state management, there cannot be specialised laws. Everything is aggregated and homogenized under the concept of a modern, efficient and rational state" (personal communication, March 15, 2015).

Concerns with efficiency and technicality were certainly present in the officialist narrative. For instance, some assembly members regarded criminalisation as a strategy to facilitate quantitative data collection. Defining clear criminal categories would allow the state to measure the incidence of each crime. Interviewees referred to the National Survey of Family Relations and Gender Violence Against Women (INEC, 2012) to explain why penalisation was needed:

> the national government carried out a survey through the INEC, which, in a way, allows to make gender violence visible by revealing statistics and numbers for each province; this allows, beyond the historical struggle of the women's movement, to locate the reality of violence, to formalise it with state data.
>
> (ministry public officer, personal communication, April 17, 2015, emphasis added)

This argument was often repeated when interviewees addressed femicide. Lawmakers considered that naming and categorising femicide would provide a mechanism to quantify the phenomenon. A historical feminist leader affirmed: "what [femicide makes] possible is for us to say: 'let us see, there are these many femicides' (feminist *histórica*, personal communication, April 13, 2015). According to Diego Vintimilla, member of the Parliamentary Group for Women's Rights:

> Regarding femicide [...], I believe that the Penal Code does not extinguish the possibility that there be women who are murdered for being women. But it makes a difference to be able to count, to be able to have a database of this, right? I say sometimes that it sounds too raw to say "we know how many women have died", but it is even harsher to say "we do not know how many women have been killed".
>
> (personal communication, April 19, 2015)

In the same line of reasoning, a prefecture public officer said:

> incorporating femicide [into the Penal Code] ultimately allows us to not have dark figures, it lets us pinpoint fundamental issues. It also lets us have numbers and end the trope of "crimes of passion" once and for all, and really speak of family violence, femicide... terms that are appropriate... and to have actual data.
>
> (personal communication, April 16, 2015)

Despite a broad agreement around the need to criminalise most forms of VAW, not many of the women's organisations agreed with the officialists that this had to be done through the general Penal Code. Such disagreement resulted in debates that I detail in the next section.

Feminists dispute the adversarial criminal justice model

While rights-based penality was widespread across feminist clusters, the older *históricas* who had promoted the 1990s reforms were less inclined to resort to the general Penal Code. In fact, a few even expressed scepticism regarding the very notion of penal guarantees. For instance, in an interview published by a national newspaper, feminist lawyer Anunziatta Valdez (a key architect of Act 103) stated that the Penal Code would lead to a regression in terms of protecting women from abuse. When the interviewer suggested that the new Code would "guarantee a better due process" she replied: "there are social problems that cannot be addressed with criteria such as those the Penal Code tries to enforce, because they are the outcome of unequal power relations. Due process does not operate here" (El Universo, 2012, para. 6).

Prior to the approval of the Code, a group of *históricas* circulated several working documents via email, with similar arguments. One of these documents disputed the idea that it is optimal to integrate all criminal laws in one major codification:

> there are rules such as those pertaining to underage offenders or to violence against women and the family, which have a decidedly protective character [...] and cannot be adapted to the unifying structure of the Penal Code, which responds to a strict model that requires the involvement of a plaintiff and a defendant.
>
> (various authors, personal communication, October 8, 2012)

One significant concern for veteran feminists was the risk of losing the protective measures of Act 103. According to the cited working document, the adversarial procedural system, that is, the model adopted by the new Penal Code, would not be as protective as the simpler model of Act 103, whereby protective measures could be made effective as soon as a complaint was filed. Act 103 framed the infractions as misdemeanours and used an older prosecutorial model known as the "inquisitorial system", which gave the acting judge some investigative competences. Conversely, the newer adversarial process, also known as the "accusatory system", emphasises confrontation between plaintiff and defendant, centring the figure of the public prosecutor. This model disallows judicial intervention during the inquest, meaning, for instance, that protective measures are to be requested by the prosecutor. Protective and precautionary measures are also subject to formal and material justifications.

Overall, protective measures are accessory and can only subsist as long as the trial advances.

In view of this, feminist *históricas* insisted that VAW requires a special treatment. Some of their arguments were included in a Minority Report presented in 2012 to the National Assembly by María Paula Romo, a lawmaker that was not aligned with the government. The Minority Report advocated for a moderate penal intervention, arguing that the official draft bill harnessed "penal populism" and "penal demagogy". The Penal Code, according to the Report, aimed at gaining notoriety through an exacerbated penal response that was neither "technical" nor addressed the roots of gender-based violence. Instead, the draft bill appealed to the scare of delinquency in order to obtain electoral profit by "responding" through harsh criminal laws:

> If the intent is to expedite women's access to justice, a criminal trial with the participation of public prosecutors, judges, and public attorneys is clearly more arduous than the one prescribed by Act 103. If we seek better access to protective measures, this will also be more complex if a public prosecutor is to request them and a judge to authorise them; today, the response of the commissariats is immediate. We should also inquire [...] whether the purpose of those who file a complaint is to obtain the deprivation of freedom of their relatives or partners, or otherwise, to have a tool that lets them sustain a less unequal and violent relationship.
>
> (Romo, 2012, p. 17)

As we see, the Report argued that incarcerating the aggressor is not paramount for complainants, a contention that was supported with data from the 2012 National Survey on family violence, which showed that 88% of women did not intend to leave their aggressor (INEC, 2012). In the Report, this was interpreted as a sign that most women would not choose to pursue a criminal trial against their partner. The Report also argued that incarceration could aggravate women's situation, for instance, by keeping the offender out of work and, therefore, leaving him unable to provide child support. In sum, the Report acknowledged that imprisonment can bring unintended consequences, and a swift state intervention, through specialised protective measures, was considered more effective.

These debates, brought in from interviews, communications and fragments of the Minority Report, demonstrate that governance feminism's stance on carcerality is more nuanced than it has been recognised in some literature. It is not always the case that feminists with access to governance address VAW in carceral terms only. Furthermore, some interviewees powerfully reflected on punitiveness as a societal feature, more than an intentional mission of mainstream feminism. Former assembly member María Paula Romo emphatically said:

> this demand of maximum penal intervention, which we usually ascribe to politicians, to representatives, to lawmakers… we cannot disregard that it probably does not rise from their wish, their beliefs, but from the pressure of the political game. […] Not that right-wing parties are punitive; society is punitive, it is fascinated by the Penal Code, by punishment, they ask you for it.
>
> (Maria Paula Romo, personal communication, April 24, 2015)

The Minority Report concluded that Act 103 should remain in force, notwithstanding the possibility of reforming it. According to a veteran activist: "in light of our experience, we wanted to preserve Act 103 as the first lifeline, but also to make [VAW] visible, to protect the life and rights of women" (personal communication, April 15, 2015). Pro-government legislator Gina Godoy observed that this was not a viable course of action, due to the reliance of Act 103 on older procedural rules, which the new Penal Code would override. From her perspective, "vis-à-vis [my] explanations, there was no understanding, there was simply a demand that Act 103 had to be preserved, period" (personal communication, April 22, 2015). Godoy further explained that she had to move forward, amongst other factors, due to the risk that the National Assembly could move ahead, leaving VAW out of the Code altogether:

> The Penal Code had a rhythm by which they pressed down the gas pedal, it was going to run, and if I was not on board, the issue [of VAW] was going to be left outside. It would have been worse if violence against women was not criminalised at all and, therefore, not penalised. So there was a breakup [with the women's movement], and I walked on… well, with those who wanted to walk with me, who were very few.
>
> (personal communication, April 22, 2015)

Dialogues were further hindered by what activists identified as a centralised governance. A prefecture public officer recounted that women's organisations had held many meetings in their localities, but could not reach the "spaces where decisions are ultimately made" (personal communication, February 27, 2015). A municipal officer from outside the capital summarised the situation:

> Many things that were debated here were not incorporated at the national level […]. I believe that this struggle to assert who has power and who is closest to power… to say who is most influential, is also a weighty issue, and many things that were [feminist] historical mottos were not acknowledged in those processes.
>
> (personal communication, April 17, 2015)

One has to wonder to what extent the resulting penal code provisions are attributable to these factors, rather than to a uniform feminist punitivity.

According to a *histórica* from the South of Ecuador, despite the considerable work carried out by the NGOs, "travelling to Quito, speaking at the assembly, discussing with the [legislative] commissions… one and a thousand formalities, lobbying, public pronouncements in the media" and preparing "texts, explanatory documents, legal backups, statistics, and so on", ultimately, "none of those were considered and, of course, Act 103 was repealed and we were left with a Code that really is a setback" (personal communication, April 15, 2015).

María Paula Romo summarised the circumstances in this way:

> The women's movement was not so keen on full criminalisation […]. I think there was a lot of understanding from the collectives that there was a setback in [relation to] what had been achieved with the commissariats. […] And so, the biggest proponents of penalisation, of [domestic violence] not being a misdemeanour but a crime, were the assembly members who identify themselves as feminists. This was not the agenda of the women's movement.
>
> (personal communication, April 22, 2015)

Success and failure: the outcome of the 2014 Penal Code

When the Penal Code finally passed, feminist proposals had suffered diverse transformations. Women's organisations were mostly unsatisfied. Table 5.1 summarises the topics that feminists introduced, how they were converted into legislative proposals by the Parliamentary Group for Women's Rights, and what the outcome was when the Code came into force.

Although Article 81 of the Constitution establishes a specialised and expeditious procedure to prosecute violence against "persons in a situation of vulnerability", including in matters of family violence, sexual offences, and hate crime, the 2014 Penal Code established general criminal proceedings for VAW. Only physical violence misdemeanours were assigned a simplified process. All remaining domestic violence infractions were treated as common crimes. This would prove problematic, given the concentration of ordinary penal courts at urban centres, and the complexity of ordinary procedures, as the NGOs anticipated. A practising lawyer explained:

> For psychological abuse [the case file] is directed to the public prosecutor, it is no longer the competence of the [specialised] courts, and then the problem is terrible because the process is delayed. The protection measures are not immediate, they lose agility.
>
> (personal communication, May 4, 2015)

Moreover, because a complaint on its own does not undermine the status of innocence, protection/restraining orders cannot be issued unless there are reasonable cues to believe that a crime has been committed, that judicial action is necessary to guarantee the defendant's attendance, and that the complainant is at "real" risk. As a result, if the complainant ceases to advance the trial, and/or does not attend a hearing, protection orders can be invalidated, as there are no legal grounds to maintain them anymore. In this context, feminist lawyers emphasised the significance of the protection orders for women who need an urgent mechanism to mitigate imminent violence:

> For many women, [the restraining order] was enough to stop violence to an extent; it was like a small weapon to tell the aggressor to be warned, maybe persuade him somehow… that is an idea that women have to control violence in that way, right?
>
> (*histórica* feminist activist, personal communication, April 15, 2015)

Another consequence of criminalisation is that the offences, including psychological abuse, were defined in a way that requires the production of ostensible damage. The Penal Code introduced what the doctrine calls a "result-driven offence" (*delito de resultado*), meaning that a behaviour is not deemed criminal unless measurable injury is substantiated. By contrast, when psychological violence was a misdemeanour, the very action of emotionally abusing a person was on its own an infraction, regardless of its effects. In practice, it is nearly impossible to prove how much damage psychological abuse has caused. A specialised psychologist affirmed: "the woman basically has to demonstrate that she is […] incapacitated to continue with her daily life, in order for [psychological violence] to be deemed a crime" (personal communication, March 15, 2015). The same professional observed that even if they managed to measure damage, it is difficult to conclusively show that the injury is the result of a specific episode of violence. Judges and advocates often ask to be informed of "pre-existing conditions" that could have impaired a person's mental health at baseline: "the difficulty is not only to demonstrate that there was psychological abuse, but also that a psychological damage resulted from that abuse", the psychologist affirmed.

Importantly, within a criminal trial, reparations are contingent on the quantification of damage. In this way, VAW comes into existence only when it is quantifiable through disciplines like medicine, psychiatry, and psychology, based on the assumption that experts can accurately measure harm. Put differently, the inscription of VAW in the Penal Code reaffirmed a positivist perspective that privileges measurability and scientific certainty over women's experiences.

As noted above, there were additional demands posited by feminists during the making of the Penal Code: to criminalise "femicide", and to decriminalise abortion in the case of rape. Each of these demands produced a different outcome: femicide became a criminal offence, while the decriminalisation of abortion was discarded. I contend that each outcome obeyed the same underlying discourses. Colonial constructions of women and the family reshaped feminist demands during the legislative process. While rights-based penality contributed to justify criminalisation, it did little to displace the narratives that produce abortion as a crime, despite the existence of frameworks which posit the elective termination of pregnancy as a human right.

Success? Femicide

The criminalisation of femicide was regarded by all interviewees as an advancement in the protection of women's rights. Assembly member Gina Godoy recalled she had attended several events in which the "organisations that work for women's right to a life free of violence" requested that "femicide be categorised as a criminal offence, independently from homicide or murder" (personal communication, April 22, 2015). The Minority Report stated:

> Although the current laws already establish hate crimes, it is an advancement that femicide is incorporated as a criminal offence, as has been done in other [countries'] laws. The change of term or its definition will not necessarily result in an immediate decrease [of murders], but it is very important because it lets us make the problem visible.
>
> (Romo, 2012, p. 21)

Pro-government legislator Rosana Alvarado also considered the creation of femicide was a significant accomplishment:

> The topic of femicide, I think, was an important achievement [...]. It is true, it is an aggravated murder, but the aggravation has to hit [the social] conscience in a way that it becomes known that the magnitude of this aggravated murder [makes it a] femicide. It is the death of a woman [...,] caused by the existence of that gendered condition, that is not tolerated.
>
> (personal communication, April 23, 2015)

Alvarado affirmed that politicians who regarded femicide as a "passing fancy" exemplified a dominant conservative stance on women's rights. Here, criminalisation is clearly portrayed as the progressive way to go: she narrated that the Mayor of Guayaquil – a veteran right-wing politician linked to the neoliberal period – had alluded to femicide as a "fad": "The 'feudal lord'...we already know what his policy on human rights has been", she commented. It was opposing criminalisation that was regarded as the regressive, conservative stance, not the other way around. Alvarado further reaffirmed the symbolic and material value of criminal law:

> Well, you already have convictions for femicide. To me, that is the most powerful message of all. There already are persons who have been sanctioned for femicide, there are investigations of femicide, very severe penalties for the killers too [...]. It seems to me that in view of this, the history of women in relation to criminal law is no longer the same.
>
> (personal interview, April 23, 2015)

Increasing the visibility of women's killings due to their gender was repeatedly pointed out as the key advantage of criminalising femicide:

> Of course, there are many good things [in the new Penal Code]; it incorporated the category of femicide, which has the advantage... Perhaps the only advantage of making the violent deaths of women by their partners, or former partners, visible. In this way a greater social awareness is possible, and maybe more... some more interest from the judge to prosecute the case. But that is all, because the sanction has not risen by even one hour [...]. That is, I have heard many interviews with assembly members who say that now with femicide the men who kill women are going to have a more severe sanction; this is not true, it is just like any other murder, the same sanction.
>
> (feminist *histórica*, personal communication, April 13, 2015)

Yet, femicide was not incorporated into the Penal Code exactly as feminists had envisioned it. Latin American scholars and activists, and the Inter-American Court of Human Rights,[1] have characterised "femincide" (*feminicidio*) as the result of structural violence, not only of interpersonal conflict. That is, *feminicidio* is not only the result of one-on-one violence, it is also a consequence of the state's negligence, and/or the direct outcome of state violence (Fulchiron, 2016; Segato, 2016); therefore, it can be considered a state crime. In this way, feminicide intends to confront the state itself: it resembles genocide more than it does homicide. A historical activist for sexual and reproductive rights observed:

> There was also a difficulty in the discussions because it is either femicide or feminicide. If it is femicide it is the crime only, if it is feminicide is the state against women. That, for instance, did not pass, and it is symptomatic that [the government] does not want to take responsibility for the deaths of women.
>
> (personal communication, April 20, 2015)

1 See, for instance, Marcela Largade's approach to feminicide, which has been very influential in Latin America (2006, 2010). For the Inter-American Court's stances, see the judgment for the 'Campo algodonero' case (Tojo et al., 2011).

Another prominent *histórica*, said:

> [Femicide] was only partially a gain, because the definition of femicide is when there are power relations within the couple and death is produced, but there is no state responsibility. In other countries [...] feminicide involves state [accountability] due to [its] negligence, when a timely response is not given, when the complaints of violence against women are not adequately treated and they finally result in femicide. We have had several cases like that, so there is state responsibility but this is not recognized.
>
> (personal communication, April 16, 2015)

Despite these considerations, "femicide" was ultimately categorised as an offence akin to aggravated murder:

> Art. 141.- Femicide.- The person who, as a result of power relations manifested in any type of violence, kills a woman for being a woman, or for her gender condition, will be punished with a custodial sentence of twenty-two to twenty-six years.

Feminists acknowledged that femicide came at a high cost. Many considered that its criminalisation allowed the government to display a false commitment to the demands of the women's movement, while dismissing other important topics, most notably, the decriminalisation of abortion. Maria Paula Romo described the criminalisation of femicide as "one of the Trojan horses of all the setbacks of the Penal Code" (personal communication, April 22, 2015). In the same vein, one *histórica* contemplated that the officialism deliberately sought to "satisfy all these women who after all even voted for the government and were eager for a change in that area". She also suggested that perhaps the legislators thought they were reassuring the women's movement because "[the decriminalisation of] abortion [was] banished, but [officialism] included femicide and elevated domestic violence to the category of criminal offence" (personal interview, April 15, 2015).

Likewise, many referred to femicide as a "consolation prize". A young municipal officer said: "this may be a subjective impression... that categorising femicide is a sort of consolation prize for not decriminalising abortion [...], and due to [the disagreements regarding] the issues of violence." She added: "Femicide is a demand of the women's movement, that is true, but it is not like in our country there has been a national debate about the content and scope of this criminal offence". Former assembly member María Paula Romo used similar expressions: "Domestic violence and femicide were the consolation prize for women; while, for instance, the issue of decriminalising abortion in case of rape was politically sacrificed including the assembly members themselves". She added:

> It seems to me that femicide and domestic violence gave [the government] a political trophy. And I think that [these offences] ended up in the code for that reason. Because they respond to a conception... their own conception of maximal criminal law, and because it gives them a political arsenal in a Code in which the other areas of the women's agenda were dead.
> (personal interview, April 22, 2015)

Failure: abortion

Decriminalising abortion[2] has long been a priority for feminist movements in Latin America. It has also been taboo in public debate: in Ecuador, decriminalisation was not formally discussed during the constituent processes of 1998 and 2008, even though it was a demand of the women's movements. According to a seasoned activist, in 1998, the term "reproductive" was intentionally excluded from the provisions on women's rights, because it was deemed a "window towards abortion" (personal communication, April 20, 2015). In 2008, despite having allies in the Constituent Assembly, women's organisations were unable to block the conservative and Christian lobbies: Article 45 of the Constitution consecrates the right to the "protection of life from the moment of conception", and this article has been often brought forward to justify that abortion remains a crime in most cases.

Moreover, for many leaders of the leftist Citizen's Revolution, decriminalising abortion was not on the table. The Executive's stance on the issue was widely known to be akin to that of the Catholic Church (RTVE, 2008). One *histórica* who had worked as an adviser for the presidency confirmed that "[the President] had, and still has, an absolutely moralist and religious stance on [sexual and reproductive rights], especially [on] the topic of abortion". *Históricas* stressed that the Executive regarded the women's agenda as an uncomfortable topic: "he told one comrade [from the women's movement] to take charge of the matter because he was tired of 'women's issues'. To him, women are an issue, a problematic issue" (personal communication, April 16, 2015).

When the new Penal Code was debated, abortion elicited a controversy that was extensively covered by the media: women's organisations demanded that it be decriminalised when pregnancy is the result of rape, not only when the survivor is a "mentally disabled woman", as was established in Article 150. One *histórica* recalled:

2 In 2021, abortion was partially decriminalised by the Constitutional Court of Ecuador via a judgment that stated that it was discriminatory and unconstitutional to allow the termination of pregnancy only when it is the result of the sexual abuse of a "mentally disabled" woman. Therefore, legal abortion was extended to all women who have been raped (Romero Larco & Salazar Páramo, 2021).

> We did everything. We brought in the UN Health Rapporteur. He sent a letter warning about the risk of introducing articles protecting the unborn. [...] That week the young [feminist activists] planned an action... With official statistics, documents, videos. We even managed to film Colombian high magistrates saying why they had [partially] decriminalised abortion in Colombia.
>
> (personal communication, April 20, 2015)

In addition, women's organisations commissioned a survey according to which 65% of Ecuadorian respondents agreed that abortion should be legal in the case of rape (Carmenati González & González, 2017). Facing this, Paola Pabón, who was part of the government coalition, presented a motion after reaching an agreement with the women's collectives, in a climate that promised the support of her fellow assembly members. She addressed the Assembly, urging the legislators to vote in accordance with their own conscience and beliefs, rather than following the officialist stance. However, this triggered a backlash: disciplinary measures for her and other feminist lawmakers who supported the motion were announced by the President, who deemed them disloyal to the party and threatened with resigning if decriminalisation was approved (El Comercio Perú, 2013). The motion was withdrawn first thing the next morning as the debate continued. Pabón then publicly addressed the President saying:

> We are the ones who defend the rights of women, we defend equal marriage, we believe in the rights of nature [...]. I want to tell you and tell the people that the ones who have promoted the thesis of defending women are not traitors. Comrade President, with the immense affection that we have for you, we tell you that this time you are mistaken. But for the unity of this legislative block, for the unity of one hundred fellow assembly members, [...] comrades, I withdraw the motion so that this block does not have the possibility of showing a rupture.
>
> (Asamblea Nacional del Ecuador, 2013, p. 4)

Pabón's intervention reveals that she and other feminists within the Citizen's Revolution identified a connection between the decolonial constitutional shifts – hence the reference to Pacha Mama – and their vindications in the field of gender, including same-sex marriage and legal abortion. Now, nonetheless, the unity of the coalition appeared to be incompatible with such a stance. When I interviewed her, Pabón acknowledged that she and the legislators who supported her felt cornered. Some of the activists who campaigned for the decriminalisation of abortion affirmed that Pabón and her group had endured political violence from the Executive's inner circle in the form of threats and marginalisation (personal communication, April 20, 2015). Ultimately, Paola Pabón, Gina Godoy, and Soledad Buendía were sanctioned by their party with a month of suspension (La Hora, 2013). Many activists interpreted this as generalised political violence: "I felt punished myself when I saw it...that is, what it is like to silence a woman, to silence a movement, to silence the historical voice of women who demanded the decriminalisation of abortion" (judge at a court for family, children and adolescents, personal communication, April 14, 2015).

Neither the decolonial elements of the Constitution nor the rights-based discourse used by feminists were sufficient to displace the colonial construction of women's sexuality regarding pregnancy, motherhood, and the family. In turn, these colonial discourses produced criminalisation. Defeating the narratives that have historically produced abortion as a crime was not attainable through any of the legal strategies that feminists resorted to. Conversely, protecting women from abuse in domestic spaces, as shown in Chapter 3, continues to be compatible with hegemonic family paradigms, and has been regarded as a necessary measure to preserve family integrity; therefore, domestic violence was successfully criminalised with hardly any opposition.

These narratives around the family have adapted to different legal frameworks through time, from nation-building in the 19th century, to the penal/patriarchal discourses that were fused with feminist narratives in the 1990s, landing in today's rights-based penality. Assembly member Diego Vintimilla observed: "And of course [the failure to decriminalise abortion] is a contradictory phenomenon, because while femicide was being criminalised, for instance, the topic of abortion had a political element that turned out to be highly critical" (personal communication, April 19, 2015).

The abortion controversy was regarded by the women's movement as symptomatic of stagnation in sexual and reproductive rights. Also, the "surrender" of the pro-government assembly members was interpreted by some as disloyalty toward the women's movement:

> we would have expected that the assembly members who championed the feminist proposal [to decriminalise abortion] would continue to do so until the end. I do not know if maybe it is romantic to say until death... what death? Political death. They would have died politically but [...] the feminist demands would have lived.
>
> (feminist judge, personal communication, April 14, 2015)

Moreover, many activists observed that demanding legal abortion had not been a strategic course of action, because the controversy led the government to discard any further discussions of feminist demands. One *histórica* observed that feminist legislators were "frightened" by the sanctions, which left the women's movement without an intermediary at the Assembly:

> No one would meet us; I myself took some actions even knowing that [the draft bill] was already in the hands of the Executive. There were

> Citizen's Outreach sessions in Babahoyo and we went with a group of women to deliver a [domestic violence] proposal... it was not allowed. I myself talked to the State Attorney General, the Public Prosecutor Office, people who were associated with the government, to grant us at least one meeting with Alexis Mera [the Secretary of the Presidency], but it never happened, and that is how it all turned out.
>
> (personal communication, April 13, 2015)

The abortion controversy had palpable consequences, not only for feminist activists and lawmakers, but for women on the ground: although abortion had always constituted a criminal offence since the first Penal Code of the Republic, it had rarely been systematically enforced. Between 2014 and 2019, organisations have documented many cases in which women have been reported by medical staff when they seek emergency attention at hospitals during an abortion in progress (Carpenter, 2019; Puente, 2020; Wambra.ec, 2019).

In the aftermath of the Penal Code, feminist groups would continue to demand a specialised law for VAW, insisting on the need for a specialised and expedited process.

Conclusion

One of the lessons we can extract from this chapter relates to the perils, for feminist theories and practices, of the universal and even "progressive" status that criminalisation and carceral punishment have attained as responses to human rights violations. As one of the interviewees put it, perhaps it is society as a whole, and legality as a system, that first needs to be interrogated for promoting punitivism. In that sense, so-called carceral feminism would be more a manifestation of the dominant legal discourse than of the "punitive ambitions" of feminist projects in particular (Halley et al., 2018). Rather than a "neoliberalised" feminism that provokes increased carcerality, what we find in Ecuador and, likely, in other Latin American countries, is a human rights-based feminism that endorses criminalisation because it has great symbolic power and is compliant with constitutional guarantees. Furthermore, an empirical look at internal feminist debates has demonstrated that even within mainstream feminism, ordinary criminal justice does not go uninterrogated nor is uncritically regarded as the main course of action. We have seen a sector of Ecuadorian feminism that opposed the integration of VAW into the general penal code; many advocated for a specialised law that could be more accessible for women on the ground.

Another important lesson relates to the role of human rights and rights-based penality in presenting prosecution and punishment as strategies that can be used harmlessly. Feminist sectors promoting criminalisation were not necessarily aligned with the right wing, conservatism, or neoliberalism. In fact, I do not recall interviewing anyone who was considered right-wing in the context of Ecuadorian politics – although not all participants were aligned with the government. Rights-based penality, portrayed as a self-limited and democratic tool, has given feminists key conceptual grounds to rely on criminalisation. The idea of a constitutionalised criminal law that condemns, punishes, and repairs human rights violations is key to adapt feminist demands to legal strategies, in a manner that does not produce an irresolvable tension with broader emancipatory goals. As we have seen, leftist feminists are able to speak about structural inequality and attempt to tackle it via criminal offences like patrimonial violence and feminicide (see Table 5.1), which aim at interrogating patriarchy as a system. At the same time, some feminists appealed to efficiency, order, and better data collection, as reasons to pursue the criminalisation of VAW.

On their side, the feminists who opposed incorporating VAW into the Penal Code did not propose inaction either, they wanted to preserve the older specialised law and make it better, likely by fully criminalising VAW but adopting simpler procedural rules. In other words, the ordinary penal apparatus was not embraced uncritically, but the imagined alternatives were still based on the idea that only criminalisation adequately responds to human rights violations. Many feminists acknowledged the subordinating effects of criminal law, but still resorted to it under the assumption that specialisation can overcome its patriarchal traits. In sum, criminalisation was seen as legitimate as long as it is modulated and specialised. Prevention, protection, and redress are still part of the feminist discourse on VAW; however, these protective dimensions have become so entangled with punitiveness that they are perceived as being undermined without the resort to criminal law.

Finally, this chapter confirms that there are still many convergences between the colonial discourses on family protection described previously, and the legislative will to criminalise domestic violence. Criminalising "violence against women *and the family*" (emphasis added) was received almost with no objection by the National Assembly, but obtaining the historical demand of decriminalising abortion was impossible. This continued defeat also indicates that governance feminism only intermittently walks "the halls of power". What I encountered was a leftist government coalition in the National Assembly, which endorsed the criminalisation of VAW but did not tolerate a disruption of colonial womanhood. Even the feminists who supported the government were marginalised by their own party when their petitions challenged hegemonic constructions of sexuality. The problem here, for feminists, is that the "siren call" of rights-based penality conceals the coloniality of criminal law, obscuring the disservice that it can do to broader feminist demands. *Which* human rights are susceptible to recognition by the dominant powers? That is a matter of coloniality. Without this insight, feminists continue to believe that the failure of criminal law lies only at the level of design and implementation, rather than the coloniality of liberal legalism itself.

To sum up, framing VAW as a human rights violation, positioning penality as the obvious response to VAW, the continuity of legal coloniality, and the prevalence of a "technical" approach to the management of social problems, are all factors that have shaped the current framing of VAW. In various degrees, rights-based penality is accepted by feminist actors, not only as a feminist strategy, but more broadly as a field of intelligibility to legally address the violations of human rights; in fact, feminist demands today become intelligible only when human rights are invoked. The price is our inability to imagine non-penal strategies to counteract VAW without feeling that this compromises our rejection of gender-based violence. Many feminists I spoke to considered that resorting to non-penal instruments would make women's injuries invisible again, and send out the message that VAW is not a violation of fundamental rights. It would, in short, be a regression. However, if feminist strategies do not challenge the coloniality of gender and law – and, as a consequence, of human rights – they are unlikely to achieve radical change. The successes of the 2014 reforms came at a very high cost.

References

Asamblea Nacional del Ecuador. (2013). *Acta 257-B*. Asamblea Nacional del Ecuador, Quito, Ecuador.

Carmenati González, M., & González, A.C. (2017). Desencanto Y Desafío De Las Agendas De Igualdad: El Caso Del Aborto En Ecuador. *Dossiers Feministes*, *22*, 139–155.

Carpenter, Z. (2019, May 27). *La represión de Ecuador al aborto está encarcelando mujeres*. https://gk.city/2019/05/27/mujeres-presas-abortar-ecuador/

El Comercio Perú. (2013, October 19). *Rafael Correa amenaza con revocación a congresistas a favor del aborto*. Elcomercio.pe. https://elcomercio.pe/mundo/actualidad/rafael-correa-amenaza-revocacion-congresistas-favor-aborto-noticia-1646954/

El Universo. (2012, July 10). *Anunziatta Valdez: "Las mujeres violentadas quedan desprotegidas con proyecto penal."* El Universo. https://www.eluniverso.com/2012/07/10/1/1355/anunziatta-valdez-las-mujeres-violentadas-quedan-desprotegidas-proyecto-penal.html

Fulchiron, A. (2016). La violencia sexual como genocidio. Memoria de las mujeres mayas sobrevivientes de violación sexual durante el conflicto armado en Guatemala. *Revista mexicana de ciencias politicas y sociales*, *61*(228), 391–422.

Gobierno de la República del Ecuador. (2009). *Respuesta al cuestionario sobre la aplicación de la declaración y la plataforma de acción de Beijing*. Comisión de Transición Hacia el Consejo de Igualdad de las Mujeres.

Halley, J. (2018). Which forms of feminism have gained inclusion? In J. Halley, P. Kotiswaran, R. Rebouché, & H. Shamir (eds.), *Governance Feminism. An Introduction* (pp. 23–53). University of Minnesota Press.

Halley, J., Kotiswaran, P., Shamir, H., & Rebouché, R. (2018). *Governance feminism: An introduction*. University of Minnesota Press.

INEC. (2012). *Encuesta nacional de relaciones familiares y violencia de género contra las mujeres*. https://www.ecuadorencifras.gob.ec/documentos/web-inec/Estadisticas_Sociales/sitio_violencia/presentacion.pdf

Kotiswaran, P. (2018). Governance feminism in the postcolony: Reforming India's rape laws. In J. Halley, P. Kotiswaran, R. Rebouché, & H. Shamir (eds.), *Governance Feminism. An Introduction* (pp. 75–148). University of Minnesota Press.

Lagarde, M. (2006). Del femicidio al feminicidio. *Desde El Jardín de Freud - Revista de Psicoanálisis, 6*, 216–225.

La Hora. (2013, October 29). *Tres asambleístas de PAIS son sancionadas con un mes de suspensión.* Lahora.com.ec. https://www.lahora.com.ec/noticia/1101584287/tres-asamblec3adstas-de-pais-son-sancionadas-con-un-mes-de-suspensic3b3n

Lagarde, M. (2010). *Preface: Feminist keys to understanding feminicide* (R.-L. Fregoso & C. Bejarano (eds.); pp. xi–xxv). Duke University Press.

Lind, A., & Keating, C. (2013). Navigating the left turn: Sexual justice and the citizen revolution in Ecuador. *International Feminist Journal of Politics, 15*(4), 515–533.

Puente, D. (2020, April 19). *Mujer es procesada por "aborto consentido"; la denuncia salió desde un hospital.* El Comercio. https://www.elcomercio.com/actualidad/mujer-procesada-aborto-denuncia-bolivar.html

Ramírez Gallegos, F. (2010). Desencuentros, convergencias, polarización (y viceversa). El gobierno ecuatoriano y los movimientos sociales. *Nueva Sociedad, 227*, 83–101.

Romero Larco, J., & Salazar Páramo, M.D. (2021, May 6). *Hasta que sea ley.* Wambra.ec. https://wambra.ec/hasta-que-sea-ley-aborto-ecuador/

Romo, M.P. (2012). *Informe de minoría para primer debate. Proyecto de código orgánico integral penal.* Asamblea Nacional del Ecuador. http://perso.unifr.ch/derechopenal/assets/files/legislacion/l_20130808_04.pdf

RTVE. (2008, September 29). *Correa, un izquierdista católico practicante.* Rtve.es. https://www.rtve.es/noticias/20080929/correa-izquierdista-catolico-practicante/166528.shtml

Segato, R.L. (2016). *La guerra contra las mujeres.* Traficantes de Sueños.

SENPLADES. (2013). *Plan Nacional del Buen Vivir 2013–2017 de Ecuador.* Secretaría Nacional de Planificación y Desarrollo.

Tojo, L., Elizalde, P., & Taboada, F. (eds.). (2011). *Herramientas para la protección de los derechos humanos. Sumarios de jurisprudencia. Violencia de género (segunda).* CEJIL.

Villagómez, G. (2013). La revolución ciudadana y las demandas de género. In J. Cuvi, D. Machado, A. Oviedo, & N. Sierra (Eds.), *El correísmo al desnudo* (First, pp. 53–69). Montecristi Vive.

Wambra.ec. (2019, September 17). *El rostro de las mujeres criminalizadas por abortar: empobrecidas y jóvenes.* Wambra.ec. https://wambra.ec/mujeres-criminalizadas-aborto/

Chapter 6

Report from the field

Women's experiences of using specialised penal courts

Introduction

Chapter 5 addressed the use, by feminists, of rights-based penality in a law reform project that criminalised violence against women (VAW); but what are, on the ground, the consequences of resorting to criminalisation? How is a rights-based penality impacting on the everyday lives of those who seek help and protection from domestic violence? This chapter presents empirical findings regarding the operation of the 2014 Penal Code. Not only did the implementation of the Code prove problematic and disorganised, it also revealed that there is more to be concerned about when criminal justice is the main field of intelligibility for human rights violations: access to protection hinges on a criminal process that very few women are willing to pursue all the way through. Furthermore, the specialised judicial system is disconnected from public services that could give women some material resources to overcome VAW, while the government continues to reduce the budget assigned to counteract gender-based violence.

The information presented in this chapter was collected at the twilight of the post-neoliberal era. Although the president that Ecuadorians elected in 2017 was supposed to be an heir of Correa's Citizen's Revolution, in practice, his government reimplemented the recipes of "structural adjustment" and the austerity programmes that its predecessor had denounced. These included major public sector cuts and the prioritisation of foreign debt payment (Telesur, 2020). Regarding VAW, in 2018, Lenin Moreno's government reduced the budgetary allocation to implement the recently created the Comprehensive Law on Violence Against Women or *Ley Orgánica Integral para Erradicar y Prevenir la Violencia contra las Mujeres* (LOIPEV) by more than 80% (Robalino, 2020).

With this backdrop, this chapter shows that rights-based penality, as a manifestation of the "postcolonial legal apparatus" (Kapur, 2015), produces a system whereby the courthouse is all but a "shadow" (Comaroff & Comaroff, 2006; Derrida, 1994) of what the state is expected to be: rather than provide services, it provides law and litigation almost exclusively. For violence survivors, the

DOI: 10.4324/9781003098799-7

state exists in the form of buildings, lawyers, and procedural rules, rather than protection, shelter, healthcare, or financial support. Although feminists have long noticed that the willingness of women to use the legal system depends on many variables that include ethnicity, class, sexuality, immigration status, relationship status, disability, geographic location, and previous experiences with the law (Goodmark, 2012; Merry, 2003), when a criminal trial is not resolved, few lawyers interrogate the legal system as such. Instead, they place responsibility on complainants for "abandoning" the trial and conclude that they are in need of "empowerment". Law itself is not scrutinised as a mechanism that coproduces inequality, often aggravating and prolonging VAW.

Although many critiques of carceral feminism have analytically linked carceral expansion to neoliberalism and governance feminism, this chapter shows that feminist discourse is not the only approach informing decision-making when it comes to the implementation of VAW laws. On the ground, familial ideologies, hegemonic masculinities, and liberal understandings of justice are at play. At the same time, specialised courts and criminal proceedings stand as a proxy for state action, which conceals women's urgent needs and the absence of services that could ensure their protection, prevent the exacerbation of violence, and allow them to overcome it.

In addition, while some authors have associated carceral feminism with a strengthening of police powers and the surveillance of underprivileged men (Kapur, 2002; Whalley & Hackett, 2017), in Ecuador, law and policy on VAW are not producing such effects. Rather, indifference and inaction characterise women's perception of interacting with police. Moreover, outspread attrition means that convictions are rare: not many people are incarcerated as a result of enforcing VAW laws. Yet, the deployment of criminal law on the ground is decidedly gendered: laws intended to protect women result in consequences that are quite distinct from what critics of penal expansion have observed in other areas of criminal policy, such as security, counterterrorism, and drug trafficking. The state and other governing agencies create a distinct form of insecurity and abandonment for women by steering them toward the legal system and offering a shallow and even counterproductive set of choices once they decide to head that way. To contextualise these findings, I will first outline the legal framework currently in force, which was reformed several times after 2014.

Sorting out chaos: law reform on VAW after 2014

After 2014, further reforms were enacted in Ecuador, in an attempt to correct the practical difficulties that surfaced when the Penal Code started to be enforced. Especially problematic was that, as criminal offences, VAW infractions were to be investigated by a public prosecutor and heard by an ordinary penal court, while, as misdemeanours, they had been in the jurisdiction of specialised judges with simpler and faster proceedings. Also, for some time, there was a conflict of jurisdiction between the ordinary penal tribunals and the specialised courts, which caused considerable confusion and delays. In 2018, the National Court of Justice issued Resolution 11-2018, indicating that specialised judges are competent to hear VAW misdemeanours, as well as the criminal offences of femicide, psychological violence, and physical violence, up to the pre-trial stage, after which, an ordinary penal tribunal takes over. Crimes against sexual integrity, including rape, fall in the jurisdiction of ordinary penal judges from the initial stages of the trial.

Another practical problem was that the descriptions of certain criminal offences in the Penal Code made them extremely difficult to prosecute: for instance, psychological violence was graded through a damage scale, meaning that the longer a person was deemed to be unfit for work due to psychological damage, the longer the conviction would be. By the same token, without any evidence of damage, the criminal offence could not be sanctioned. As mentioned in Chapter 5, it is difficult to demonstrate that psychological damage is caused by one particular form of abuse, or to determine the resulting number of inability days. Also, the new procedure to obtain a protection order was far more complicated than that of the extinct Act 103: "upgrading" misdemeanours to crimes and, therefore, assigning them to the ordinary process, entailed that public prosecutors were to prove that there was merit to grant them, before a judge. In view of these bottlenecks, feminist and women's organisations insisted that a specialised law was necessary.

The 2018 Comprehensive Law to Prevent and Eradicate Violence Against Women (LOIPEV)

In January of 2018, the Comprehensive Law to Prevent And Eradicate Violence Against Women (*Ley Orgánica Integral Para Prevenir Y Erradicar La Violencia Contra Las Mujeres*, LOIPEV) passed, with the support and input of women's organisations, mainly from Quito.[1] Some of the gaps left by the Penal Code were filled in: for example, patrimonial violence was incorporated into the new law. The LOIPEV also abolished the damage scale for psychological violence, and misdemeanours were broadened to include forms of abuse that do not produce measurable damage (such as insults, hostility, and other forms of emotional abuse), as well as physical violence that does not cause measurable injury.

1 In my experience, this process was less participative than the one for the making of the 2014 Penal Code. I was not aware of many women's collectives from outside the capital who were heard at the National Assembly. A small group of colleagues and myself even sent a text suggesting guidelines to create a protective procedure that did not subordinate the protection order to the progress of the criminal trial, to no avail.

In June of 2018, the General Regulation for the Comprehensive Law to Prevent and Eradicate Violence Against Women was issued. These rules modified some procedural aspects: for instance, local administrative authorities, such as the Cantonal Boards for the Protection of Rights and the Political Lieutenants in smaller locations, are now competent to issue protection/restraining orders. However, the orders have to be validated by a judge afterwards, because they restrain fundamental rights, such as the defendant's freedom of movement. In addition, because penal guarantees entail the presumption of innocence, the duration of the protection order cannot be indeterminate. Protection orders are issued *ex parte*, that is, immediately after a complaint is filed and without a hearing, but they are temporary, and last while the criminal trial is progressing. They only become permanent with a conviction.

The latest reforms to the Penal Code

In the 2014 Penal Code, VAW offences were prosecuted using ordinary procedural rules, which comprise several stages: investigation, instruction, evaluation, preparatory trial, and trial. These phases can last several years. In view of this, a group of feminist lawyers presented a lawsuit against the National Assembly and the Presidency of the Republic for breaching the constitutional mandate to establish a "specialised and expedited" procedure for intrafamilial and sexual violence (Art. 81 of the Constitution). In its decision, the Constitutional Court stated that it had not found "in the provisions contained in the Penal Code, that the National Assembly has implemented a uniform, special and expeditious procedure for the prosecution and punishment of the crimes of intrafamilial violence, sexual violence, hate crimes, and those committed against girls, boys and adolescents, youth, people with disabilities, older adults and people who, due to their particularities, require greater protection" (*Sentencia 133-17-SEP-CC*, 2017, p. 27). Hence, the Court ordered the National Assembly to issue new legal provisions to instrumentalise an expedited procedure for VAW.

In December of 2019, the Penal Code was reformed again, this time introducing a "unified, specialised and expedited procedure for the prosecution and punishment of crimes of violence against women or members of the family unit" (*Ley Orgánica Reformatoria Al Código Orgánico Integral Penal*, 2019, p. 16). The reform ordered judges to issue protective measures immediately after receiving any notice of VAW. The new rules also enable public prosecutors to request an "abbreviated procedure", which is a faster track to judge crimes when the defendant pleads guilty. Another "alternative exit" from the trial consists of suspending the process at the request of the complainant, and with the authorisation of the prosecutor, when the resulting injury does not cause more than 30 days of disability. In the case of psychological violence, the trial can be suspended when the sanction would not have exceeded a year of imprisonment.[2] While these changes indicate some decentring of carcerality and a greater focus on reparations, it remains uncertain what the implementation of these rules will look like in practice.[3] As I show below, most processes are dropped at very early stages. Lastly, the reform introduced an optional "restorative justice" phase in the trial, which offers complainants who are over 12 years of age the possibility of demanding that the defendant recognises the damage, apologises, and commits to deliver reparations.

Still, most aspects of the new "expedited" procedure remain the same. The rules are different up to the point of the "intermediate stage" of the trial, meaning that the largest part of the process follows the ordinary rules. Further, the reformatory law mandates that all stages of the trial, including the hearings "are to be held in accordance with the general rules of the Code" (Art. 6511.1 N. 14). It also indicates that "in matters not provided for in these rules, the provisions of this Code shall apply" (Art. 651.1 No. 16). In fact, the feminist networks I contacted more recently consider that the reform did not entail a true fulfilment of the Constitutional Court's mandate to create a specialised and expedited procedure.

At any rate, together with the changes introduced by the LOIPEV, the Penal Code categorises VAW as indicated in Table 6.1.

Having outlined the current legal framework, I now introduce my empirical findings, foregrounding the lived experiences of women who approach the specialised courts to report violence.

The abandonment of women: beyond carceral expansion

Marilu,[4] 38, survived a violent relationship of 18 years. Her husband repeatedly kicked her on the abdomen when she became pregnant, causing a miscarriage. He later attempted to kill her. A municipal social worker, who was guiding her to obtain medication for a chronic health condition, directed her to an NGO that assisted battered women. There, a specialised psychologist provided therapy and eventually encouraged Marilu to report her abusive partner.

After leaving her violent husband, Blanca, 32, sells cosmetics by catalogue to support herself and her three children; but she rarely purchases stock, and can only place an order when someone pays in advance. She came to

2 This option is only applicable when the defendant has not been convicted of any other VAW offence, has not already used a rapid pathway in another criminal trial, and commits to accept the reparation measures established by the judge.

3 Soon after the passing of these reforms, the Covid-19 pandemic hit, greatly interrupting and suspending the functioning of the entire judicial system, including in VAW processes. As a result, it is difficult to assess, at the moment, the practical efficacy of the new provisions.

4 The names used in this composite story are pseudonyms. While all the facts are real, they have been adapted to avoid the potential identification of the protagonists.

Table 6.1 Crimes and misdemeanours of violence against women or members of the family unit (2014 Penal Code, after the 2018 and 2019 reforms)

Definition of Violence

Art. 155.- Violence is any action that consists of physical, psychological, or sexual abuse carried out by a member of the family against the woman or other members of the family unit. Family members are the spouse, the common-law partner, cohabitant, ascendants, descendants, sisters, brothers, relatives up to the second degree of affinity and people with whom it is determined that the accused maintains or has maintained family, intimate, affective, conjugal, cohabitation, courtship, or cohabitation ties.

Criminal Offence of Physical Violence

Art. 156.- Physical violence against women or members of the family unit.- The person who, as a manifestation of violence against women or members of the family unit, causes injuries, will be punished with the same penalties provided for the crime of injuries, increased by a third.

Criminal Offence of Psychological Violence

Art. 157.- Psychological violence against women or members of the family nucleus: The offence of psychological violence against women or members of the family unit is committed by the person who carries out threats, manipulation, blackmail, humiliation, isolation, harassment, persecution, control of the beliefs, decisions or actions, insults, or any other conduct that causes psychological damage, and will be punished with imprisonment from six months to one year.

If, on the occasion of psychological violence, a mental illness or disorder occurs to the victim, the sanction will be a custodial sentence of one to three years.

If the offense is committed against a person from one of the priority care groups, who is in a situation of double vulnerability or with a catastrophic or highly complex disease, the penalty will be the maximum penalty, increased by one third.

If the offense falls on the person of one of the priority care groups, in a situation of double vulnerability or with catastrophic or highly complex diseases, the penalty will be the maximum penalty, increased by one third.

Criminal Offence of Sexual Violence Against Women or Members of the Family Unit

Art. 158.- Sexual violence against women or members of the family unit.- The person who, as a manifestation of violence against women or a member of the family unit, imposes himself on another and forces her to have sexual relations or other similar practices, will be sanctioned with the maximum of the penalties provided for crimes against sexual and reproductive integrity, in the case of boys, girls, and adolescents, older adults, and people with disabilities.

Misdemeanours

Art. 159.- Misdemeanour of violence against women or members of the family unit. The person who hurts, injures, or hits the woman or members of the family unit, causing damage or illness that limits or conditions their daily activities, for a period not exceeding three days, will be punished with a custodial sentence of fifteen to thirty days.

The person who physically attacks the woman or members of the family unit, by means of kicks, slaps, shoves, or any other way that entails use of physical force without causing injury, will be punished with imprisonment of five to ten days, or community work of sixty to one hundred and twenty hours and comprehensive reparation measures.

(*Continued*)

Table 6.1 (Continued)

The person who carries out acts of theft, destruction, retention of objects, work instruments, personal documents, or property of the de facto or conjugal society, in the cases in which it does not constitute an autonomous crime established in this Code, will be sanctioned with community work from forty to eighty hours and the return of the goods or the payment in monetary value of the same, and comprehensive reparation measures.
The person who, by any means, utters expletives, expressions in disrepute or dishonour against the woman or members of the family unit, in the cases in which it does not constitute an autonomous crime established in this Code, will be punished with fifty to one hundred hours of community work, and psychological treatment will be provided for the aggressor and the victims, as well as comprehensive reparation measures.

Table designed and produced by the author. Source: Penal Code of Ecuador, Lexis Finder database.

our interview, like many other survivors, with her children. Blanca too had decided to look for help outside her own family circle. She was also sponsored by a pro bono attorney from a women's NGO. The resident psychologist reassured her that filing a complaint could help protect her from her aggressor.

Like Blanca, Marilu had never thought of her abuser as a "criminal" until she started a trial. Right after filing the complaint, she received a protection order that required the aggressor to leave the family home. She was happy to have reported him, because her former husband left: "the miracle of my life was when [the aggressor] left the house" (personal communication, February 14, 2019). When she first started living on her own, it was hard. She could not make enough money to feed her children. She was at some point tempted to move back in with her ex-husband.

Blanca also obtained a protection order, but she still allowed the father of her children to visit them. She did not call the police even when he came against her will: "if he goes to jail, who knows where they will take him, what they will do to him". For her, who sometimes convinces her ex-husband to pay child alimony, it would not have been wise to have him arrested: "when husbands go to jail, they do not work", she said.

On her part, Marilu followed the NGO staff advice and filed for a divorce. When the sentence came, she cried with joy. The criminal trial for domestic violence was a different story: the judge had set a date for a hearing on two occasions, but Marilu did not attend. At last, the court dismissed the proceedings due to lack of evidence.

Blanca too stopped contacting the attorney that was sponsoring her after she obtained the first protection order – she would later file another complaint to obtain a new order. She deleted all the voice notes she and the NGO lawyer had exchanged. She wanted to forget. At home, Blanca and her family still avoid using ceramic crockery: her ex-husband used to throw it around during his fits of rage.

Marilu and Blanca's stories are the "successful" ones. They survived, left their abuser, and started anew with their children, despite critical economic difficulties. At the same time, their stories illustrate the many gaps that separate women's expectations from law's representations of justness. Like all other survivors I interviewed, Marilu and Blanca did not obtain a conviction in their cases. They did not really want their abuser incarcerated; they wanted violence to stop. For Marilu, the comfort that law brought her was the divorce, which resulted from a civil process, not a criminal trial. For Blanca, what she valued from filing the complaint was not related to the judicial system; she cherished the support and services offered by the NGO that sponsored her, including therapy, capacity-building workshops, and support groups.

The stories of Marilu and Blanca offer a glimpse into the operation of criminal justice in matters of VAW: many trials start, but few are resolved. After speaking to 12 survivors of intimate-partner violence, I realised that the door that criminal law opens is little more than an entrance to a cluttered room where the exit cannot be spotted: while procedural rules abound, rarely does a criminal trial end with a judicial decision. Also, the legal instrument that women request the most – the protection/restraining order – has more of a symbolic value than an actual power to make violence stop. It is the police who are responsible to execute protection orders, but more often than not, they are indifferent or inoperative when women request help.

I conducted fieldwork in Cuenca, over a period of eight months, from January of 2019. Cuenca is the capital of Azuay, the Ecuadorian province with the highest incidence of VAW, at 79.2% (INEC, 2019). The goal of the study was to observe how the specialised apparatus for VAW responds to the needs of violence survivors. The methodology comprised in-depth interviews with 12 women who had filed a complaint at a specialised court, 6 specialised judges (of 7 in the jurisdiction), 6 case workers from a university pro bono law clinic (all of those assisting VAW cases at the time), and 3 first-contact judicial officers (the entirety of those working in this capacity) who attend to women when they first approach the courts. In addition, 80 case files from a Pro Bono Law Clinic were analysed in order to compile a dataset organising and quantifying the outcomes of the criminal proceedings. I also obtained statistics from the Judicial Council of Ecuador, to understand the proportion of cases that receive a resolution against those that are dropped. Qualitative data analysis paid particular attention to women's motivations to report violence, what they expected to obtain, and why they withdrew from the trial.

The meanings of justice: litigation is not protection

Traditionally, all definitions of access to justice include an element of access to litigation: TH Marshall, for instance, referred to the right to justice as "the right to defend and *assert all one's rights* in terms of equality with others and *by due process of law*" (Sommerlad, 2004, p. 346 emphasis added). The previous chapters have chronicled how activists and legislators have sought to ensure the prosecution of VAW and facilitate litigation. In the following sections, I show that the possibility of filing a complaint and initiating a criminal trial is meaningful for women only to the extent that it enables them to obtain a protection/restraining order, which they hope will halt ongoing violence. Most violence survivors want to be safe, rather than to obtain a conviction. As shown in Table 6.2, the available protective measures are established in the Penal Code and the LOIPEV.[5]

The protection order (*boleta de auxilio*) is a key instrument to illustrate the downsides of inscribing VAW within rights-based penality, and of equating access to justice to access to litigation. Protection orders appeared in Ecuador and Latin America in the 1990s, during the "boom" of anti-VAW laws. These can be requested from a judicial or administrative authority to restrict the aggressor's possibilities of coming in contact with the complainant. Research at the global, regional, and national level has shown that protection/restraining orders are actively sought for by survivors when they report violence (Camacho & Hernández, 2011; De Aquino, 2013; Jácome Villalba, 2003; Jubb, 2008).

While none of the participants I spoke to had received a judgment for their case, they had all requested a protection order, which was the primary reason why they filed a complaint in the first place. When asked about their motivations, expressions like "I wanted to feel safe", "I wanted help", "I wanted violence to stop", "I wanted to protect myself", and "I wanted [the aggressor] not to approach me", were common responses. Moreover, the interviews revealed that women would not have initiated a criminal trial if not to obtain the protective measures. There were some cases in which, after finding out that a criminal trial would start, women left court empty-handed:

> We told [a woman who came to court] what the procedure was like, so she was one of the people who said "I don't want to, I don't want to, I don't want the hearing, I just want the protection order [...]". It was impossible for her to file the complaint here, so she refused... [...] The girl did not want to file the complaint because [the aggressor] had blackmailed her: "if you present a complaint against me, I will publish our intimate videos".
>
> (Judicial Officer 2, personal communication, July 1, 2019)

5 In case of conflicting interpretation, the specialised LOIPEV prevails; however, some Penal Code provisions also describe measures that are applicable to VAW only and are, therefore, specialised. Constitutional principles mandate that, ultimately, the provision that better ensures the materialisation of fundamental rights, should prevail.

Table 6.2 Immediate protection measures available in Ecuador's specialised legal system for VAW

Law to Prevent and Eradicate VAW (Art. 51)	*Penal Code (Art. 558)*
A. Issuance of a protection/restraining order prohibiting the aggressor to approach the complainant in any public or private space. B. Order to restitute the complainant to her habitual residence, when she has been removed from it due to VAW. C. Insertion of the complainant and her dependents in a protection program. D. Prohibition for the aggressor to change the residence of common children. E. Prohibition for the aggressor to perform acts of intimidation, threats or coercion to the complainant or her family, by himself or third parties. F. Order for the aggressor to leave the shared home when his presence is a threat to the physical, psychological or sexual integrity of the complainant or the family unit. G. Order to make an inventory of the property of the complainant and/or common property. H. Arrangement for the installation of emergency warning devices in the home of the complainant. I. Arrangement for the activation of the protection and care services provided in the Comprehensive National System to prevent and eradicate violence against women. J. Provision for the insertion of women and their dependents in programs of social and economic inclusion, health, education, employment and care. K. Provision to verify the rectification of behaviors of VAW by technical units and governing bodies. L. Prohibition for the aggressor to hide or withhold property or documents belonging to the complainant or persons who depend on her. M. Order, when necessary, to allow the flexibility or reduction of the working hours of complainants. N. Order to suspend the activities carried out by the alleged aggressor in sports, arts, care or formal and informal education institutions.	1. Prohibition for the defendant to attend certain places or meetings. 2. Prohibition for the defendant to approach the victim, witnesses and certain persons, in any place they are. 3. Prohibition for the defendant to perform acts of persecution or intimidation of the victim or members of the family unit, on his own or through third parties. 4. Issuance of a protection/restraining order for the victim or members of the family unit, in the case of VAW. 5. Order for the defendant to leave the shared home or residence, if cohabitation involves a risk for the physical, mental or sexual safety of the victim or witness. 6. Reinstatement of the victim or witness to the home and simultaneous departure of the processed person, in the case of a common home and it is necessary to protect their personal integrity. 7. Deprivation, for the defendant, of the custody of the victim, child, adolescent or person with a disability and, if necessary, appointment of a suitable person as their guardian, in accordance with the specialised laws for childhood and adolescence, or civil law. 8. Suspension of the permit to possess or carry weapons for the defendant. 9. Order therapy for the defendant, victim and their children under eighteen years of age. 10. Order to immediately suspend the damaging activity that is affecting the environment when there is a risk of damage to people, ecosystems, animals or nature. 11. Eviction orders, to prevent invasions or illegal settlements. 12. In case of VAW, the judge shall set an alimony that allows for the subsistence of the people harmed by the aggression. If the presumption of innocence is ratified, the measure will be revoked.

Table designed and produced by the author. Source: Penal Code of Ecuador, LOIPEV, Lexis Finder database, and the author's field notes.

For their part, judges, judicial officers, and case workers with legal training put much emphasis on persuading women to sustain the trial until the sentencing stage, not least because withdrawing from a trial can entail the loss of the protection order:

> This is the common denominator during the hearing: given that innocence has been ratified, the protection measures are reversed. The victim does not come [to the hearing], so there is no evidence [of violence]; therefore, protection measures are cancelled and the status of innocence is ratified.
> (Judge D, personal communication, February 16, 2019)

In view of this, first-contact officers tried to "empower" women to file a complaint:

> There are people who refuse [to file a complaint], who say "no". That lady did not want to [file the complaint], we had to empower her for one hour… it took us one hour to empower her to agree to file the complaint, but she said "no, this is the first time [the aggressor hurts me], I just wanted the protection order".
> (Judicial Officer 2, personal communication, July 1, 2019)

Correspondingly, survivors narrated the doubts and fears that emerged when they were about to file a complaint:

> I was thinking: "do I do it or not?… Do I file the complaint or not?" because [the aggressor] told me that if I did anything to him, it would be worse. So I was already sitting there, that is, with a [court] appointment […]. I was scared to death and at the same time I was afraid that [the judicial officers] would not listen to me, because there are many times when one is not heard, they do not pay attention, and that has already happened to me.
> (Carolina, personal communication, February 15, 2019)

Many judges knew that the central motivation for women to go to court is to obtain the protection order, not necessarily to win at a trial:

> I would think that the woman who comes here is satisfied in the first instance, because she leaves the court with her protection measures. [The protection order] is like a protective shield for them […], and I think that they leave with a satisfaction level of 80%, in the sense that their request is answered as soon as possible. But later, when a final sentence is to be given, I think that [there is] dissatisfaction, because many times it does not depend on the judge, but on [women's] abandonment of the process.
> (Judge C, personal communication, September 23, 2019)

Legal professionals repeatedly used the word "abandonment" (*abandono*), to refer to the attrition of the criminal proceedings due to the complainant's "failure" to move the trial forward (field notes, February 14, 2019). "Abandoned" is also the term caseworkers at the Law Clinic employed to label the files that are archived due to loss of contact with the complainant. Most interviewed legal professionals worried that after filing a complaint and receiving the protection order, women would not return to court:

> The greatest difficulty to advance the legal process comes at the time of the hearing, and it is the key moment when [complainants] withdraw. It may be due to factors… As I have already told you, economic, or strongly emotional factors that have the victim in some way tied to the aggressor […]. Suddenly they talk, she forgives him, etc., and [women] do not attend the hearing, and that is where [the process] is truncated, because the public attorney may be there, he may have already talked to the victim, informed her of when the hearing is, at what time she has to be there… they could have prepared all the evidence and all the things, and in the end, on the day of the hearing, she does not turn up.
>
> (Judicial Officer 1, personal communication, July 1, 2019)

> because these are infractions that involve cycles of violence… there is the decision not to participate in the processes; then [women] do not come to the hearing, there is no accusation, there is perhaps no evidence and the result is a sentence ratifying the innocence [of the plaintiff].
>
> (Judge B, personal communication, April 16, 2019)

> It is […] that feeling of sadness for the fact that that aggressor will face [a criminal trial], which turns into a problem and an obstacle wherein justice cannot go further. [When] the victims abandon the process, it is precisely because of that feeling. And fundamentally, due to that circle of violence, the injured victim comes and seeks protection but with the passage of time this generates a logical emotional reaction.
>
> (Judge D, personal communication, February 16, 2019)

These representations of women, foregoing their own right to justice by reconciling with the aggressor, is commonplace amongst lawyers and other professionals. Such ideas are connected to the concepts of "battered woman syndrome", "learned helplessness", and "cycle of abuse" described in Chapter 3 (see Figure 3.1). The model suggests that domestic abuse develops in three cyclical stages: (1) Tensions building; (2) Acute incident; (3) Loving-contrition or honeymoon, when there is no abuse and the incident is forgotten, only for the cycle to start again (Walker, 2000). Many interviewed professionals believed that it is during the last phase of the cycle of abuse that women abandon the proceedings:

> Considering precisely the circle of violence, [women] access justice when they are in the explosion stage. So they go and start the judicial process. Later, as they walk through the process, they are told how it is supposed to be, what the procedure is like. No matter how agile we try to be, when they find out what the consequences are, that perhaps [the aggressor] is going to be deprived of freedom, they abandon the process.
>
> (Judge C, personal communication, September 23, 2019)

This narrative has multiple effects: first, it places the "blame" for not securing protection on women, and, second, it oversimplifies the reasons why they withdraw from the trials. In fact, my interview data showed that various forms of fear were major factors persuading women from advancing a criminal trial (see Figure 6.1). Qualitative content analysis brought to light six distinctive forms of fear.

Some judges did acknowledge that fear is a factor that discourages women from carrying on with a trial:

FEAR

1. Of **not being believed** by police or judicial authorities.
2. That **violence will worsen** when the aggressor finds out that a complaint was filed.
3. Of getting involved in an **onerous and complex trial.**
4. That the father of the children will be **arrested and incarcerated.**
5. Of **losing the financial support** provided by the aggressor to the family.
6. Of being **ostracised by family and friends** for breaking up the marriage/partnership.

Figure 6.1 Forms of Fear. Source: designed and produced by the author.

> [one problem] is also the fear of what can happen to [women] if they report [violence]. There are not many incidents of femicide, but women always feel threatened. If not by the aggressor himself, by the family [who says]: "don't report it, something could happen to you".
>
> (Judge C, personal communication, September 23, 2019)

Another common answer, from survivors, to the question "why did you not continue to attend court?" referred to difficulties regarding the submission of evidence: "the evidence from the [forensic] psychologist never came back"; "I could not find any witnesses to testify", interviewees said (fieldnotes, February 2019).

Still, the problem of attrition is regarded by the majority of legal professionals, not as a matter of deficient protection, insufficient financial resources, or difficulties related to judicial evidence. Rather, they tend to attribute attrition to lack of individual "empowerment". One specialised judge considered that "it is that empowering factor that is lacking for the victims to come and sustain a judicial process" (Judge D, personal communication, February 16, 2019). According to another judge:

> Although the procedure applied to misdemeanours is specialised [...] we have to consider the circle of violence. [...] What happens is that no matter how fast the proceedings are, many times those cycles are closed before the hearing and, if there is no empowerment or assistance for the victims, many times they do not attend the hearing to complete the criminal trial. That is a flaw that we have in the system, we do not have a team that helps us to empower women to continue with the process.
>
> (Judge A, personal communication, April 16, 2019)

That protection orders are invalidated when proceedings lapse is a major problem: the interviews and the case file data suggest that, in most cases, women report violence when they are at high risk. Several complaints described extremely violent events, including attempted femicide. In Case 013-A01-13,[6] the complainant had been hit in the face by her husband while she was on the phone, as he accused her of cheating. The aggressor then threatened her with a kitchen knife, attempted to strangle her, ripped up her clothes with his hands, and locked her in a room for over five hours. Although the forensic report confirmed the severity of the injuries, the file shows that the complainant never returned to the clinic after receiving the protection order, which was

6 The original case file number has been replaced by the research project's own serialisation, to avoid the identification of the parties involved.

eventually invalidated due to the "abandonment" of the trial. In other cases, complainants were persons in a situation of augmented vulnerability: Case 046-T08-3 contains a complaint by a disability card holder (45% disability), who was pregnant at the time of the aggression. In this case, the judge erroneously declined jurisdiction, stating that the defendant was the complainant's brother-in-law and, therefore, was not part of the "family unit".

Finally, another area where the gaps between women's expectations and what a trial actually offers are evident, is the work of attorneys in guiding complainants and ensuring that the proceedings yield the results they expect. While I did not interview any private attorneys, most judges manifested that, in their experience, lawyers were often inefficient and encouraged a reconciliation between the aggressor and the complainant:

> [regarding private attorneys] a lot is lacking, a lot… because lawyers come with many… I don't know if taboos, or a lot of patriarchal burden… familial roles that must be maintained above anything else, regardless of whether the woman is harmed. So it is more like "let's preserve the family", and that has been seen in many hearings.
>
> (Judge C, personal communication, September 23, 2019)

> Well, the issue of measuring how professional and how technical a lawyer is can be perceived in the hearings. I see that there is a lot of work to be done on gender issues.
>
> (Judge D, personal communication, February 16, 2019)

Overall, the data confirms that, from a lawyer's perspective, access to litigation equals access to justice. This equation is unfamiliar to violence survivors, whose testimonies convey an urgent demand for effective protection from ongoing violence, and reliable mechanisms to overcome it. Instead, criminal law, procedural rules, and the will to establish criminal responsibility are the central signifiers of the state's obligation to protect women's rights, while social interventions have lost their relevance as pressing courses of action.

Police are indifferent, ineffective, or unskilled

As noted before, a documented effect of penal expansion is the increase of police surveillance, especially over underprivileged sectors (Amar, 2013; James, 2007). However, in the domain of VAW, gender produces particular effects. While women rarely pursue a criminal conviction, they do expect police to assist them during an emergency, and/or when a protection order needs to be enforced. Barring one interviewee, who was assisted by an agent who happened to be her personal acquaintance, all survivors who had interacted with police considered their attitude and intervention inadequate.

When women called the emergency number to alert police of the violation of a protection order, they either did not respond, or arrived too late: "I called the police, but they did not arrive; they answered the phone, yes, but they did not arrive. They came later, when [the aggressor] had already left" (Veronica, personal communication, May 14, 2019). Other survivors recounted:

> When I have had problems with my aggressor, I have called the police, and they have never arrived. What I wanted has never been fulfilled; that is, sometimes one wants to say "I want justice", and it is never fulfilled.
>
> (Angelica, personal communication, May 14, 2019)

> After I filed the complaint, they gave me the protection order, but really that has not been useful for me at all because the police… when you call them, they arrive at whatever time they want to arrive; the [aggressor] was attacking me, he did something to me, but [police] simply arrived when the aggressor had already done everything.
>
> (Carolina, personal communication, February 15, 2019)

In other cases, police agents arrived but, instead of assisting the caller to get out of the violent situation, they tried to encourage her to reconcile with the aggressor. Survivors' accounts reveal that police reproduce hegemonic masculinities linked to women's role as mothers and homemakers, as well as the preservation of the family at all costs:

> So what do the police do? [They say:] "ma'am, look at your children, they are crying, poor things". Then I told [the police agent] "no, my children are not the problem, that is not the issue here, my case is the issue here; you have to enforce that protection order".
>
> (Carolina, personal communication, February 15, 2019)

A specialised judge recognised: "we hope to optimise the training of police. Police have a very important role because they are the ones to whom [survivors] first turn to for help, but sometimes they try to bring the couple back together" (Judge D, personal communication, February 16, 2019). As if this was not bad enough, I was appalled to learn about a case in which the agents had made friends with the aggressor and shared a couple of beers with him, leaving the scene without providing any help to the caller.

Admittedly, there is also a growing problem of staff shortage. Although there is a (small) specialised police division working alongside the specialised courts to provide assistance and protection to survivors, when the operators answer emergency calls they usually assign the cases to non-specialised agents.

Police intervention is also required to notify the defendant with the protection order, and it has been a common practice to ask survivors' themselves to deliver the notification. Sometimes, when available, they are accompanied by a police agent. For many women, who are understandably reluctant to confront the aggressor, insufficient staff can translate into the impossibility of delivering the summons, which means that the protection order will be invalidated:

> I filed the complaint [...]. At that time, they told me that they had to give the father of my children the notification, for him to leave our home [...]. They told me that I had to wait for a policeman to accompany me, but I did not wait. They told me to come back at three o'clock in the afternoon because... the policeman who had to accompany me was not there at that time. It was twelve o'clock [...] and I did not return, and he did not receive [the notification].
>
> (Veronica, personal communication, May 16, 2019)

The practice of asking the complainant to notify the defendant had become so frequent that the 2018 General Regulation for the LOIPEV specifically instructed: "Under no circumstances should the victim be responsible for conducting the corresponding summons" (Art. 49).

There were many other cases of inadequate police intervention. For instance, one participant had been forced to ride in the same police car as the aggressor when he was arrested during a flagrant offence. Another participant told me that her husband was arrested in front of their children, which was very distressing for them. Therefore, not only is the penal approach to VAW masking women's lack of access to material resources, it also potentially aggravates the complainant's already difficult situation by exposing her to mechanisms that fail and can result in a worsened state of affairs.

No carceral expansion on the ground

As expected, fieldwork did not produce any evidence that carcerality is expanding due to the criminalisation of VAW. One specialised judge estimated that 90% of complaints are not resolved with a judicial decision, an assessment that is not too distant from the numbers shown by the Judicial Council and the dataset from the Law Clinic (see Table 6.3). Only 11.1% of all cases heard by the specialised courts between 2014 and 2019 resulted in convictions. Almost 56% never reach a resolution.

Difficulties arise as soon as women report violence: as mentioned above, summoning the defendant is indispensable to start the process, and the judges coincided in pointing out that the summons are an early obstacle that often results in the dismissal of the proceedings, either because the defendant's whereabouts are unknown, because he asks the people he is staying with to

Table 6.3 VAW complaints filed in Cuenca from 2014 to 2019 (Judicial Council data)

Total number of complaints	14826	
Case files redirected to the public prosecutor	6530	
	Number	**Percentage**
Cases processed by the specialised courts	8296	100 %
Number of sentences issued between 2014 and 2019	3652	44.02
• Convictions	927	11.1[i]
• Acquittals	1952	23.5
• Other[ii]	773	9.3
Cases without a judgment/sentence	4644	55.98

Table designed and produced by the author. Source: The Judicial Council of Ecuador.
[i] Percentage based on total cases processed by the courts (8296).
[ii] This category corresponds to miscellaneous, non-typical forms of judicial resolution, such as when a judge declares lack of jurisdiction due to the conflict being unrelated to VAW. The Judicial Council did not provide a detailed explanation of each one of these cases.

hide him, or the complainant does not have enough resources to ensure that a police officer delivers the notifications (it is common, although not legal, to ask the complainant to pay for the transportation of the police agent).

According to the database compiled at the Law Clinic, 47% of cases were "abandoned". The case files are labelled with expressions such as "abandoned due to lack of interest from the user"; "complainant does not attend hearing despite being telephoned and searched for"; "complainant leaves the process and states that she does not want to continue". Altogether, the amount of complaints that never received a sentence within this dataset is 69%.

The open door that leads to nowhere

> The victims are truly abandoned. We have not worked as a state to see what happens next. What happens next?
>
> (Judge D, personal communication, February 16, 2019)

By enacting penal laws on VAW to protect women's human rights, the state has opened an almost flamboyant door to litigation. Specialised courts exist and laws have been reformed on multiple occasions to "correct" each new difficulty that emerges when institutions start applying the law. However, this open door does not lead to any meaningful place for violence survivors: complaints, as shown above, do not bring about effective protection, let alone reparations, social services or any resource that women could in practice use to overcome violence.

There are many reasons why women are unable or unwilling to advance a criminal trial: most interviewees did not have financial resources to cover the direct and indirect costs of a trial, even with a law clinic or NGO as a sponsor.

Although the Constitution grants free access to justice, and there are some public attorneys to assist those who cannot afford a private lawyer, staff always falls short at the Public Defender's office. A large portion of women likely do not have access to legal advice. Resources are also scarce to cover day-to-day expenses, such as transportation to the courthouse (which is more difficult for rural women), childcare, photocopying, and the time required to meet lawyers, consult the status of the proceedings and attend hearings. Sure enough, one survivor considered that money was the reason why many women she met at the NGO had ceased to attend court: "[women] hear what the procedure is like, and they say 'no, I will have to spend [money] on a lawyer, and I don't even have the means to feed myself'" (Marilu, personal communication, February 14, 2019).

Admittedly, I set the interviews up through institutions whose services were oriented to low-income sectors, therefore, I cannot accurately attest to middle- and upper-class women's experiences. However, the testimonies did unearth how the system treats underprivileged people. For instance, in one case (018-A02-3), the complainant was the main caregiver of a child living with disabilities and was not receiving any alimony from the aggressor (the child's father): one must wonder how a person in such circumstances is expected to sustain care work and advance criminal proceedings at the same time. Unsurprisingly, this case was also "abandoned". Moreover, one interviewee assured me that she had felt mistreated by some public servers due to being poor, which discouraged her from attending court.

Judges and officers agreed that most women who file complaints are poor: when asked what factors may affect women's distancing from the criminal trial, besides procedural aspects, some responses were:

> The economic factor. What happens is that, well, most of the cases that we have, I would say 70%, are people with limited resources. So, what does transportation entail for them? Perhaps, from the place where they live to here, sometimes 25 cents for the bus... many women do not have that much.
>
> (Judge C, personal communication, September 23, 2019)

> The economic factor, it would seem to me, is the preponderant factor for people to abandon the legal process. Why? Because, not all, but I could say, most of them do not have a job, they do not have any way to defend themselves economically and they are dependent [...] on the husband who is often the alleged aggressor.
>
> (Judicial officer 1, personal communication, May 14, 2019)

Likewise, in two other cases (032-T04-1 and 045-A07-1), complainants were living with their in-laws and did not have a place to go if they left the abuser.

Some were migrants without relatives or friends in the country. Surely these factors weigh in when a person thinks about reporting violence and/or moving forward with the proceedings. Despite these insights, judges and judicial officers did not mention economic redistribution or a better access to social services as critical to counteract VAW.

Even women who have some resources and "succeed" at obtaining protection, regard the process as a grim experience. Three of the participants I spoke to had a stable job and relative financial autonomy when they reported violence; yet, as one of them said, the process was utterly unpleasant. In one case, for instance, several neighbours witnessed how the aggressor was taken away by police, and the complainant felt embarrassed and humiliated. Criminal policy can bring about consequences that women do not expect nor want.

As we see, protection for women hinges on the progress of the trial, not on the existence of risks. At no point does a risk assessment take place, nor is it possible for judges to appreciate the situation of the complainant, given that, until the hearing, there is no contact between them. In fact, the courthouse departments are distributed in a way that impedes communication between users and judges: "we are completely separate from the unit itself. We are now on the fifth floor, and the front office is on the first floor" (Judge C, personal communication, September 23, 2019). In addition, most judges consider that having contact with the complainant would make their intervention less objective:

> We cannot make contact with any of the process' subjects [before the hearing] because this is what the [applicable laws] have established, and I believe that this is done with a view to not diminish the trust that society needs to have in the system, hoping that our response is impartial, independent and timely.
>
> (Judge D, personal communication, February 16, 2019)

Ultimately, it is highly possible that, even when a high risk exists, women are unable to secure lasting protection or help.

Conclusion

In this chapter, I have unearthed the concrete effects, on survivors of violence, of addressing VAW through rights-based penality. In connection with the previous chapters, I elucidate the nature of the "collateral damage" caused by penality in the realm of gender-based violence. In Chapter 1, I explained that *mestizaje* largely entails the rejection of non-whiteness, and that becoming a citizen is in many ways the process of becoming white-like. These insights are useful to understand today's neglect of women by the state. While the state may offer colonised subjects the formal resources that liberal understandings of citizenship prescribe (namely, the possibility of litigating), it does little to provide the material resources that give access to citizenship in practice.

In Chapter 4, I argued that rights-based penality, which introduces a "new" constitutionalised criminal law, is a discourse that, paradoxically, authorises and even encourages penal expansion. The image of criminal justice as a humane apparatus underlies many feminists' justifications of the resort to penality. This embracement of criminal law reauthorises penal power – albeit a version that allegedly respects and guards human rights. However, criminal law is largely failing women when it comes to delivering what they envision as justice and protection, and often making their situation more difficult.

Altogether, my findings reveal that a rights-based penality results in diminished protection for women and increased opportunities for the state to display its "preoccupation" with VAW. Today's strategies to address VAW reproduce women's subordination and abandonment. Human rights framings are building and concealing the barriers for women who seek protection from gender-based violence. The mechanisms created to support the state's rhetoric of non-impunity are obscuring women's material needs. Still, promoting a non-penal strategy is equated to disregarding the seriousness of VAW.

The important lesson, for me, is that criminal proceedings are precarious mechanisms that open a door that leads to nowhere or takes women to a place where they do not want to be. The possibility of reporting violence is there, but not much more is offered, and what is delivered potentially worsens the situation. Most aspects of the criminal trial are at odds with women's necessities. When violence survivors, understandably, prefer not to walk the halls of criminal justice, the state and its agents allege that access to justice exists but is not seized; therefore, what women need is empowerment.

Clearly, the effects that rights-based penality produces on the ground are gendered: no increase in incarceration or the surveillance of stigmatised men is resulting from Ecuador's VAW laws; however, the law-centric state is delivering fewer and fewer services and offering more and more law. As a result, women are materially abandoned but also legally protected, with the added irony that giving access to litigation passes as progress in gender equality. In the eyes of liberal law, it is women who abandon justice, not the other way around. The alliance between penality and human rights is begetting a phantom state that can produce little more than legal rules and judicial systems, claiming, at the same time, that it is protecting women, even as survivors remain at a high risk of losing their lives.

References

Amar, P. (2013). *The security archipelago: Human-security states, sexuality politics, and the end of neoliberalism*. Duke University Press.

Camacho, G., & Hernández, K. (2011). *Comisarías de la mujer y acceso a la justicia en Cuenca* (L. Pásara (ed.); pp. 229–282). Ministerio de Justicia y Derechos Humanos, Naciones Unidas.

Comaroff, J., & Comaroff, J.L. (eds.). (2006). *Law and disorder in the postcolony*. University of Chicago Press.

De Aquino, S. (2013). Organizing to monitor implementation of the Maria da Penha law in Brazil. In M. Al-Sharmani (ed.), *Feminist activism, women's rights, and legal reform*. Zed Books.

Derrida, J. (1994). *Specters of Marx: The state of the debt, the work of mourning, and the new international*. Routledge.

Goodmark, L. (2012). *A troubled marriage: Domestic violence and the legal system*. New York University Press.

INEC. (2019). *Violencia de Género*. Instituto Nacional de Estadística Y Censos. https://www.ecuadorencifras.gob.ec/violencia-de-genero/

Jácome Villalba, N. (2003). *Estudio cultural de la práctica jurídica en las comisarías de la mujer y la familia* [MSc]. Facultad Latinoamericana de Ciencias Sociales.

James, J. (ed.). (2007). *Warfare in the American homeland: Policing and prison in a penal democracy*. Duke University Press.

Jubb, N. (2008). *Mapeo regional de las comisarías de la mujer en América Latina*. CEPLAES.

Kapur, R. (2002). The tragedy of victimization rhetoric: Resurrecting the "native" subject in international/post-Colonial feminist legal politics. *Harvard Human Rights Journal*, 15, 1–37.

Kapur, R. (2015). Precarious desires and ungrievable lives: Human rights and postcolonial critiques of legal justice. *London Review of International Law*, *3*(2), 267–294.

Ley orgánica reformatoria al código orgánico integral penal, Asamblea Nacional del Ecuador, Suplemento - Registro Oficial N. 107 (2019). www.registroficial.gob.ec

Merry, S.E. (2003). Rights talk and the experience of law: Implementing women's human rights to protection from violence. *Human Rights Quarterly*, *25*(2), 343–381.

Robalino, J. (2020, January 13). *Víctimas de violencia de género se quedan sin presupuesto y sin atención*. Pichincha Comunicaciones. http://www.pichinchacomunicaciones.com.ec/victimas-de-violencia-de-genero-se-quedan-sin-presupuesto-y-sin-atencion/

Sentencia 133–17-SEP-CC, 0288–12-EP 1 (Corte Constitucional del Ecuador 2017). http://sgc.corteconstitucional.gob.ec:8494/FichaRelatoria.aspx?numdocumento=133-17-SEP-CC

Sommerlad, H. (2004). Some reflections on the relationship between citizenship, access to justice, and the reform of legal aid. *Journal of Law and Society*, *31*(3), 345–368.

Telesur. (2020, April 6). *Denuncian a pdte. de Ecuador por pagar deuda en medio de Covid-19*. teleSUR. https://www.telesurtv.net/news/ecuador-denuncian-presidente-pagar-deuda-medio-covid-20200406-0043.html

Walker, L. (2000). *The battered woman syndrome*. Springer Publishing Company.

Whalley, E., & Hackett, C. (2017). Carceral feminisms: The abolitionist project and undoing dominant feminisms. *Contemporary Justice Review*, *20*(4), 456–473.

Conclusion

> When we speak about the past and the future, these exist now.
>
> (Kapur, 2018, p. 219)

In their recent book, Schenwar and Law (2021) argue that introducing alternatives to incarceration is not enough to challenge the dominant carceral logic: reforming the system does not disrupt its foundations. Ben-Moshe's (2020) account of the US mental institutions' closure in the 1960s as a form of abolition, suggests that a non-carceral society may not be just a utopia. Along these lines, this book has not advocated for reforming the existing penal apparatus to make it "human-rights-compliant" or more "efficient". Instead, it has shown how, despite the many attempts made by diverse political actors to rationalise and humanise penality, it remains oppressive, exclusionary, and inadequate to protect and redress women. I have provided empirical evidence to dispute the idea that it is possible to "constitutionalise" a system that is based on colonial violence, economic inequality, and a Western episteme that rules out non-liberal understandings of justice and social life. In offering this evidence, I invite us, as feminists, to radically transform our common sense of justice. With other critics studying Latin America (Fulchiron, 2017; Gómez Vélez & Gómez Gómez, 2018; Hernández Castillo, 2017; Pérez, 2019), I am committed to "rethinking all our forms of social interaction, and to rethink them not only as tools of patriarchy, but also of cissexism, racism, ableism, among so many other forms of violence that traverse us" (Periódicas, 2019, para. 12).

Simultaneously, within such a radical critique, I believe that there is room to nuance and broaden the meaning of what we are calling governance and carceral feminism and how these categories may or may not be of benefit to social justice struggles in different contexts. A significant sector of scholarship has argued that mainstream feminism collaborates with the carceral state by centring criminal law as a "solution" to gender-based violence (Bernstein, 2012; Halley et al., 2018; Richie, 2012; Whalley & Hackett, 2017). While I sincerely encourage self-critique, researching feminist networks has taught me not to lose sight, in that self-critical endeavour, of who and what should not be excluded as targets of our scrutiny.

DOI: 10.4324/9781003098799-8

In that sense, this book has augmented the body of literature on governance and carceral feminism, to point at some perils that we may not be sufficiently aware of, either due to their apparent innocuity, or to our own omissions. For instance, contextualising governance and carceral feminism in Ecuador reveals that feminists' actual impact on governance, in many places and periods, is so slight and impermanent that we need to rethink the concepts themselves. Moreover, when feminists have made an impact on governance, whether through the state or NGOs, their proposals have continually been reshaped by non-feminist actors who reproduced coloniality – despite, or even due to, the adoption of a human rights discourse. In Ecuador, even when feminists were part of the governing coalition, they were not able to attain some key law reforms they had pursued for decades.

My search for the origin and development of the legal discourses that feminists commonly use, has led me to address what some critics have identified as "coercive human rights" (Lavrysen & Mavronicola, 2020). From there, I had to grapple with other overarching questions, such as "what happens when we frame our political demands in the post-political idioms of human rights?" (Golder, 2014, p. 78). To this, I added: what happens when human rights reproduce penality but present it as democratic and constitutional? What do these legal fields of intelligibility mean for feminists, and what happens when they use them to voice their demands? To answer these questions I historicised liberal legality from the perspective of the women's movements and observed the effects of rights-based penality by listening to violence survivors. Historicising power networks, I believe, is key to understanding the opportunities and limitations of political/legal action. I thus opted for a strategy that scrutinises the coloniality of liberal legalism and also acknowledges the tensions and struggles within and among feminist networks. This search also took me to a place where I could see that the effects of criminalisation do not always amount to carceral expansion, but can indeed be harmful and should lead us to a revision of tactics.

From a Latin American perspective, and through the case of Ecuador, I have shown that we have yet to come to terms with how many legal discourses organising our social world are colonial, especially when, as it happens with human rights, they are afforded the presumption of benignity. Ecuador provides an example of the extent to which human rights are entangled in the punitive feminist agenda: penality is inextricably interwoven with the protection of women's human rights, and it is this discursive association that primarily animates today's appeals to criminalise, rather than, say, an "ambition" to inflict suffering on violent men. If prosecution and punishment are construed as the only legitimate responses to human rights violations, opposing penality would equate to opposing human rights, and opposing human rights equates opposing the greatest achievement of the modern, democratic (Western) world.

Besides, it would be unfair not to recognise that despite these limitations, many Ecuadorian women have disputed the violence of law and the resort to the state. From indigenous leaders like Dolores Cacuango and Tránsito Amaguaña, to the collectives meeting at the Latin American *Encuentros*, to those feminists still swimming against the current, like Marena Briones, resistance has always been there. It was present in the debates that led to the 2014 Penal Code, and the Minority Report is a testament to feminist interrogations of penality. Hence, it would be reductionist to say that women's and feminist movements in Ecuador and Latin America have "downloaded" most of their ideas and strategies from North American and European feminisms. Moreover, groups and institutions that have organised mainly from Latin America (such as the Inter-American Commission on Women), have strongly influenced the rest of the world's understanding of violence against women (VAW). Of course, across history, those who tend to invest more in law reform are those who have more reasons to believe that they will not be the target of state violence.

This historical inquiry has shown me that rights-based penality is seldom questioned, largely due to human rights' universal status as non-ideological devices to fend for dignity. Human rights are presented as a defence against power (Kapur, 2018; Tulkens, 2011); however, in order to contain power, they have to define and legitimise power: asserting what degree and type of state violence is acceptable is still asserting that state violence is acceptable, and once accepted, carceral violence can, and does, expand. Consequently, I do wonder whether it is high time we recognised that the "redemptive return to human rights" (Golder, 2014) is conducive to penal expansion. Perhaps it is not too provocative to say that today, in order to interrogate our investment in criminal justice, we should first interrogate our investment in human rights.

In addition, the case of Ecuador demonstrates that penality, as a governmental technology to regulate race, gender, and sexuality, was around long before the start of neoliberal globalisation and the entry of feminists into the circles of legal power. Penality has been an interpretive framework entrenched in the legal imaginary of Latin American societies since colonial and early republican times. This is not to say that late capitalist trends have not enhanced penality; but it is difficult to understand Latin American and other Southern feminist networks without acknowledging the synergy between coloniality, liberal legalism, and criminal law. In Ecuador, the feminists who have promoted the criminalisation of VAW have also demanded the decriminalisation of abortion and endorsed social redistribution and decolonisation. Yet, they were obstructed in their efforts to disrupt the coloniality of power, gender, and law. This obstruction was in part possible because human rights were never interrogated as an element of colonial power. Instead, they were considered a good ally to challenge the status quo. Thus, the language of rights is key in masking the most problematic aspects of penality and also facilitates the displacement of legally plural perspectives. As feminists, we should not lose sight of the convergence between rights-based penality and the coloniality of gender: human rights and penality limit our ability to imagine and prefigure a decolonial justice.

Clearly, coloniality entails the impossibility of being otherwise, thinking otherwise, conceiving justice otherwise. Because feminist proposals need to be intelligible within the colonial/liberal paradigm, they have revolved around widening the scope of legal provisions – e.g. demanding that the category "criminal offence" includes violence against women – rather than challenging law's inherent liberal values. At the same time, whether it is indigenous understandings of communal living, or women's demands for effective protection, the Other's justice is seen as deviation, as non-justice; not full, proper justice. From the viewpoint of violence survivors, law is designed by someone else, for someone else, and demands resources that very few have.

A rights-based criminal law is still criminal law. Its dynamics respond first and foremost to the state goal of establishing criminal responsibility. Despite so many attempts to transform criminal justice into a human rights-compliant system that delivers protection *and* reparations, criminal law's structure and categories cancel non-penal aims, including women's demands to halt ongoing violence and obtain material resources to alleviate their situation. While some feminist literature on decriminalising domestic violence highlights the importance of individual agency (Goodmark, 2018), I have also put emphasis on how penality disguises women's lack of access to social services and tools like financial help. My sense is that, as important as enhancing women's agency is, this would be a shallow goal if the gendered economic inequality that is the norm in Latin America is not combatted.

Rights-based penality has imposed, on survivors, a penal logic whereby they are compelled to trigger state coercion if they want to gain a legal safeguard, despite the risks they run in doing so. To access justice, women have to be an adversarial subject; a self-sufficient, self-interested individual who is willing to disrupt most aspects of her and her children's lives in order to litigate. Colonial family-oriented policy has taken different shapes: sometimes it manifested as the penal prosecution of "adulterous" women and alcoholic men, other times it condemned violence against women *and* the family, but, throughout history, the design of criminal laws has had a common denominator: its disregard for women's lived experiences.

By now we should know that power relations are complex and multiple, often intertwined, imbricated, and dispersed, and that oppressive discourses are also reproduced through progressive projects. In Ecuador, liberal legality did not cease to be colonial when Andean cosmovision principles were incorporated into a largely liberal constitution. Indigenous movements know this very well. Thus, how can we challenge the idea that criminal responsibility is an individual matter, that punishment is a deserved evil, that it is morally just to inflict pain, and that this pain is the measure of justice and redress? We have a duty to address the coloniality of rights-based penality. This is one pathway to reclaim justice. Human rights have been of advantage to many people and have signalled political and legal shifts that we can and should celebrate. Yet, human rights have only allowed us to make change happen at certain moments, on certain topics, and using a certain language. In other words, human rights achievements have come at a high cost. A post-neoliberal future, and more so, a "decolonial feminist abolitionism" of sorts, requires an epistemic break that may render our demands difficult to articulate in legal terms. Doing away with liberal law is a radical political project that involves the enormous challenge of unlearning colonial penality and Western human rights.

References

Ben-Moshe, L. (2020). *Decarcerating disability: Deinstitutionalization and prison abolition*. University of Minnesota Press.

Bernstein, E. (2012). Carceral politics as gender justice? The "traffic in women" and neoliberal circuits of crime, sex, and rights. *Theory and Society*, *41*(3), 233–259.

Fulchiron, A. (2017). Actoras de Cambio en Guatemala: poner el cuerpo y la vida de las mujeres en el centro de la justicia. *Género Y Justicia Transicional. Movimientos de Mujeres Contra La Impunidad*, 65–112.

Golder, B. (2014). Beyond redemption? Problematising the critique of human rights in contemporary international legal thought. *London Review of International Law*, *2*(1), 77–114.

Gómez Vélez, M.I., & Gómez Gómez, D. (2018). Capítulo 1. Abolicionismo decolonial: repensando las maneras de abordar el castigo. In M. Gutiérrez Quevedo & Á.M. Olarte Delgado (eds.), *Política criminal y abolicionismo, hacia una cultura restaurativa* (pp. 25–74). Universidad Externado de Colombia.

Goodmark, L. (2018). *Decriminalizing domestic violence: A balanced policy approach to intimate partner violence* (1st ed.). University of California Press.

Halley, J., Kotiswaran, P., Shamir, H., & Rebouché, R. (2018). *Governance feminism: An introduction*. University of Minnesota Press.

Hernández Castillo, R.A. (ed.). (2017). *Resistencias penitenciarias. Investigación activista de espacios de reclusión*. Juan Pablos Editor.

Kapur, R. (2018). *Gender, alterity and human rights: Freedom in a fishbowl*. Edward Elgar Publishing Ltd.

Lavrysen, L., & Mavronicola, N. (eds.). (2020). *Coercive human rights: Positive duties to mobilise the criminal law under the ECHR (hart studies in security and justice)*. Hart Publishing.

Pérez, M. (2019). El antipunitivismo como utopía cotidiana. XIX Congreso Nacional AFRA, Mar del Plata. https://www.aacademica.org/moira.perez/59

Periódicas. (2019, September 20). *Moira Pérez: "El castigo no repara, no previene, no sana."* Periódicas. https://periodicas.com.ar/2019/09/20/moira-perez-el-castigo-no-repara-no-previene-no-sana/

Richie, B.E. (2012). *Arrested justice*. New York University Press.

Schenwar, M., & Law, V. (2021). *Prison by any other name: The harmful consequences of popular reforms*. The New Press.

Tulkens, F. (2011). The paradoxical relationship between criminal law and human rights. *Journal of International Criminal Justice*, *9*(3), 577–595.

Whalley, E., & Hackett, C. (2017). Carceral feminisms: The abolitionist project and undoing dominant feminisms. *Contemporary Justice Review*, *20*(4), 456–473.

Index

Note: Page numbers in **bold** reference tables.